Morton Beckner

THE EXPLANATION OF BEHAVIOUR

International Library of
Philosophy and
Scientific Method

EDITOR: A. J. AYER
ASSISTANT EDITOR: BERNARD WILLIAMS

THE EXPLANATION
OF BEHAVIOUR

by

Charles Taylor

Associate Professor of Philosophy,
University of Montreal

LONDON
ROUTLEDGE & KEGAN PAUL
NEW YORK : THE HUMANITIES PRESS

First published *1964*
by Routledge & Kegan Paul Ltd
Broadway House, 68–74 Carter Lane
London, E.C.4

Second impression *1965*

Printed in Great Britain by
Fletcher & Son Ltd, Norwich

TO ALBA

CONTENTS

vii

CONTENTS

ACKNOWLEDGEMENTS

THIS book was written while I was a Fellow of All Souls College. I am very grateful for the opportunity that this provided me to complete the work.

I would also like to thank Isaiah Berlin, Stuart Hampshire, Roy Holland and Bernard Williams who helped by advice, and even more by criticism, to make this book somewhat less inadequate to the subject than it would have been.

PART ONE

EXPLANATION BY PURPOSE

I

PURPOSE AND TELEOLOGY

IT is often said that human behaviour, or for that matter the behaviour of animals or even living organisms in general, is in some way fundamentally different from the processes in nature which are studied by the natural sciences. This opposition is variously expressed. It is sometimes said that the behaviour of human beings and animals shows a purposiveness which is not found elsewhere in nature, or that it has an intrinsic 'meaning' which natural processes do not. Or it is said that the behaviour of animate organisms exhibits an order which cannot be accounted for by the 'blind accident' of processes in nature. Or again, to draw the circle somewhat narrower, it is said of human beings and some animals that they are conscious of and direct their behaviour in a way which finds no analogue in inanimate nature, or that, specifically in an account of human affairs, concepts like 'significance' and 'value' play a uniquely important part which is denied them in natural science.

Against this view stands the opinion of many others, in particular of many students of the sciences of human behaviour, that there is no difference in principle between the behaviour of animate organisms and any other processes in nature, that the former can be accounted for in the same way as the latter, by laws relating physical events, and that the introduction of such notions as 'purpose' and 'mind' can only serve to obscure and confuse. This is in particular the point of view of the widely spread school of thought in psychology known as 'behaviourist'.

Now the issue between these two views is one of fundamental

and perennial importance for what is often called philosophical anthropology, the study of the basic categories in which man and his behaviour is to be described and explained. That this question is central to any science of human behaviour—if such a science is possible—needs no showing. But this does not by any means exhaust its importance. For it is also central to ethics. Thus there is a type of ethical reflexion, exemplified for instance in the work of Aristotle, which attempts to discover what men should do and how they should behave by a study of human nature and its fundamental goals. This is the attempt to elaborate what is often called a 'humanism'. The premiss underlying this reflexion, which is by no means confined to philosophers, is that there is a form of life which is higher or more properly human than others, and that the dim intuition of the ordinary man to this effect can be vindicated in its substance or else corrected in its content by a deeper understanding of human nature. But this premiss collapses once it is shown, if it ever is, that human behaviour cannot be accounted for in terms of goals or purposes but must be explained on mechanistic principles; for then the concept of fundamental human goals or of a way of life more consonant with the purposes of human nature—or even the existentialist notion that our basic goals are chosen by ourselves—will be shown to have no application.

A similar premiss, that a purpose or set of purposes which are intrinsically human can be identified, underlies all philosophical and other reflexion concerning the 'meaning' of human existence, and this, too, would collapse if the mechanistic thesis were shown to hold.

These brief remarks, which still do not exhaust the ramifications of this question, are enough to show why it has been of perennial interest to philosophers and laymen. And yet in spite of, or perhaps because of this, it still awaits resolution. We might try to explain this simply by pleading lack of evidence. In fact the sciences of man are in their infancy. But this cannot be the whole explanation. In fact, it seems simply to put us before the same question in another form. For we might just as truly say that the sciences of man, and particularly psychology, are in their infancy because this question remains unresolved. It is not enough, therefore, simply to invoke research. In fact the trouble is deeper: we have first to know where to look. And when we ask ourselves *this* question, we find ourselves well and truly at sea.

In fact there has never been agreement among philosophers or other students as to what is at stake here, that is, on the meaning of the claim that human behaviour is purposive, or, what is the same thing, on what the relevant evidence is which would decide it. As a matter of fact, it is not even generally agreed that it is a matter of finding evidence in the first place, for some thinkers hold that the issue is not in any sense an empirical one, but rather that it can be decided simply by logical argument.

This confusion might tempt us to say that the question is insoluble, or even that it is a pseudo-question. But this radical 'solution' would itself have to be established by some argument about the nature of the putative issue involved. Before finally turning our backs on the matter in this way, therefore, it is worth trying once more to define what is at stake. This is what will be attempted in the first part of this book.

I. TELEOLOGICAL EXPLANATION

What, then, does it mean to say that human, or animal, behaviour is purposive? Central to this claim would seem to be the view that the order or pattern which is visible in animate behaviour is radically different from that visible elsewhere in nature in that it is in some sense self-imposed; the order is itself in some way a factor in its own production. This seems to be the force of the rejection of 'blind accident': the prevalence of order cannot be accounted for on principles which are only contingently or 'accidentally' connected with it, by laws whose operation only contingently results in it, but must be accounted for in terms of the order itself.

The point, then, could perhaps be put in this way: the events productive of order in animate beings are to be explained not in terms of other unconnected antecedent conditions, but in terms of the very order which they produce. These events are held to occur because of what results from them, or, to put it in a more traditional way, they occur 'for the sake of' the state of affairs which follows. And this of course is part of what is meant by the term 'purpose' when it is invoked in explanation. For to explain by purpose is to explain by the goal or result aimed at, 'for the sake of' which the event is said to occur.

Explanation which invokes the goal for the sake of which the explicandum occurs is generally called teleological explanation, and thus at least part of what we mean by saying that human or animal behaviour is purposive is that it is to be accounted for by a teleological form of explanation.[1]

But does this take us any further ahead? What is meant by teleological explanation and how can we establish whether it holds or not of a given range of phenomena? The remainder of this chapter will be devoted to an attempt to answer this question, and to cut through the skein of confusions which usually makes it difficult to bring this question into focus.

2. AN EMPIRICAL QUESTION?

Now a first difficulty arises straight off with the objection that this question, whether or not a teleological explanation holds, is not an empirical one at all. In fact many theorists, and particularly students of what can roughly be called the behavioural sciences, would hold that the claim that animate behaviour must be explained teleologically or in terms of purpose is a meaningless one, empirically empty or 'metaphysical', that the whole question is a 'pseudo-question'. This is especially true of many theorists in the field of experimental psychology, those of the behaviourist school, on which the discussion later in this book will mainly centre. These thinkers, extremely hostile to the claims of teleological explanation, make short work of it by purporting to expose, in summary fashion, its non-empirical character.

If this objection is a valid one, then our whole enquiry is stopped before it starts. But, as a matter of fact, it is not. In fact, it reposes on an interpretation of the notions of purpose and teleological explanation which is arbitrary and by no means imposed on us.

Thus the claim that we must explain the behaviour of a given system in terms of purpose is often taken to mean that we must

[1] That this is not all that is meant by 'purposive' will be made clear in Chapters II and III. But it will help as a simplifying assumption for the discussion in this chapter if we forget this and treat 'explanation by purpose' and 'teleological explanation' as interchangeable.

6

explain it by laws of the form $x = f(P)$, where 'x' is the behaviour and 'P' is the Purpose considered as a separate entity which is the cause or antecedent of x. Of course the view that an explanation in terms of purpose involves the postulating of a special entity is by no means confined to those who are hostile to the idea. Many who were on the 'vitalist' side of the controversy in biology made use of a hypothetical entity of this kind. (Cf. Driesch's 'entelechy'.) But there is no doubt that the end result of this is to create a handy Aunt Sally for the mechanists. For a theory of this kind can neither be confirmed nor add in any way to our power of predicting and controlling the phenomena.

This can be readily seen. In fact, the only empirical evidence for the operation of the purpose is the behaviour which its operation is used to explain. There is thus no conceivable evidence which could falsify a hypothesis of this kind because whenever the behaviour is emitted, the purpose responsible is *ex hypothesi* assumed to have been operating. And at the same time we would never be able to predict behaviour with the aid of such a hypothesis. For if x having a value of x_1 is due to P having the value P_1, and if the only evidence for P_1 is the occurrence of x_1, then we have no way of knowing beforehand what the value of x will be.

Now, of course, we might find some antecedent conditions for P, such that we could determine the value of P *ex ante* by means of a function such as $P = f(a)$. But then we would be turning P into what is often called an 'intervening variable',[1] that is, a term useful in calculation which is nevertheless without empirical content, which is not itself an empirical descriptive term. For in this case the entire empirical content of the two functions $P = f(a)$ and $x = f(P)$ could be expressed in one more complex function linking a and x directly, $x = F(a)$. What is meant by saying that 'P' is not an empirical descriptive term is that no single proposition about P is open to empirical confirmation or infirmation. Thus, in the case above, neither of these functions can be verified singly. We have seen above that this is true of $x = f(P)$, but it is equally so of $P = f(a)$. The proposition

---

[1] Cf. K. MacCorquodale and P. E. Meehl, 'On a Distinction Between Hypothetical Constructs and Intervening Variables', *Psychological Review*, 1948, although the sense of the term here differs slightly from their interpretation.

formed by the conjunction of both is open to empirical confirmation, but then the evidence for this is the same as the evidence for $x = F(a)$ which makes no mention of P. That is, no empirical sense can be given to the supposition that $x = F(a)$ be true and the conjunction of the two functions false. Thus the question whether or not the functions containing 'P' are to be accepted is not an empirical but purely a stipulative question, to be determined by the convenience in the calculation. 'P' is therefore not an empirical descriptive term.

Thus those who hold that 'purpose' is essential to the explanation of the behaviour of animate organisms are left with the unattractive choice either of making an unverifiable claim of no explanatory utility in science or of winning their point at the expense of making the laws true by stipulation. This view of the matter is very common among behaviour psychologists who are unsympathetic to this claim. Their view seems to be that their opponents adopt the first position, that of positing an unobservable entity, propositions about which cannot be verified. Thus Hebb in the first chapter of his *The Organization of Behaviour* speaks interchangeably of 'animism' (the view that animate behaviour must be explained in terms of 'purpose') and 'interactionism' (the view that behaviour is the result of the interaction of observable physical and unobservable 'inner' or mental processes) and of course 'mysticism' (which doesn't seem to have a very clear sense in Hebb's usage but which means something counter-empirical, unscientific and generally nasty). Similarly, Spence[1] speaks of animistic theories as those in which the relation of the (unobservable) constructs to the empirical (observable) variables is left entirely unspecified (and hence they are unverifiable as in the first alternative above).

The upshot of this view, then, is that the claim that animate organisms have a special status is undecidable, or rather that even to make it is to say something which cannot be verified. If the question is not to be closed here we shall have to examine explanation by purpose more closely in order to determine whether it must involve the postulating of an unobservable entity which is the cause or the antecedent condition of behaviour.

Now, as we have said, explanation by purpose involves the

---

[1] 'The Nature of Theory Construction in Contemporary Psychology,' *Psychological Review*, 1944.

use of a teleological form of explanation, of explanation in terms of the result for the sake of which the events concerned occur. Now when we say that an event occurs for the sake of an end, we are saying that it occurs because it is the type of event which brings about this end. This means that the condition of the event's occurring is that a state of affairs obtain such that it will bring about the end in question, or such that this event is required to bring about that end.[1] To offer a teleological explanation of some event or class of events, e.g., the behaviour of some being, is, then, to account for it by laws in terms of which an event's occurring is held to be dependent on that event's being required for some end.

To say that the behaviour of a given system should be explained in terms of purpose, then, is, in part, to make an assertion about the form of the laws, or the type of laws which hold of the system. But *qua* teleological these laws will not be of the kind which makes behaviour a function of the state of some unobservable entity; rather the behaviour is a function of the state of the system and (in the case of animate organisms) its environment; but the relevant feature of system and environment on which behaviour depends will be what the condition of both makes necessary if the end concerned is to be realized. Thus for instance, we can say that the conditions for a given action, say a predator stalking his prey, are (1) that the animal be hungry, and (2) that this be the 'required' action, i.e., the action in his repertoire which will achieve the result—catching his next meal. The condition of an event B occurring, is, then, not a certain state of P, but that the state of the system S and the environment

---

[1] The difference is small between these two formulae. To say that an event is required for an end is to say more than that it will bring it about; for it adds that no other event, or none other in the system concerned can bring it about. A sufficient condition of a teleological kind can only be found for an event if it is in this unique position; if there are several possibilities we cannot account for the selection between them unless we add another teleological principle, e.g., of least effort. Since the putative teleological systems whose behaviour we shall be discussing in later parts of this book, i.e., organisms, seem to manifest some such principle, or else to select between alternatives when these are available in the repertoire on some other teleological principle, e.g., by certain standards which are norms to be observed, we shall generally assume the selection as made, and speak elliptically of 'the event required for' the goal or end.

9

E be such that B is required for the end G, by which the system's purpose is defined.

Now the fact that the state of a system and its environment is such as to require a given event if a certain result is to accrue can be perfectly observable, and the fact that this antecedent condition holds can be established independently of the evidence provided by the occurrence of the event itself. This type of law, therefore, does not suffer from the disabilities of functions of the type $x = f(P)$. On the contrary, whether laws of this kind hold can be verified or falsified, and, if true, they can be used to predict and control the phenomena like any others. To say that a system can only be explained in terms of purpose, then—at least insofar as this is an assertion about the form of the laws—does not involve making an unverifiable claim any more than it involves postulating an unobservable entity. The element of 'purposiveness' in a given system, the inherent tendency towards a certain end, which is conveyed by saying that the events happen 'for the sake of' the end, cannot be identified as a special entity which directs the behaviour from within, but consists rather in the fact that in beings with a purpose an event's being required for a given end is a sufficient condition of its occurrence. It is not a separable feature, but a property of the whole system, that by which it tends 'naturally' towards a certain result or end. It is this notion of a 'natural tendency' towards a certain result or end—which we shall discuss at greater length in the next section—which lies behind the notion that, in systems whose behaviour must be accounted for by laws of this kind, the order which results cannot be attributed to 'blind accident', that is, to principles which are only contingently connected with the bringing about and maintenance of this order; for the principle underlying the laws by which the behaviour is explained is itself a tendency to produce this order.

3. ASSUMPTIONS OF ATOMISM

What considerations, then, led to the belief held by mechanists and vitalists alike that the claim to some special status involved the postulating of some special entity? The background to this belief is very complex and exploring it would involve unravelling a skein of connected questions which surround this subject, some of which we hope to return to in the fourth chapter. But at this stage one of the causes can perhaps be laid bare.

We can readily see that, in any explanatory functional law, the antecedent and the consequent must be separately identifiable. Thus it cannot be a logical condition for the occurrence of the antecedent that the consequent occur. Something like this was what was the matter with our $x = f(P)$. True, it was not a condition (logically) of P having a certain value that x have the corresponding value demanded by the function, but since the latter was the only evidence for the former, it came to much the same thing. Similarly, the antecedent's occurring cannot be a logical condition of the consequent's being held to occur. Now teleological laws meet this requirement. For the antecedent may occur independently of the consequent, and vice versa.

But there is a stronger requirement which teleological laws cannot meet. This not only demands that the two terms which are linked in a law be identifiable separately from each other, that is, that it not be a condition for identification of either term that it be linked to the other term in the law,[1] but also that each term be identified separately from *any* law in which it may figure, i.e., that it not be a condition for the identification of any term that it be linked to any other. Now this more stringent requirement arises from the atomism which is part of the tradition of empiricism, and is ultimately founded on epistemological grounds. The notion is that the ultimate evidence for any laws we frame about the world is in the form of discrete units of information,[2] each of which could be as it is even if all others were different, i.e., each of which is separably identifiable from its connexions with any of the others. Our knowledge of the world is built up from the empirical connexions which are found to hold (contingently) in experience between these units. Thus the evidence for any law can ultimately be given, although perhaps with great tedium, in terms of connexions between such discrete units. Thus

[1] We can, of course, decide to make this a condition of identification, but then we cease to have an empirical law which can figure in explanation. This may, however, be more convenient. Thus, e.g., we can consider it to be among the defining properties of a chemical that it melt at a certain temperature.

[2] E.g., Hume's 'impressions' to which all 'ideas' must be ultimately referred.

if a given chemical C, with defining properties x, y and z, is held to produce a certain result R in some conditions, although we may usually for convenience sake speak of this law as $C - R$, the ultimate evidence for it is the concomitance of x, y, z and R, each of which is identifiable separately from the others.

Now teleological laws cannot meet this stringent requirement of reduction to the basic type of evidence required by atomism. In this way, teleological explanation is, as has often been re-marked, connected with some form of holism, or anti-atomistic doctrine. The first term of a teleological correlation violates the stringent requirement since it identifies the antecedent condition of the event to be accounted for, B, as a state of affairs in which B will lead to G. Thus the antecedent is identified in terms of its law-like connexions with two other events, B and G, i.e., as that state of affairs in which, when B occurs, G will follow. This law, therefore, is elliptical as it stands, and, on atomist assumptions, we should be able to restate it in a more satisfactory way. But this cannot be done, or at least it cannot be done without transforming the law into a non-teleological one.

This might seem odd. Surely that state of affairs which is such that B will lead to $G(B - G)$ can also be identified intrinsically, that is, without reference to its relation to other states of affairs. Thus to return to the examples above of the predator stalking his prey: instead of describing the environment in which the animal is now beginning to stalk as one which requires this action for the goal of getting food, we could characterize it intrinsically, without making any reference to his goals, e.g., by simply enumerating the components, or by mentioning certain key stimuli which are impinging on his receptors. Let us call this intrinsic type of characterization E. Then for any teleological law we can state a new law $E - B$ and this, together with a law to the effect that E and B together produce G will convey the content of the original teleological law. We will assume that E, B and G are all separably identifiable from each other (and either that they are separably indentifiable from all other terms or that they could be further broken down). But now a startling result has occurred. We no longer have a teleological law, but instead two laws of a non-teleological kind, $E - B$ and $E + B - G$, from which can be deduced a third, also non-teleological law $E - G$; for none of these characterizes the antecedent as requiring the consequent if some result is to accrue. The teleological explanation has disappeared like the morning dew.

It is commonly assumed among empiricist philosophers that such a translation-out-of-existence can always be effected. Thus Nagel[1] assumes that a non-teleological account can always be given of a system which, like the living organism, shows 'goal-directedness'. He imagines a system S which maintains state G and has three components A, B and C, which operate in such a way that if A undergoes a change which will carry the system out of G, B and C will compensate so as to maintain the system in this condition. Such a system is recognizably like living organisms in their 'homeostatic' functions, e.g., if the temperature of the air falls, the body will 'compensate' to maintain 'G', in this case the body temperature normal for the species. Of course, as I have stated it, the account is still teleological in form, for the changes in B and C were characterized as 'compensating' so as to maintain the G-state. But there is no reason, thinks Nagel, why we should not characterize the functions linking changes in B and C to those in A in a non-teleological way, by laws of the form, whenever A changes from Am to An, then B changes from Bx to By and C . . . , etc.[2] Thus, for instance, we would be able to express the antecedent for a given change in B, say, which in fact produces G, in terms other than that this change is required by the system for G, namely in terms of the states of A and C. This would correspond, in our above example, to the E-term.

But we have no right to make this assumption. Of course, any given antecedent condition of B which fulfilled the conditions for the description 'requiring B for G' (let us call this T) would also fulfil some other 'intrinsic' description, E. But this is not to say that B's occurring is a function of E's occurring, i.e. that B depends on E. For it may be that in other circumstances a situation which fulfils the description E is not followed by B, the circumstances being precisely those in which the situation does not also fulfil the conditions for the description T; whereas all cases of T may be followed by B. Thus in our above example, it

---

[1] 'Teleological Explanations and Teleological Systems' in Feigl and Brodbeck, (Eds), *Readings in the Philosophy of Science*.

[2] I have paraphrased and greatly compressed Nagel's account, but I hope done no violence to it.

may be that the key stimuli we isolate in one case may impinge on the receptors of our predator in other contexts without inducing stalking behaviour; and this may happen in just those contexts where such an action would not bring about the goal of getting food. Now in such circumstances we would not say that B depended on E, but rather on T. The correlation $E - B$ would be explained by means of $T - B$, and could be derived from this law together with a statement of the conditions in which $E - B$ holds, $E = T$. When the antecedent in a teleological type law T is replaced by a non-teleological antecedent E, the assumption is that all cases of T which are followed by B are cases of E. But whether this is so or not is an empirical matter. We have no guarantee *a priori* that we shall discover an 'intrinsic' characterization E which will apply to all cases of T (assuming for the sake of simplicity that $T - B$ holds invariably[1]), and which will never apply to a case which is not followed by B. Of course, we might be able to discover a disjunction of such descriptions, E, F, G, etc., but there is no reason *a priori* why this list should be finite. A similar objection applies to Nagel's proposed translations. There is no guarantee that a finite list of laws of the form, $An - By - Cq$, etc., which will cover the phenomena, i.e., enable us to make the predictions which we now make with teleological laws, can be found. Whether this is so or not must be discovered empirically. But if it is not, we cannot be held to have replaced the teleological law. On the contrary we will have to explain the fact that these rules of thumb hold when they do in terms of this law.

The belief that the regularities cited in teleological type explanations must also be accountable for in terms of non-teleological laws is a manifestation of the tendency on the part of those who are opposed to the view that organisms have a special status to assume the problems away and to close an empirical question with a logical clasp.[2] And once we see that this assumption is

---

[1] By 'invariably' is meant here not necessarily every time, but such that the exceptions can be cogently explained by interfering factors.

[2] Something of the same features may perhaps be observed in Braithwaite's account, *Scientific Explanation*, Chapter X. Braithwaite, too, speaks of a variety of chains which, starting from different points, all end in the same final state. But the point of teleological explanation is not the co-incidence of different antecedents having the same consequent, but the type of antecedent involved.

an empirical one, we can see what is wrong with the atomist position. For the proposed translation using only intrinsic terms is not another, epistemologically sounder, way of stating the evidence for the teleological law; it is a rival account of the matter; it differs in meaning and in the evidence required to substantiate it. For what is claimed by the teleological explanation is that what occurs is a function of what is required for the system's end, G, that an event's being required for G is a sufficient condition of its happening, whereas the proposed 'translation' offers us a quite different sufficient condition. And which claim is correct is an empirical question, that is to say, the evidence required for the one is not the same as that required for the other. Whether the stringent atomist requirement can be met by all valid laws, then, is itself an empirical question, which hinges partly on the question whether all teleological explanation—or any other type of explanation which involves holistic assumptions —can be done away with. It cannot be decided by epistemological fiat, by a rule to the effect that the evidence for teleological laws must be such that it can be stated by means of non-teleological laws.

But we have perhaps discovered part of the answer to our question. It would seem plausible to conclude that one of the reasons for the widespread belief that explanations involving 'purpose' required the postulation of some special entity is the hold of atomist assumptions. For atomism in effect rules out teleological explanation and thus also the possibility of construing purposiveness as a feature of the whole system and its manner of operation. On the contrary, since all laws hold between discrete entities intrinsically characterized, then to invoke a purpose must be to postulate some new discrete entity as a causal antecedent. This seems the only interpretation of explanation by purpose which can fit the epistemological requirements. But, of course, it violates these requirements in another way, for this entity is unobservable, and so the whole enterprise is doomed from the start. But once we examine the assumptions on which this rests we can see that this interpretation is not forced on us.

The influence of atomism can also be seen in the common misinterpretation of teleological explanation as explanation in terms of a correlation between intrinsically characterized terms which has the peculiarity that the antecedent comes after the consequent.

Thus while an ordinary type law is of the form $A - B$, where A, the antecedent, comes before B, the consequent, a teleological law is of the form $G - B$, where the occurrence of B is explained by the result G which follows from it. Thus Hull, in his *Principles of Behaviour*, holds that:

> In its extreme form teleology is the name of the belief that the *terminal* stage of certain environmental-organismic interaction cycles somehow is at the same time one of the antecedents determining conditions which bring the behaviour cycle about.[1]

And, thus interpreted, teleological explanations can be shown to be of no value because we cannot determine whether the antecedent conditions of behaviour obtain until after it has happened. Thus:

> In effect this means that the task of deduction cannot begin until after it is completed! Naturally this leaves the theorist completely helpless.[2]

Thus once again the whole enterprise can be shown to be misguided. And once again this demonstration is based on an arbitrary interpretation. For this is, of course, a travesty of teleological explanation. In a teleological law the antecedent of an event is not the result which follows but the state of affairs obtaining prior to it in which this event is what must happen if the result is to ensue. The whole idea that teleological explanation is like causal explanation in that it uses correlations between separate events but unlike it in that the time order is reversed, i.e., the antecedent comes after the consequent[3] is mistaken. Because it is not necessarily a counter-example to a teleological correlation if the event first in time (the B-event) does not occur, while that second in time, G, does; that is, comes about by accident or through some cause outside the system. And a case where the first (B) occurs without the second (G) may still be taken as evidence for the correlation if, say, some factor interferes to prevent G at the last moment; whereas this case would have no relevance to a correlation of the form $G - B$. This misrepresentation of teleological explanation seems to be based on atomist assumptions which involve the rejection of what is in fact the antecedent

---

[1] P. 26. Hull's emphasis. [2] Loc. cit.
[3] Cf. Braithwaite, *Scientific Explanation*, p. 337.

term in teleological laws, and the construction of these as holding between discrete entities, i.e., entities which meet the stringent requirement for independent specifiability. The peculiarity of teleological explanation, that it accounts for the events by final causes, by that for the sake of which they happen, is then construed as a reversal of the usual time order. The goal or final cause is cast as an ordinary antecedent causal condition which happens to come after what it brings about. The whole thing has a most bizarre air, and the temptation to reject it out of hand becomes overwhelming.

Both here and in the interpretation above of purpose as an 'unobservable entity', atomism has stacked the cards against those who maintain that animate beings show a type of behaviour radically different from other processes in nature. The only way to make any progress in this question is to reject its assumptions and start afresh.

4. THE ASYMMETRY OF EXPLANATION

Some progress has, perhaps, already been made. The claim is that animate beings are special in that the order visible in their behaviour must itself enter into an explanation of how this order comes about. This can in part be expressed by the claim that the events which bring about or constitute this order are to be accounted for in terms of final causes, as occurring 'for the sake of' the order which ensues. Now this claim is not inherently 'mystical' or non-empirical in nature, and nor does it entail postulating any unobservable entities. It involves, in part, the thesis that the laws by which we explain the behaviour of these organisms are teleological in form, and whether the laws which hold of a system are or are not of this kind is an empirical question.

But although not inherently 'mystical', this claim does involve some features which are *prima facie* at variance with certain common views about scientific procedure. Thus an explanation of a teleological type does involve the assumption that the system concerned 'naturally' or inherently tends towards a certain result, condition or end; for the principle of laws of this kind is that an event's being required for this end is a sufficient condition of its occurring. But in this we seem to be reverting (some would say, regressing) to a pre-Galilean form of explanation in terms of 'powers'. Much discredit, not to say ridicule, has been cast on this form of explanation. One has only to think of the merciless attack by Molière on the medical profession of his day in *Le Malade Imaginaire*. On being asked for the

> 'causam et rationem quare
> opium facit dormire',

the protagonist replies:

> 'quia est in eo
> virtus dormitiva,
> cujus est natura
> sensus assoupire';

this to the applause of the assembled 'doctors'.

But these very just strictures on verbal non-empirical explanations do not show that this way of talking is always absurd. It is so, as we have seen, if the reference to 'powers' is meant as the identification of a causal antecedent. And this was the kind of case which Molière chose. For the supposed antecedent, like Purpose or Entelechy, can never be observed. But, as we mentioned above, the appeal to 'powers' or 'natural tendencies' can be a way of attributing certain properties to the system as a whole and its manner of operation, and this can be empirically verified.

But the appeal to 'natural' or 'inherent' tendencies, although not empty, does involve some of the other traditional features of pre-Galilean explanation which have been no less frowned on. It involves, for instance, the assumption that the basic level of explanation has been reached. For the claim that a system is purposive is a claim about the laws holding at the most basic level of explanation.

The distinction between levels of explanation can be made in the following way: If explanation is conceived here as explanation in terms of a functional law, then an explanation can be considered as less basic than another when the regularities which the laws cited in the first describe are themselves explained in terms of the laws cited in the second. Thus if the behaviour of a system can be explained by the laws $y = f_1(z)$ and laws $y = f_2(x)$, where 'x' and 'z' range over different domains, we can call the second explanation more basic if the fact that laws $y = f_1(z)$ hold of the system can be explained in terms of $y = f_2(x)$. Thus the behaviour of gas in a container can be explained by Boyle's

Law, and also in terms of the Kinetic Theory of Gases, but it is the second explanation which is the more basic.

Why we should be concerned with explanation at the more basic level is clear once we see what it is for the regularities described in one set of laws to be explained by another. This is sometimes interpreted as meaning that the first set of laws can be deduced from the second which are at the same time more general in their application.[1] But this interpretation obviously cannot apply here because a set of laws which are purposive in character, i.e., describe the behaviour as tending towards a certain condition, cannot be *deduced* from a set of laws which are non-purposive. We are dealing here with 'explanation' in a stronger sense, in which the less basic laws $y = f_1(z)$ can be derived not from the more basic $y = f_2(x)$ alone, but from these together with some other contingent statement of 'initial conditions' which ensure that z is related in some way to x. What this strong type of explanation gives us which the weaker one did not is the set of conditions on which the behaviour of the system depends, and this increases our ability to exercise control over it or, at least, if our technology is inadequate, to predict changes in it.[2] Thus we can say that the set of laws $y = f_2(x)$ is more basic than $y = f_1(z)$, for the former provides us with the conditions in which the latter will apply or not apply, so that we know how to construct systems exemplifying it, or at least when to predict of any system that it will exemplify it.

[1] I.e., other laws can be deduced from them or other evidence is relevant to them. Cf. Braithwaite; *Scientific Explanation*, pp. 300–3.

[2] This feature of explanation seems to be ignored by many philosophers of the empiricist school, who tend to confine their account to the weaker sense of the term. Thus Braithwaite: *Scientific Explanation*, pp. 302–3, accepts the proposition 'all animals are mortal' as an explanation of 'all men are mortal,' because the second can be deduced from the first, and at the same time the evidence for the first is not confined to the second; for we also know that horses, dogs, etc., are mortal. But this is only an explanation in the weaker sense, for it adds nothing to our knowledge of the conditions for men dying. For the statement of 'initial conditions' which permits the derivation of explicandum from explicans is itself a necessary proposition, 'all men are animals'. But this is surely a caricature of explanation in science where the type of discovery implied in the stronger form has been so much in evidence with such amazing results in control over our environment. (If all scientific explanation had been of the form suggested by Braithwaite's example we would still be living in a pre-technological age.)

Now it is clear that the claim that the behaviour of a system must be accounted for in terms of purpose or 'natural' or 'inherent' tendencies concerns the laws which hold at the most basic level of explanation. For a more basic explanation can be said to set out the regularities on which those cited in the less basic depend. $y = f_1(z)$ is true because $y = f_2(x)$ is true of the system, that is, the former can come to apply or not to apply to the system because the latter constantly applies to it. But if $y = f_1(z)$ is teleological in character and $y = f_2(x)$ is not, then the tendency towards a certain condition or state described in the first set could itself be shown to depend on the fact that the behaviour of the system is a function of those factors set out in $y = f_2(x)$. Thus we could construct a mechanical dog, programmed to behave like a real one. In this case the laws descriptive of his external behaviour $[y = f_1(z)]$ would be teleological like those of his real counterpart, they would characterize the behaviour as 'goal-directed', but the more basic explanation $[y = f_2(x)]$ would not. With systems of this kind we can hardly speak of an account in terms of 'natural' or 'inherent' tendencies. What we have in effect is the fact of the convergence of events towards a certain result which in turn is accounted for on quite different principles. We could account for the behaviour of such a system without using anything like the notion of purpose or tendency and without losing at all, but on the contrary gaining, in explanatory or predictive power or the capacity to control it. Those who claim a special status for animate organisms on the grounds that the order evident in their behaviour must be accounted for in terms of a tendency or 'purpose' of the events to realize this order could hardly hold that their claim had been vindicated by an explanation of this kind, where the tendency to realize the given order could itself be accounted for by other factors.[1]

---

[1] The issue is confused in this way by some thinkers in the field of cybernetics research who adopt a usage of 'purposive' and 'teleological' such that it can be applied without change of sense to animate beings and to machines which have been designed to imitate them. Thus Rosenbleuth and Wiener, in their discussion with Taylor, *Philosophy of Science*, 1950: 'if the notion of purpose is applicable to living organisms, it is also applicable to non-living entities when they show the same obervable traits of behaviour.' But if this is the only sense given to 'purpose' then the claim that animate organisms are radically different cannot be stated, or else it must be interpreted as the obviously untrue claim that machines cannot be devised which show the

Thus the claim that 'the purposes' of a system are of such and such a kind affects the laws which hold at the most basic level. In other words, it is incompatible with the view that the natural tendency towards a certain condition can itself be accounted for by other laws. Thus the function of an explanation invoking powers or natural tendencies can be precisely to shut off further enquiry. And this is why it is absurd when it is taken as an attempt to state some antecedent. For the fact that a tendency towards a given condition results in this condition neither requires not admits of further explanation. It is, rather, the break-down of such a 'correlation' which stands in need of explanation. And this logical feature of an account in terms of powers which makes it a block to further enquiry is also the one which unfits it to serve itself as an empirical law linking two terms. On the contrary, it can serve only to characterize the type of laws which hold of the system.

Now this claim to have reached the rock bottom of explanation is not one which is usually made in scientific theory, the possibility always being left open, however unlikely it may seem, that another set of laws will be discovered which are more basic. In this way, therefore, teleological explanation represents a deviation from the modern norm and a throw-back to an earlier type of explanation.

The block to further enquiry is connected with another feature of pre-Galilean forms, viz., their assumption of an asymmetry of explanation. This is implicit in what has been said above. In holding that the most basic laws are such that a sufficient condition of an event's happening is that it be required for a certain goal, that the tendency towards this result cannot be accounted

---

same 'observable traits'. And this is not part of what is meant when people say that human and animals are different from non-living entities. The distinction concerns not certain features of the observable behaviour but rather the laws which account for the behaviour at a more basic level. There is a widespread belief that just this distinction holds between animals and machines imitating them. Whether this is so or not is, of course, the point at issue. But this question is prejudged if we apply the notion 'purposive' to either case indiscriminately. This redefinition of 'purposive' would be permissible only if it were true that the class of systems of which the notion in its ordinary sense, that in which it refers to the most basic laws, holds was the null class, which, of course, is exactly what Rosenbleuth and Wiener assume. In fact our usual notion of purpose cannot properly be applied except in a metaphorical way to machines, as we shall see in the next chapter.

for by other, more basic, laws, teleological explanation places one result among those which are ideally possible for the system in a special position. For that the system achieves this result-condition neither calls for nor admits of explanation; but should it achieve any other condition, we are bound to give an account. For the second type of result, being at odds with the tendency of the system, must, if the theory is correct, be accounted for by some special interfering factor. Thus we usually explain abnormal behaviour by invoking fatigue, sickness, alcohol, nervous strain, or some such special condition. The adducing of an interfering factor here differs from the ordinary cases, not involving teleological laws, where this is done. If we explain a breakdown in the correlation $A - B$, by adducing the interfering factor I, both the correlations $A - B$ and $A + I$—not-B can be accounted for by the same set of laws. But in this case, the fact that the system brings about the result towards which it tends cannot be further accounted for, and *a fortiori* not by the same set of laws by which we account for the link between the interfering factor and some other result. Thus, if we were dealing with some non-teleological system, say, a machine designed to imitate animal behaviour, then the difference between normal and non-normal operation could be explained by the same set of laws in terms of different programming of the mechanism. But if we are dealing with a species of live animals (according to the usual hypothesis) then there is no set of more basic laws by which we can explain their tendency to emit the behaviour in question. In other words, granted the existence of animals of this species, there are no antecedent conditions for their normal behaviour—unless one wants to count the absence of all lesions, drugs, and any other factors producing abnormality as an antecedent—but any abnormal result has some special factor to which it is traceable. And thus the normal operation of the system, i.e., the occurrence of events which result in the normal condition is accounted for by teleological laws, while any abnormal functioning must bring in a set of laws linking interfering factors and non-normal conditions which are not teleological.[1] And this is the basis for the distinction between 'normal' and 'abnormal' itself, between the

[1] For the specification of an intervening factor would be different from that of an antecedent in a teleological law, i.e., the factor would not be characterized as a state of affairs requiring B for G.

'natural' result and the 'unnatural' ones, that the two must be accounted for in quite different ways; that there exists, in other words, an asymmetry of explanation.

Now this is recognizably a pre-Galilean feature; one has only to think of the distinction between 'natural' and 'violent' movement in pre-Galilean physics.[1] And this is often enough to discredit this form of explanation with many thinkers, for whom the principles laid down by Galileo are binding on all scientific thought. And, indeed, the gap between teleological explanation and that in vogue in modern physical science can be seen if we compare principles of asymmetry with their modern analogues. The term 'principle' is apposite here because asymmetry plays something of the kind of role in a teleological science of behaviour that Inertia does, for instance, in Newtonian physics. In both cases the principles serve to make clear the kinds of event for which an antecedent must be adduced and the kinds of event for which this is not the case. For Newton's first Law, the continuation of a body at rest or in uniform rectilinear motion did not admit of explanation in this sense, only changes in velocity were to be accounted for. Continued rest or rectilinear motion could be spoken of in this sense as 'natural'. This represented, of course, a radical change from Aristotelian science which held that continued motion must always be accounted for by a mover.

But this analogy serves to show the importance of the disanalogy. For the Principle of Inertia is 'neutral' in an important sense in which a principle of asymmetry is not. That is, it is not part of what is asserted by the Principle of Inertia that, for any system, one particular condition or set of results is natural. The Principle of Inertia does not single out any particular direction in which bodies 'naturally' tend to move or any constellation which they tend to move towards. And thus it can be said to be neutral between the different states of any system of which it may be invoked to explain the behaviour (that is, where the theory of which it is one of the foundations is invoked). But this cannot be said of a principle of asymmetry, whose function is precisely to distinguish a privileged state or result.

[1] Perhaps we should say here 'pre-Newtonian', for Galileo did not entirely free himself from the language of his predecessors. His reputation as a pioneer, however, has taken on such a symbolic importance among those who discuss these questions as to justify the use of his name in this context.

The point could be put in this way: The analogy between the Principle of Inertia and the various principles of asymmetry which preceded it, specifying the 'natural kinds' and their natural tendencies, lies in the fact that both are used to define the type of event which requires an explanation; for the latter motion, and for the former only changes in velocity. But there is another sense of 'requiring an explanation', that is, an explanation in terms of external forces, in which a principle of asymmetry distinguishes between the types of movement a given body can make, so that only movement in certain *directions* requires an explanation. And this is the disanalogy: That a principle of asymmetry does distinguish between different states of a system where it is invoked in explanation, that it is not neutral between different results.

'Natural' movements are only a sub-class of those requiring explanation. In this sense the natural course of events is reversible. And yet it is the 'natural' course, that is, that this goal or condition is reached does not admit of further explanation, but on the contrary, the tendency towards it must be itself invoked in explaining the system's behaviour. Thus teleological explanation gives us a notion of 'tendency towards' a given condition which involves more than simply the universal and exceptionless movement of events in that direction. For, like Inertia, it concerns not so much how the events move as how they must be accounted for however they move. And yet unlike Inertia it holds that a particular result in a given system is privileged, that, in other words, this result will be brought about unless countervailing factors arise. And thus the notion arises not just of an empirically discovered direction of events, but of a bent or pressure of events towards a certain consummation, one which can only be checked by some countervailing force. This, then, is the force of the notion of 'power' or 'natural tendency', not the *de facto* trend of events, but rather a press of events, which lies behind the view that order exhibited in the behaviour of living organisms does not come about by 'accident', but is somehow part of their 'essential nature'.[1]

---

[1] The principle of asymmetry seems to be invoked in a doctrine held by some thinkers: e.g., R. S. Peters, *The Concept of Motivation*, pp. 9–16; cf. also D. W. Hamlyn, *The Psychology of Perception*, about the role of causal explanations in terms of the physiological substratum in accounting for behaviour.

We can see, then, why this view is resisted, for the result of the Galilean revolution was precisely to sweep away all the asymmetries of Aristotelian science, between 'natural' and 'violent' movement, between sub- and supra-lunar events, and so on, and to replace them by a homeogeneous science of nature in which all the differences could be accounted for in terms of the same set of antecedent variables. But, although understandable, the resistance is not thereby necessarily justified. For whether or not an explanation of a teleological sort holds is plainly an empirical matter. And therefore whether the principle of asymmetry is valid and whether the most basic laws are of this sort are also empirical questions. The inadequacy of Aristotelian physics lay not in any inherent absurdity, but in its gross inadequacy in accounting for natural events. But to assume from the superiority of Galilean principles in the sciences of inanimate nature that they *must* provide the model for the sciences of animate behaviour is to make a speculative leap, not to enunciate a necessary conclusion.

These causal factors are held to be *necessary* but not *sufficient* conditions of behaviour. They do provide, however, '*sufficient* conditions for breakdowns in performance, as in the case of brain lesions, by indicating a necessary condition which was absent'. Peters, op. cit., p. 16. This might be interpreted as the thesis that the normal operation of the organism follows teleological laws. We can therefore never give sufficient conditions for normal behaviour in terms of 'casual' (i.e., non-teleological) antecedent conditions, whether these be physiological or of any other kind. But we can so account for breakdowns or non-natural functioning. The negations of these causal conditions for breakdown, then, are conditions for the normal functioning. But these being 'causal' (i.e., non-teleological) are not sufficient conditions, but only conditions *sine qua non*.

Thus the existence and freedom from damage of certain organs may be a necessary condition for certain behaviour. But a sufficient condition would be a state of these organs together with states of others and the environment which constituted together an antecedent of a teleological type. Without the existence and capacity to function of these organs such a global state couldn't exist, but the existence of the organ is not the cause of the state (its sufficient condition) and therefore not the cause (the sufficient condition) of the behaviour either. The widespread assumption that, because certain physiological states are *necessary* conditions of behaviour, behaviour must be accounted for by non-teleological physiological laws involves an illegitimate inference.

II

ACTION AND DESIRE

IN the last chapter, we tried to give an account of teleological explanation, and specifically to refute the charge that explanations of this kind were non-empirical or 'metaphysical' in a pejorative sense of that term. The purpose was to make clearer what is meant by explanation in terms of purpose, which, as we saw, involves a teleological type of explanation. To simplify the discussion, we treated these two as equivalent, but, in fact, there is more to explanation by purpose than simply the teleological form; it is, one might say, a form of teleological explanation with special features of its own. It is time, then, to lift the simplifying assumption of the last chapter and to attempt an analysis of these special features.

In order to do this it will be best to turn to the paradigm of all explanations by purpose, which is the form of explanation implicit in our ordinary everyday account of human behaviour. In this chapter, we shall try to show that our language does presuppose that our behaviour should be explained in a certain way, and to outline what this is. In the next chapter, we shall try to state more clearly what this form is and how it is related to teleological explanation in general.

We shall thus examine the ordinary notions 'action' and 'desire' and the related notions by which we describe and explain our own behaviour and that of others. There will, however, be one disadvantage involved in this procedure which we should make clear at the outset. For our discussion will be centred around human behaviour, to which these concepts are primarily applied.

But we generally want to claim a special status, as 'purposive' beings, for animals as well as men. If 'explanation by purpose' is to be taken in its wider sense, the discussion in this chapter may narrow our scope unduly. We shall turn, therefore, in the latter part of the next chapter to discuss whether, or the extent to which, the features noted in our examination of human behaviour can meaningfully be attributed to the behaviour of animals. But, for the present, our discussion will deal, for the most part, with the behaviour of men.

I. ACTIONS AND GOALS

Let us look first at the notion of action. Implicit in our everyday notion of action is that of 'direction' to a goal or end. That is, our ordinary action concepts generally pick out the behaviour they are used to describe not just by its form or overt characteristics or by what it actually brings about, but also by the form or goal-result which it was the agent's purpose or intention to bring about.

This is part of the force of the notion 'goal'. When we say that actions are classified by their goals, we mean not only that they are classified by the result which in fact is brought about by them, but also by that end to which they are aimed; and that is why we speak of a 'goal'. But the term 'goal' may mislead in another way; for the phenomenon of 'directedness' is in evidence in a wider range of behaviour than that which we usually speak of in terms of goals.

We usually speak of a goal when there is a certain end-condition or change aimed at by an action; and a wide range of actions, from 'jumping the fence' to 'seizing power', are classified by their goals in this sense. But there are many other actions which we shall also want to speak of as directed where there is no such end-condition by which they are characterized separately identifiable from the action itself, as, for instance, 'being on the other side of the fence' and 'being in power' are in relation to the actions instanced above. Such are, for instance, dancing, walking, running, and so on. Now we often want to speak of behaviour classified in this way as directed, but what is being aimed at in these cases is not some end-condition but simply the emitting of the behaviour of the required type; and the end is not a result separately identifiable from the action but simply the action's having a certain form or fulfilling a certain description. In these cases it would perhaps be less misleading to speak of a 'criterion' being fulfilled rather than a 'goal' being aimed at in the action, but it will simplify matters if we can adopt one term to apply to all cases of directed behaviour, and we shall therefore speak, in what follows, of 'goals' in a special extended sense in which any action can be said to have a goal.[1]

Thus our ordinary action concepts generally pick out behaviour as 'goal-directed' in this extended sense. But we have to qualify this thesis with the term 'generally', because in fact the borderline between the behaviour we call action and that to which we refuse the name is very ill-defined. And this in turn arises from the fact that there is no sharp demarcation between directed behaviour and that other range of an organism's movements which cannot be described in this way. There are of course clear cases of both kinds. Blinking is clearly not directed, while running for president is; but between these there lies a whole gamut of intermediate cases many of which cannot unambiguously be put in one category or the other. The scale runs from blinking, shivering and sneezing, through yawning and laughing, to fidgeting

[1] Of course, these two classes of action are not exclusive. Any action may bear many descriptions, and some of these may be of different types. Thus a professional dancer is not only dancing but also earning his living or making money. An activity not itself identified by its result can be undertaken for an 'ulterior motive' and thus also have a goal in the usual restricted sense. It can also itself be the goal of other actions, as when I put on tails, hail a taxi, etc., all in order to go dancing. But there is also the opposite case of play, where an action usually done for an 'ulterior motive' is undertaken for its own sake. Thus I may jump fences all afternoon, not in order to get anywhere, but 'just for fun'. In a sense, we can say in such a case that 'being on the other side' isn't the goal of the action any more, for it isn't the 'point' of what I am doing; that is, if I were miraculously translated to the other side, I wouldn't have achieved what I set out to do or was aiming at in undertaking the activity and might even feel frustrated. But in another sense being on the other side is part of the point, since if I weren't on the other side of the fence after the jump my action wouldn't have reached the criterion, fulfilling the description 'jumping the fence', which I set myself as my goal in the extended sense. Much of the 'pointless' activity of play is action where the goal-state which is usually also what is being aimed at in the action, or the goal in our extended sense, is this no longer, but the goal is simply the performance of the action itself. Play is thus often an imitation of 'serious' activity with the serious 'point' removed.

and doodling, then to walking, writing, speaking, where we come
to behaviour which is virtually always directed. Much of the
behaviour on this scale might be called 'action' in a loose sense,
even where we would not wish to speak of 'direction'. But it
would not deviate too much from the normal sense of the term
if we used it in a strong or restricted sense, according to which
only directed behaviour can be spoken of as action, and this is
what we propose to do in what follows.

How, then, can we tell what is directed behaviour? It is, as
we mentioned above, that it is characterized by terms the criteria
for whose application are two-fold. Thus for something to be an
action in the strong sense, it is not only necessary that it end in the
result or meet the criterion by which actions of this kind are
characterized, but it must also be the case that the agent's intention or purpose was to achieve this result or criterion. In other
words, the agent must not only make the appropriate movements,
it must also be his intention or purpose to do so. It is this second
criterion which gives its point to the language of 'attempt' and
'achievement', which can only, therefore, be used in connexion
with action in the strong sense. For when a piece of behaviour
fails to meet the first criterion for an action of type X, i.e., when
the result doesn't occur, or the criterion is not achieved, we can
still speak of it as an 'attempt at X' if it meets the second criterion,
i.e., if it was intended or aimed to achieve this result or criterion.
Where the second criterion is irrelevant, on the other hand, we
cannot speak of 'trying'. Similarly, when the action comes off,
we can speak of 'achievement'. For this implies that some
standard aimed at has been met, and here the standard is provided
by the goal aimed at. If this were not the case, 'achievement'
could not be used. The notions 'goal', 'attempt', 'achievement'
are closely linked, and this complex of notions applies where-
ever we have to do with action in the strong sense.

Now it is clear that most of what we normally call action meets
both these criteria, that, in fact, we usually require that both be
met before we will speak of action. Thus, when a given piece of
behaviour meets the first but not the second criterion for X, we
often refuse to call it an X. It is necessary to be cautious here
because there are two types of cases. It may be that the piece
of behaviour will not meet the second criterion for any action
at all, as in the case of a man undergoing an epileptic fit. In this

case the behaviour is not 'directed', that is, there is nothing that the man meant or intended to do. And here we withhold all action descriptions, and therefore description X, even if the behaviour meets the first criterion for X (which might be, say, a step in the latest dance-form of some youth sub-culture). But there are other cases where a man meant or intended to do something, but not this action which is attributed to him. And here our ordinary practice is less clear.

Sometimes we withhold the description. Thus we would deny that Socrates had corrupted the youth, even though we might agree that the effect of his teaching in that social context on many of his pupils was bound to be destructive of a sense of moral restraint. At other times we maintain the description but qualify it with such terms as 'unknowingly', 'out of ignorance', 'by mistake', 'by accident', 'by inadvertence', and so on. There are many reasons why we treat the different cases differently. One of the principal ones, which arises out of the Socrates case above, is their connexion with the attribution of responsibility. Thus it is possible for me to be held morally or legally responsible for something I didn't intend to do. I may do something by accident or unwittingly in circumstances where I should have taken precautions or taken the trouble to find out. In these cases I may be blamed or punished, although the sentence may be mitigated. And since I am responsible for the event it is naturally attributed to me as an action, although with qualification. On the other hand, in cases, say, of genuinely non-culpable ignorance, such as to remove from me all blame, the action is usually not attributed to me. Thus, if in passing the salt to my table companion in the dining-car of the Simplon Orient, I am passing him a receptacle which contains NATO's secret plans, I cannot be blamed for the resulting disclosure to the other side. We would certainly not say that I had given away the secret. If however I, too, were an agent and knew the custom among Balkan spies of transmitting information through salt-cellars: If I passed this one because I thought that, for a change, it just contained salt, and I could have and didn't check, then I am rightly blamed for what ensues, and in this case we say that I *did* disclose the information, although I am not a Bolshevik agent and didn't do it deliberately but unknowingly. We can attribute responsibility, then, outside the paradigm context where a man commits an action in the un-

qualified sense because the gap between intention and performance should have been overcome by him, and therefore he is still
to blame. But the notion of responsibility is closely linked to
that of action; if a man is rightly attributed responsibility for an
action, then it follows that he did it; so we attribute the action to
him, but with qualifications.[1]

Sometimes again we attribute to someone an action which he
didn't intend to commit if it resembles what he did intend in some
essential respect. Thus, in those cases where the behaviour is
such that we can distinguish between act and object, and where
the intention was to do the action but not to this object, we
often attribute the actual result to the agent. Thus the innocent
in the Simplon express might be held to have *handed the plans* to
the agent, because he did intend to hand him something, the
salt-cellar, and this happened to include the plans.

Again, we sometimes attribute actions to people where the
results concerned are what we could call 'causally close' to what
they intended. Thus, if in doing something intentionally, I inadvertently bring about some other result—as when in rising
from my seat, I clumsily knock over the lamp—the action
defined by this result is often attributed to me, although in a
qualified way; for instance, in this case, I am said to have knocked
over the lamp, although accidentally. But we only do this when
the causal link between the action I performed intentionally and
the unintended result is relatively direct and obvious, or when
the link has been set up by human agency directly to produce this
result, as when in pressing the appropriate button, I am held to
have rung the bell, even though I expected some other result. But
if the link is longer, more complex or more uncertain, the attribution cannot be upheld. Thus the assassin Prinzip cannot be said
to have brought on the First World War, nor the incompetent
electrician who installs faulty wiring to have set fire to the house.[2]

---

[1] We can therefore see what separates us from Socrates' accusers. Let us
suppose that the gap here between intention and performance could only be
closed by silence, i.e., the only way that the resulting unintended moral
corruption of Critias, Alcibiades, etc., could have been avoided would have
been for Socrates not to teach at all. Then the validity of the accusation hangs
on the question whether the gap should have been closed, whether the price
—Socrates' silence—is not too high.

[2] There are also cases where we may attribute an action to someone in spite
of his disclaimer. Thus a man may vigorously disclaim that what he is doing

Thus the notion of action normally involves that of behaviour directed towards a goal. For action terms generally cannot be applied at all unless behaviour is directed to some goal, and specific action terms cannot be applied in an unqualified manner unless behaviour is directed towards the specific goal concerned. In many cases where this condition is not met we do not apply the action term even in a qualified way. And where we do, there seems to be usually some link between intention and performance; either the act intended and that attributed are similar in some essential way, or they are joined by some close causal link, or the gap between the two itself falls into the range of the responsibility of the agent, i.e., the fact that there is a gap can itself be considered the result of the agent's action or inaction. In any case, enough has been said to show that the normal notion of an action is of a piece of behaviour which not only brings about a certain condition but is directed towards bringing about that condition as an end.

2. ACTION AND DIRECTION

But why do we speak of the second criterion, that concerning intention or purpose, as the requirement that behaviour be 'directed'? What is the justification for speaking of the 'direction' of behaviour? The justification lies in the fact that whether or not the second criterion applies has something to do with the way we account for behaviour. Using this notion 'behaviour', as we have done above, in a general non-committal sense in which it can range over both action and non-action, we can say that in classifying some behaviour as an action, we are accounting, in a sense, for the fact that it meets the first criterion for an action of this sort, i.e., has a certain overt form or brings about a certain result, by the fact that it meets the second criterion, i.e., was

---

can be described as avenging himself, but only seeking justice. And he may not be lying. And yet we may want to attribute the action to him. But, in this type of case, it is not that the second criterion, that concerning the goal towards which the action is aimed, has been relaxed. For an essential part of the hypothesis that the man was really doing the action is the claim that, in some unconscious way, he intended to. For the question here hinges on motive. Should this claim be shown to be mistaken, the hypothesis falls to the ground. Cf. below, pp. 58–61.

meant to do this by the agent. For that something is an action in the strong sense means not just that the man who displayed this behaviour had framed the relevant intention or had this purpose, but also that his intending it brought it about. That is, it is not a sufficient condition of an action's occurring that a man intend to do something and that behaviour answering to the relevant description occur. For it is perfectly conceivable—and, indeed, happens in rare cases—that the two be unconnected, and the behaviour occur for some other reason. And in these cases we do not characterize the behaviour as an action in the strong sense. Thus I may decide, for a joke, to jump as if startled when something occurs, and when it does I may really be startled and jump involuntarily. Or I may decide to stab someone, and, before I can execute my intention, my arm may be pushed. In these cases we would not say that I had acted, i.e., that I had committed the action of jumping or stabbing; and this fact might be of the first importance, e.g., in the latter case, because of the connexion of 'responsibility' with 'action' and the legal and moral consequences which flow from this.[1]

Thus the distinction between action and non-action hangs not just on the presence or absence of the corresponding intention or purpose, but on this intention or purpose having or not having a role in bringing about the behaviour. With action, we might say, the behaviour occurs because of the corresponding intention or purpose; where this is not the case, we are not dealing with action. But to use the expression 'because of' here might mislead. For we could not say that the intention was the causal antecedent of the behaviour. For the two are not contingently connected in the normal way. We are not explaining the behaviour by the 'law', other things being equal, intending X is followed by doing X, for this is part of what we mean by 'intending X', that, in the absence of interfering factors, it is followed by doing X. I could not be said to intend X if, even with no obstacles or other countervailing factors, I still didn't do it. Thus my intention is not a causal antecedent of my behaviour.

But to call something action is like citing a causal antecedent

[1] There are, of course, borderline cases, where we use such expressions, e.g., as 'accidentally on purpose', but as the paradoxical nature of this expression implies, these do not undermine the validity of the distinction which can be clearly applied in most cases.

in that it rules out other such antecedents and sets the type of explanation which is appropriate. We have already seen this in the examples above, where accounts of behaviour in terms of reflex or the agent's being pushed are enough to disqualify this behaviour as action. Thus to call something an action, while not to subsume the behaviour under any law, does involve ruling out certain rival accounts, those incompatible with the implied claim that the intention brought about the behaviour. Now a rival account must be one according to which changing the intention, other things being equal, would have no effect on the behaviour; that is, a rival account of some behaviour event B would be an account according to which B would occur[1] on this antecedent condition, whether or not the agent intended to do B.[2] Thus, if a given piece of behaviour is rightly classified as an action, then we cannot account for it by some causal antecedent, where the law linking antecedent (E) to behaviour (B) is not itself conditional on some law or rule governing the intention or purpose. For if the law linking E to B were not dependent on some law linking E and the intention or purpose, I, to do B, then $E - B$ would hold whether or not $E - I$ held. But then B would occur on E whether the corresponding intention was present or not. And then, even when it is present, it cannot be said to bring about the behaviour, so long as this is done by E.

[1] B would occur, that is, in the absence of counter-vailing factors. This qualification is necessary, for it is always possible that a reflex could be inhibited by a contrary intention, as, e.g., shivering sometimes can, but this behaviour when uninhabited would still not be called 'action' for intention does not enter into the account of its occurrence. That is, that it tends to occur on this antecedent condition is a fact which holds of it independently of the state of the agent's intention.

[2] One might cite against this reasoning cases where an action is 'over-determined', that is cases where there is more than one motive for an action, such that if one didn't hold the other would suffice. But this concept only makes sense in talking of action. One could not say that a given movement could be *both* determined as a reflex and motivated as an action; for the one characterization excludes the other. There are, of course, apparent counter-examples; e.g., where we hold a man responsible and blame him for some 'reflex' behaviour. But in these cases we either mean that he could, perhaps with great effort, have inhibited the behaviour, or that he knew that this behaviour would follow from this antecedent and still did nothing to avoid the latter. But neither of these cases show the behaviour itself to be *action*. I may be held responsible for the damage done by an avalanche or fire that I negligently start, but this doesn't make the avalanche or the fire action.

Thus to account for B in terms of E would be to offer a rival account, to disqualify B as an action.

Thus to classify behaviour as action is to rule out a certain type of account. It is to set the type of laws by which it can be explained. The difference between the two types of law can be seen from an example. If I say of someone that he struck me, it is compatible with this claim that his behaviour be accounted for by some such law as, 'he strikes whoever contradicts him', or even on some more wildly irrational hypothesis, such as, 'he strikes every fifth person he meets'. But it could not be explained by some law to the effect that, e.g., whenever a light flashes, his arm moves in this way. For in the former cases, these are the conditions of his behaviour because they are conditions of his intending or having the purpose of behaving in this way. It may be that he wants to strike those who contradict him because they make him angry, or that he has adopted a policy, which he sticks to whatever the unpleasant consequences, or however big the fifth person may be. In this second case, he can be said to have formed a conditional intention beforehand. But in both these cases, the regularities in his behaviour are regularities in his intentions or desires, and we can alter his behaviour by inducing him to change his policy or accept opposition with greater tolerance. In the latter type of case, however, we are saying that the tendency to lash out is independent of any intentions or desires which are conditional on or arise from the light flashing. And for this reason we cannot class this movement as an action.

There are, of course, lots of borderline cases, some of them pathological. But to the extent that we discovered that the tendency to strike was resistant to changes in his desires or intentions, to that extent we would hesitate to call this 'action.'[1]

The notion 'action' is linked in this way with 'responsibility'. When we speak of action, we are accounting for the behaviour in terms of the man's desires, intentions and purposes. And this is why we hold him responsible. Here, too, there are, of course, gradations. The adoption of some policies, e.g., our example above, may itself be a pathological sign. Certain purposes or desires may be resistant to changes in other long-term and

---

[1] The more likely case would be, of course, that the desire be repressed, but continue to appear in the aggressive behaviour which would now be 'rationalized' in some way. In this case we would still want to speak of action.

important goals and policies by which we guide our lives, and to the extent that this is true we are judged less responsible for having them and acting on them than others might be. But an attribution of responsibility is cancelled out altogether if we can show that the behaviour concerned was not an action, that intentions were irrelevant to it.

Thus the laws by which we explain action must be such that the antecedent is the condition of the agent having a certain intention or purpose, whether because it gives rise to a desire, or is the object of a certain policy, so that the regularity in his behaviour is conditional on the regularity of his intentions or purposes. A behaviour law which fulfils this condition can be called a 'law governing action', while one which relates antecedent to behaviour unconditionally can be called a 'law governing movement'. The point could then be put in this way, that action can only be accounted for by laws governing action; that once we can explain behaviour by laws governing movement, we are no longer dealing with action.

Thus part of the reason why we speak of actions as 'directed' is that actions are to be explained by laws governing action, and thus to be accounted for in terms of intentions or purposes. But the notion of direction is given its specific force by the fact that explanation in terms of intentions or purposes is explanation in terms of goals. For in characterizing a man's intention in doing something we are characterizing the goal, in our extended sense of this term, which the action was meant to fulfil, and if we account for his behaviour by the fact that he intended X, then we are accounting for it by the fact that X was his goal.

It is because of the role of 'intention' and similar concepts in explaining action that we can frequently offer as an explanation of someone's behaviour a redescription of this behaviour as an action of some kind. Thus, if a man is groping about in the dark and reaching for the ceiling, 'he's trying to fix the light' is an answer to the question 'what is he doing?', but also to the question 'why is he doing that?'. For in characterizing the action we are characterizing his intention, and in characterizing the intention we are accounting for the behaviour. And it is because of the connexion between 'intention' and 'goal' that the answer which redescribes the behaviour can often be replaced by a simple statement of the goal. Thus to the question, 'why do you work?', it is equally appropriate to answer by identifying the goal ('to make money') or by redescribing the action ('I'm earning my living').

In short the *redescription* of an action can be an *explanation* of that action because it gives the goal for the sake of which the action was undertaken, because the fact that something meets the second criterion for an action of a certain type means that it is to be explained by the goal which defines actions of that type. And this is the case whether it meets the first criterion for this type of action or not. For where it does not we speak of the action which occurred, Y, as an attempt at some other action, X, and this means that the occurrence of Y is to be accounted for by the goal of X.

And this is why, in redescribing some behaviour as an action of type A, or as an attempt at A, we are saying that this behaviour will, in the situation—or in the situation as seen by the agent[1]— bring about the goal of A. If this is not the case, then the attribution of A will have to be withdrawn. If, for instance, the behaviour is not adequate to the goal of A, we can only maintain our claim that it is an 'attempt at A' by upholding the claim that the agent has certain (false) beliefs according to which his action will reach this goal. But this redescription of behaviour in terms of a goal it achieves or is thought to achieve is also an explanation, as we have seen, and this means that the behaviour is held to occur because of its adequacy or believed adequacy to the goal. And this is what allows us to speak of that behaviour which meets the second criterion for action as 'behaviour directed to a goal'.

3. ACTION AND ITS EXPLANATION

Our ordinary account of behaviour as action, therefore, usually involves characterizing it as behaviour directed to a goal. And this means that it also involves a form of teleological explanation. For to account for behaviour in terms of its goal is to say that it occurs 'for the sake of' that goal. Our ordinary account is thus, insofar as it makes use of the notion of action in the strong sense, teleological in form. But this teleological form is not only

---

[1] This qualification is obviously very important in any account of the behaviour of animate organisms. We shall raise it again in the next chapter.

provided by 'action', it is also implicit in other explanatory notions of common speech, notably that of desire or wanting. For part of what is meant by 'desire' is the disposition to bring about what is desired. That is, to say that someone wants something is to say that he is disposed to do it or get it, in this sense, that his desiring it issuing in the appropriate action neither requires nor admits of explanation, while the action's not ensuing demands that we adduce some counter-vailing factor if we are to maintain the claim that he wants the thing concerned. Explanations in terms of desire, therefore, introduce the type of asymmetry into our account of behaviour which we noticed above, for they assume a press or tendency in the behaviour of the being which desires towards a certain consummation.

Our ordinary language account is teleological, then, because at the basis of much of our everyday explanation of action is the notion of desire. This notion is involved whenever we attribute a 'motive'. For attributing a motive is often stating the end which was wanted in undertaking the action (e.g., 'he was after the money'). Then in some cases we name the motive by characterizing the 'psychic energy' behind the act, i.e., by citing what are usually called feelings or emotions, such as fear, envy, greed, pride, anger, shame, guilt, or desire (in the sense of sexual desire). But the citing of these emotions is only explanatory of behaviour insofar as they are linked to certain desires, so that to anyone to whom they can be truthfully ascribed there can be ascribed the tendency, albeit perhaps inhibited, to display behaviour of a certain type. Thus fear is linked to the desire to escape, and therefore it can serve as a motive-term. Similarly, if I explain the fact that many people who are entitled to it do not resort to the National Assistance Board by invoking pride, i.e., because the action or the experience would be humiliating to them, this can function as an explanation because part of what we mean by something being humiliating is that people generally and normally desire to avoid it.

It seems, then, that our ordinary account of behaviour is teleological in form. But it is not yet clear exactly what is meant by 'teleological form'. Does it mean simply that everyday explanation makes use of teleological concepts? Or are the implications more far-reaching: Does the use of these concepts imply in some way that *only* a teleological explanation is appropriate, and that the basic-level laws are teleological in form? Behind this question, however, lies a further one: Does the fact that we use these notions in daily speech mean that the implications of their use, whatever these may be, must be true? It is sometimes held that this must be so, that if one could show that such concepts could only be correctly applied in their present sense to beings whose behaviour followed teleological laws (that is, where the basic level laws were teleological) this would be sufficient to show that the beings to which they are commonly applied are of this kind. This premiss is at the root of many arguments which purport to show, from the nature of our ordinary concepts, that a non-teleological or non-purposive explanation is impossible.

But first we shall try to answer the first question, and discover what the implications of our ordinary concepts are. One line of enquiry might be to ask whether our ordinary language offers an account of behaviour in terms of natural or inherent tendencies, an account, that is, where the basic level laws are teleological in type. But this question, as it stands, is badly posed. For our ordinary explanation does not offer any particular account of our behaviour. In other words, there is no such thing as the common sense theory of behaviour. When people speak of some scientific theory of behaviour as 'conflicting with common sense' they are generally speaking of a view commonly held in their society or milieu. But this notoriously differs from the views which are commonly held in other societies, and so if we wish to speak of a 'commonsense view' in this sense, we must say that there is not one but several.

Of course, these views, although not theories, generally have certain features which are analogous to theories of a teleological kind. Thus commonsense views often contain 'stopping points' beyond which further questioning is inappropriate or unintelligible. And since these often invoke a desire or goal, which is thought of as 'natural', they play an analogous role to the 'inherent tendencies' of teleological explanation. Thus an example of a stopping point of this kind would be if someone replied to the question, 'why are you doing that?', by saying 'my life depends on it'. This is a stopping point because, unless some special factors are adduced (such as, 'after the disasters you have suffered, life should be nothing to you', or 'what is life without honour?'), we do not know how to go about answering the question, 'why do you want to preserve your life?'. The end of self-preservation is thought of as inherently desirable, as something that men 'naturally' desire, so that no further explanation can be offered.

But the features of common-sense views provide us evidence only about what most men have believed about themselves, whereas we are trying to discover what the form of explanation is which is implicit in our everyday account, whatever theory we accept of human motivation, or whatever view has wide currency in our society. And we want to know in particular whether this form is compatible with an explanation in terms of basic laws which are non-teleological in type. Our question is, then, whether the concepts we use in our everyday account can be applied without change of meaning to beings whose behaviour could be explained by non-teleological laws.

The answer to this question, as far as the concept 'action' is concerned, must be in the negative. Let us suppose that we had discovered a set of non-teleological laws by which we could account for our behaviour. By these, the ordinary rough and ready correlations and laws governing action by which we account for what we do at present would be explained on a more basic level. This is roughly what is imagined by some thinkers in the field of cybernetics research.[1] Thus the fact that the mechanism (or, in this instance, the human being) is emitting a particular type of behaviour at this moment can be accounted for by the way it has been programmed, the correlation between this programming and this behaviour being an instance of some general law. In this way the behaviour can be accounted for by this law or laws, which constitute a level of explanation more basic than our everyday account since we shall now be able to derive our observed correlations between behaviour and its antecedent conditions from this law.

Now since these basic laws are to be non-teleological, they must be laws governing movement and not laws governing action, i.e., they must not make use of the notion of 'direction'. This might be thought enough to end the matter, since actions can only be accounted for by laws governing action, and therefore an explanation of this kind would show that we are no longer

[1] Cf. Rosenbleuth and Wiener, op. cit.

dealing with action. But the matter is more complicated. First, it might be claimed that these were also laws governing action, that, in other words, our distinction breaks down at this point. For the laws linking programming conditions to behaviour will also link these conditions to intention, or what we now might call intention, if these laws are really such that we can derive our present correlations governing action from them. That is, these laws will have not only to explain why we emit the behaviour we do but also why we desire or intend to emit this behaviour. Thus the antecedent condition of programming will be an antecedent both of intention and behaviour.

Now it is perfectly true that the distinction between these two types of laws was not framed to fit this case, that, indeed, as we hope to show, it presupposes that this case does not arise. But this does not mean that the distinction breaks down here, that these basic laws govern both action and movement. For the criterion for a law governing action is that the regularity it outlines in behaviour is conditional on a regularity in the intentions or purposes of the agent, and our putative basic laws certainly do not meet this. For *ex hypothesi* the connexion between antecedent and behaviour cannot be changed by altering that between the antecedent and intention, for the intention cannot be changed without the antecedent being changed also.

But this is still a misleading way to put it. It sounds as though the difficulty were simply that we could not test the hypothesis that these laws governed action. But this misunderstanding arises from the assumption that the notion 'intention' and related notions would have the same meaning in an account of a non-teleological kind as it has in ordinary speech. But this is not the case. In fact, 'intention', for instance, could be given two senses both of which differ from its normal one. Thus behaviour would be explained by some antecedent condition of programming which determined that the mechanism should be guided, say, in a certain way, i.e., such that this behaviour would be emitted. In this way we could account for some common-sense law to the effect that environmental condition E leads to behaviour B, by the fact that E leads to programming condition P which is the antecedent condition for B according to the law. But now let us say that $E - B$ is a law governing action; what sense could be given to the notion of 'intention' here? We could either identify intention as some

41

subjective state, that is, the thoughts or feelings which accompanied B, or what the man said to himself when doing B; but this would deviate from our normal sense, for this allows us to say that we are deceived or mistaken about our intentions, i.e., about what is actually bringing about our behaviour; or we could preserve the role of intention in accounting for behaviour by identifying it by the programming condition itself, such that a man's intending B meant simply that condition P obtained, where P was the antecedent of B; but this would deviate from our normal use in that the 'intention' would be a causal antecedent of the behaviour.

Now if one adopted the first meaning, then the connexion between P and the intention would be a contingent one, and the fact that the intention (I) could not be changed without P being changed would rest simply on the fact that P was the causal antecedent of I. But in this case, $P - B$ would not be conditional on $P - I$. That is, we could interfere with $P - I$ without interfering with $P - B$. And therefore $P - B$ and the more general law from which it was deduced would be laws governing movement purely and not action. And if one adopted the second meaning, the connexion between P and I would be necessary, the impossibility of altering the second without altering the first would be a logical one, and then, in this case also, $P - B$ could not be conditional on $P - I$ in a causal sense. Thus, once more, $P - B$ (or $I - B$) would be a law governing movement only and not action.

Thus the basic laws of such a non-teleological explanation would not be laws governing action, and as such we would be tempted to deny any behaviour which fell under them the title of action. This is, indeed, the way the problem has often been seen. This is evident in what one might call the 'Canute view' of behaviour. Many fear or hope that the gradual progress of scientific explanation of behaviour will bring more and more of our actions under laws of this kind, with the consequence that, one by one, they will be deprived of this status and relegated to the category of non-action. Along with this—and this is often the principal ground of interest in the subject—the area in which we can attribute responsibility, deal out praise or blame, or mete out reward or punishment, will steadily diminish—until in the limiting case, nothing will be left; the courts will be closed or become institutes of human engineering, moral discourse will be relegated to the lumber-room of history, and so on.

The prospect—even if based on a rather shaky extrapolation from our greater understanding of pathological cases—is frightening, or at least awe-inspiring, according to the way one looks at such matters. But it will already be evident that this way of putting it is rather misleading. For the distinction between action and non-action, like many other fundamental distinctions, could not survive unchanged the discovery that all the phenomena it ranged over in fact fell on one side of it. And we have already seen that notions like 'intention' suffer some distortion when we try to apply them to our hypothetical case of a systematic non-teleological explanation. In fact we would still be able to, and presumably want to, distinguish falling off a cliff, and blinking, from earning our living or running for president, and the first class would be accounted for by the law of gravity or some reflex law, and the second by our basic laws of programming. But the distinction would differ from our present one between action and non-action for it could no longer hang on whether or not it is the intention which brings about the behaviour. For if the claim that this is so can be defeated, as at present, by offering a rival explanation; and if a rival explanation is one where the behaviour is held to follow from an antecedent according to a law which is not itself causally dependent on a law linking antecedent and intention; then nothing qualifies as an action. And, if we drop this interpretation and take the most suitable one in the new circumstances, such that behaviour is action when it can be subsumed under the laws about programming, then we are using 'intention' in a new sense, in which its link with the corresponding behaviour is purely contingent.

Thus our present distinction would be of no use to us. It assumes that we can oppose explanation by intention to explanation by laws governing movement. But in the new dispensation this would be impossible. For, on the most likely interpretation, explanation by intention would itself be a form of explanation by laws governing movement. (And, on the less likely interpretation, where 'intention' meant some accompanying subjective state, it would explain nothing at all.) The distinction is thus not framed to meet this case. It requires that we be able to identify as intention or purpose something which is not a causal antecedent in that it is not contingently linked with the behaviour it brings about, and yet is like an antecedent in that it excludes other ones, i.e., excludes all explanation by antecedents in normal causal laws, i.e., laws governing movement. We have to identify, as it were, an 'antecedent' which is non-contingently linked with its consequent. For otherwise there will be nothing called intention to oppose to explanation by laws governing movement. There is thus a factual premiss at the basis of this distinction, of the belief, that is, that it can be applied. And this premiss would be shown to be wrong if an explanation by non-teleological laws were shown to hold. Thus, in this case, our present distinction between action and non-action, and hence our present notion of action could not be applied.

This point can be put in another way. Because explanation by intentions or purposes is like explanation by an 'antecedent' which is non-contingently linked with its consequent, i.e., because the fact that the behaviour follows from the intention other things being equal is not a contingent fact, we cannot account for this fact by more basic laws. For to explain a fact by more basic laws is to give the regularities on which this fact causally depends. But not being contingent, the dependence of behaviour on intention is not contingent on anything, and hence not on any such regularities. The conditions can only be specified in such phrases as 'other things being equal' or 'in the absence of countervailing factors' which can only be given meaning by reference to the 'law' itself, that behaviour follows from intention. Thus the only scope left for more basic laws of behaviour lies in discovering the determinants of intention, that is, the laws must be laws governing action. For if we introduce a more basic law governing movement $B = f(p)$, this can only be compatible with the behaviour being brought about by the intention (I) if $I - B$ can be derived from $B = f(p)$. But $I - B$ cannot be derived from anything, for it is not a contingent correlation. It follows that our accounting for behaviour by a law governing movement is incompatible with its being brought about by the intention or purpose concerned, and therefore with its being action in the usual sense of the term.

Thus our notion of action would have to change with a systematic non-teleological explanation of behaviour. It could no longer hang on the role of intention in the present sense of the term. The difference would be this: That to say that something was an action, that is, was brought about by intention in the new sense, would be to say that its occurrence could be explained by the law, $B = f(p)$. To classify something as an action would be to subsume it under a law. But this is not what we normally mean when we attribute an action to someone. Thus when I say of someone that he struck me, I am not saying that this bit of behaviour was an instance of a certain law. No doubt this action can be explained by some law or law-like statement, such as our example above, 'he always strikes people who contradict him', but to classify it as an action is not to subsume it under this or any other law. Similarly to identify something as a particular action, that is, to characterize the intention from which it flowed, would be to say that it followed from a particular antecedent P; whereas to identify a particular action in our ordinary use does not involve picking out the antecedent from which it follows (contingently). It is a peculiarity of an action that its having a given direction or being an action of a certain kind is a fact which holds of it independently of the antecedent conditions which give rise to it. We first identify the action and then search for the conditions which brought it about. But this would not be the case in our new dispensation; for, if we are to characterize an action by the nature of the intention, we should have to characterize it by the antecedent condition from which it followed, so that to say that something was an action of type B would be to say that it followed from an antecedent of type P.

4. IS MECHANISM CONCEIVABLE?

Thus, of our ordinary concepts, 'action' at any rate cannot be applied without change of meaning to beings whose behaviour could be explained by non-teleological laws. But does this mean that a non-teleological explanation of human behaviour is impossible? At first sight this might seem a plausible conclusion from the fact that we apply the notion, and very successfully, in describing our behaviour. Surely the fact that we can use it to distinguish between action and non-action is enough to show that the premisses at the basis of this distinction hold, and if they are incompatible with systematic non-teleological explanation, then so much the worse for this.

But this conclusion would be too hasty. The fact that a distinction is made and agreed on does not show that it has been properly understood, that the criteria on which it is putatively made are valid. The history of thought shows this. Thus we can all understand the Aristotelian distinction between 'natural' and 'violent' movement, and will all admit that the things distinguished here really do fall into different categories, but this does not mean that we can accept the criteria on which it was putatively made, can accept that it is really the 'natural' and the 'violent' that are being distinguished. What happened here is that a distinction was in fact made on certain criteria which were wrongly characterized, and the wrong characterization was linked with certain very deeply rooted features of the conceptual scheme of the day. The discovery of the error upset this scheme very considerably.

Our case presents more than one analogy. Among others, our ordinary explanation of action bears a similarity, as we have seen, to the Aristotelian explanation by 'natural movement'. But the important analogy for our present purpose is the general one. If a systematic non-teleological explanation is correct, then we shall be shown to have mischaracterized the distinction between action and non-action. It will not hang on the role of intention as we now understand it, but rather on the laws by which different sorts of behaviour are explained. But as in the case above, it will not be that the things distinguished are not really distinct. On the contrary. It will simply be that we have mischaracterized the criteria on which we have been making it. In fact the ways which we now tell whether we or other men have a given intention, purpose or desire will turn out to be reliable guides to the nature of the laws which are operating. But it will be shown that we are not distinguishing between what we think we are distinguishing between. The putative criteria will not be the real ones.

This may sound odd. Surely, we might say, the criteria on which we distinguish will be in a sense the same, both before and after, although our new knowledge might give us more direct neurophysiological ways of telling. Only the rationale of the distinction, what we think hangs on the criteria, will differ. In other words, the distinction between action and non-action will remain, only the 'metaphysical overtones' will be dropped. Now in a sense the criteria are the same. But this way of putting it is misleading. For this distinction between criteria and their rationale will only appear after the discovery that we have been mistaken. Then we shall be able to distinguish a certain physiognomy of action or certain feelings or thoughts as *signs* of a certain neurophysiological condition of programming. But we will call them 'signs' because observing them will be contrasted with observing the condition itself, or because this way of telling will be contrasted with more reliable and direct ways. Then, having distinguished sign from signified, we shall be able to say that these phenomena were misinterpreted as signs. But, today, your angry expression or action, or my thoughts and feelings cannot usually be called 'signs' of desire or intention. For there is no more direct way of observing or telling what we or others intend to do. In observing these we are observing our desires and intentions. Or so we think. We cannot at this stage distinguish between sign and signified, between the criteria and their interpretation or rationale.

This is in the nature of the case. That is, it follows from our rationale of this distinction that we should not be able to distinguish the criteria from their rationale. For our mischaracterization of these criteria, if it is one, will have been linked, like the one above, with certain deeply rooted features of our conceptual scheme. And it is a requirement of this scheme that sign and signified be not separated. For the scheme requires that we identify, in intention or purpose, a condition which is noncontingently linked with what follows from it. But then it is essential that we be able, at least in some cases, to identify this condition directly, that is, not merely via signs, i.e., phenomena which are only contingently linked with it.[1] For the signs, in this sense, will only contingently be linked with intention and hence with the action. And if we could only observe the signs, we would only be able to observe the antecedents of action, that is, conditions only contingently linked with it. But then our conceptual scheme would collapse; for the only way we could identify something as a sign of the intention to X would be to observe that it was usually followed by X. And then there would

---

[1] Of course, dualism, either of the Cartesian or empiricist kind, did assume just this for all mental phenomena, with the well-known consequences, similar to the ones raised here, that an intelligible account of our use of psychological terms could not be given, and with the inevitable by-products of scepticism and solipsism.

be no way we could distinguish a 'sign of intention to X' from a 'causal antecedent of X'.

In order for us to identify intention, therefore, and hence action, it must be that we can be said to observe it directly, that is, not merely through signs. Intention must have what we can call 'direct expressions' by contrast with the indirect indications afforded by signs. Now in the normal case the behaviour itself which the intention brings about is considered an expression of it in this sense. Uncertainty may arise in borderline cases, but generally speaking observing the behaviour is taken to be observing the intention or purpose pursued. Thus we can read a man's purposes in his actions. And this must be the case if we are to have our present notion of action and identify an action independently of its antecedent conditions. It is only if the systematic non-teleological explanation is shown to hold that the physiognomic features of action by which we identify it as such would be shown to be merely signs of a generally reliable kind that a certain antecedent condition holds, that the 'machine' is programmed in a certain way. But this distinction between sign and signified would accompany, and could not precede the change in the notion of action. The two would be part of the same profound and far-reaching change in our conceptual scheme.

Thus it is a requirement of our conceptual scheme that the criteria of the distinction between action and non-action be not separable from their rationale, that the distinction cannot be separated from its 'metaphysical overtones'. If we have made a mistake it is not that of having misread the signs. It is much deeper. For the singling out of these phenomena as *signs* will only be possible when our present conceptual scheme is overthrown, that is, when the mistake is already behind us.

Thus the fact that we make the distinction that we do between action and non-action offers no guarantee that the type of explanation which it presupposes is the correct one, that the conceptual scheme in which it is embedded is beyond revision. For it is possible that we are making an invalid distinction while still distinguishing things which are really different. The fact that 'action' can't be applied in its present sense to beings whose behaviour could be accounted for by non-teleological laws does not of itself prove that we are not such beings. The issue remains open.

5. MECHANISM AND DESIRE

But what we can say is this: should we discover that we are after all such beings, we would have to alter our notions considerably. And 'action' would not be the only one affected. If 'action' is to be changed, then all the related concepts must be too.

Let us take the notion of desire which includes that of a disposition to action. Here we can see an analogous shift of meaning. The difference which we noticed in the case of 'action' lay in the fact that we would have to identify actions by their causes, that is, to class a given piece of behaviour as action would be to say that it followed from an antecedent of a certain type. But now we recognize action without making any claim about its antecedent conditions.

Now this change comes about through the notion of intention and related notions. For, as we have seen, 'intention' cannot survive the discovery that there is nothing which brings behaviour about and is nevertheless non-contingently linked with it. The notion thus splits apart in the way we described above. Either we take it to mean the subjective state, or the physiognomic signs, but then it is no longer what brings about the action. Or we use it for the antecedent condition of action. And in the latter and more likely case classing something as an action would simply be to subsume it under a certain law.

Now 'desire' would necessarily split apart in the same way as 'intention'. For desiring something is also non-contingently linked with doing it, as we have seen above. That is, that the action follows the desire neither requires nor admits of explanation, whereas its not following does. But now the only sense which could be given to 'disposition to X' which is part of the force of 'desire for X' would be that of an antecedent condition of programming which was the antecedent for X.[1] But this would be contingently linked with X. But then we would be faced with the same choice: Either we could identify desire by certain

---

[1] The antecedent would have to be a condition of programming and not just any antecedent. For we could only distinguish action from non-action by the fact that the former was subsumed under the laws of programming; so that other antecedents, e.g., those of reflex laws, would not be held to determine action, and could not therefore be called desires.

physiognomic characteristics or subjective states,[1] but at the cost of shearing the concept of the force of 'disposition to do', of denying desire its role in bringing about behaviour; or we could retain this force by identifying desire as an antecedent condition contingently linked with the behaviour it brought about. But then to attribute a desire to someone would be to say that the antecedent condition for the corresponding behaviour existed (which would be the condition also for the subjective symptoms of desire). And this is not the force of our present notion at all. For to say of someone that he desires something is not to say anything about the antecedent conditions for the corresponding behaviour. We first identify the desire and then try to discover why the man wants and does this.

And an analogous shift would occur in the status of our criteria for applying the two notions. Just as what we now call seeing what a man's intentions are, or—as we say in our own case—knowing our intentions, would be downgraded to merely observing signs which were a usually reliable guide to 'intention', or the antecedent of action, so what we now call recognizing desires or wants in ourselves or others would be simply observing certain generally reliable physiognomic or subjective signs for 'desire'. Or alternatively, if we still wished to call this 'recognizing desire' then 'desire' itself would be downgraded to designate merely a sign that the antecedent held. Our present scheme requires that we be able sometimes to identify our desires directly, that what we or others want should sometimes, indeed normally, be an open fact. The phenomena by which we identify them, then, must be transparent, as it were, so that the desire can be read through them directly, without having to decode signs according to some correlations established in experience. Thus our scheme is such that we can recognize in ourselves or in others a desire for something (in the sense of a disposition to do something before action has occurred) without our having to recognize it first under some other description, as feeling or behaviour

---

[1] It is hard to find terms to characterize these because of the shift involved in our conceptual scheme. We might want to speak of feelings, but the terms of our present vocabulary for feeling usually carry the force of disposition in one way or another. Thus the feelings which accompany desire are usually characterized as the 'feelings of desire to do so-and-so', e.g., feelings of sexual desire, and hence by what the person who has them is disposed to do.

of a certain sort.[1] Indeed we may be able to give no such description of the feeling or behaviour which usually precedes certain actions beyond saying simply that it is the feeling or behavioural expression of desire. To discover that these phenomena are really only signs of 'desire' in the new sense would be to discover, as it were, that what we thought was transparent was opaque; and this would involve a far-reaching conceptual shift.

The importance of this shift in the notion of desire can also be seen in another way. For 'desire' in the sense of 'disposition to do' would be indistinguishable from intention, since both would be antecedent conditions for behaviour. But, if these two are indistinguishable, then the distinction between things done reluctantly and enthusiastically, between what we do '*malgré nous*' and what we do willingly, will break down, or rather, will have to be drawn in a different way. This distinction is possible on our present scheme because the identification of both desire and intention is independent of the identification of the antecedent conditions for the corresponding action. Thus we may be said not to want to do what we nevertheless are doing or intend to do, and what, presumably, therefore, the antecedent conditions are present for our doing. And thus a distinction is possible between intention and desire, between what we are simply disposed to do and what we also relish, or at least want to do. For not all our dispositions are desires. 'Desire' contains more than the notion of disposition, it contains that of a 'spontaneous disposition', one which 'comes from us', as against one which is imposed by fate or by others, or by convention, or whatever.

But with a systematic non-teleological explanation, this distinction would have to be drawn in a different way. It would have to rest on the presence or absence of those physiognomic or

---

[1] 'Desiring X' can thus be called a 'primary characterization' of a 'mental state', in that this latter doesn't need to be identified first as something else before being identified as a desire. This is what distinguishes a disposition in the sense which is involved in 'desire' from that which is attributed to certain material objects. Thus we can say that something is 'brittle' or 'soluble', and by this mean simply that in certain conditions it will shatter or dissolve. But this can only be a secondary characterization, in this sense, that before something has shattered or dissolved we can only recognize it as brittle or soluble by first identifying it as an A, where A is a class of things (e.g., glass or sugar) which has been found to shatter or dissolve.

subjective states[1] which would be produced by certain programming conditions and not by others. In other words, a desire would be that kind of antecedent which also produced these by-products, and that an action was done willingly would be a fact about its attendant symptoms, and not the way it was brought about. Thus the distinction would no longer have anything to do with the way we *explained* the action, and would no longer have the force of a distinction between what comes from us and what is imposed.

This argument might be contested in the following way. We might imagine a cybernetic system, for instance, with a fairly complex repertoire, which could be placed in situations which conditioned two incompatible results. The stronger would win out; but we could say that one 'tendency' or 'disposition' was inhibited, the weaker one, and therefore that the mechanism acted against desire. Thus we could say that although the antecedent conditions for a given 'action' were present (and hence the machine was 'disposed' to undertake it) it did not occur because the antecedents were present for another act. In this way we could account for action against inclination in terms of conflict. But of course there are many cases of action against inclination that this could not cover; for it is not true that a disposition is always over-ruled by another disposition. Thus I may stay home for the holidays because I have no money, and in a clear sense I do what I don't want. But there is no conflict. In a clear sense I am disposed to do an action the antecedent conditions for which are not present.[2]

But even considering cases which are analogous, which do involve conflict, we could have no grounds for speaking of *desire*

---

[1] Once more it is hard to think of terms to describe these. What we would need is a sense of 'feeling' shorn of its force of 'disposition'. It is a 'feeling' of this sort which seems to have been invoked in Cartesian and empiricist dualism. E.g., men are pushed by pleasure and pain. Here the feeling is a causal antecedent. But like all such it is only contingently the antecedent of the action, i.e., a disposition to do it. Thus feeling and disposition are split. It is only a step to the mechanistic account in which feeling ceases to play even a causal role.

[2] But surely, one might say, the antecedent conditions are present for this, all I lack is the money. But then it may be that the 'antecedent conditions are present' in *this* sense for me to eat mud; all I lack is (enough) money. In one case the disposition comes with the cash, in the other it precedes it. But the whole problem is how we can distinguish these two cases, if we are allowed to speak only of antecedent conditions.

here. The fact that such a mechanism could be said to act against its dispositions would not warrant us in saying that it was acting against inclination. For this we would have to be able to class its dispositions as inclinations. But we would have no grounds for doing this, for the only criterion for the thing having a disposition for X would be that the antecedent conditions for X were present. We would thus not be able to distinguish those 'dispositions' or tendencies which were desires from those which were not.

And, besides, not all cases of conflict are cases of action against inclination. Thus, if I have trouble deciding whether to take my holiday in England or France, whatever the outcome we will not say that I did what I did not want to do. Thus we cannot analyse the distinction between acting willingly and acting reluctantly in terms of conflict alone, even if many cases where we do the latter are cases of conflict. And thus the distinction would have, in a non-teleological system, to rest on the attendant symptoms, and would therefore not be a distinction based on the way we account for the action. And this is where it would differ from our ordinary distinction, and hence where the notion of desire would differ from our ordinary notion.

III

INTENTIONALITY

1. ACTION AND MOVEMENT

THE upshot of this discussion has been that the account of our behaviour implicit in our ordinary language is teleological in form. And this must be taken in a strong sense. It is not just that such notions as 'action' and 'desire' are teleological notions; it is also that their use carries the implication that no non-teleological account is valid. But the discussion of the last pages has clearly shown more than this: It has shown that our everyday account is more than teleological, that it has as well some special features not shared by other such explanations, that it is marked off from others essentially in that it deals with a special type of event.

We can easily see this by an imaginary example. Thus we might conceive of a teleological physical system in which there was a natural tendency towards a certain constellation of elements. The tensions in such a system would be measured in terms of force, and so on. But we would not want to speak of 'action' here. For here too the 'direction' that the events had would be defined by the laws holding of the system of which these events were instances. We would, of course, unlike with non-teleological systems, be able to distinguish between events which were directed and events which were not, between those which followed the bent of the system and those which did not; and this would bring us closer to the distinction between action and non-action. But we still would not be dealing with action because the only evidence conceivable for an event's having a given direction would be that laws held of the system which defined this as the direction, and that this event was an instance of them. Thus we would still be identifying an event's direction by the laws under which it could be subsumed.

Thus something more than teleological explanation is required for us to use the notion of action, and, it follows of course, the notion of desire as well. And this something more is, as we have seen, that we be able to identify the 'direction' of an action, i.e., what kind of action it is, independently of its antecedent condition or the laws by which it is explained. It must be the case that to make an action attribution is to make a statement about this event itself, that is, not one the verification for which lies in laws or regularities which this event instances. But then to describe a given piece of behaviour as directed in a certain way, that is, to characterize it as an action or attempted action, is to ascribe a certain *nature* to this piece of behaviour and not just to subsume it under certain laws.

Thus the directedness of actions has to do with their nature; they are not marked off from other events simply by the way we account for them, by the laws they instance. In this sense actions constitute a type or category of event, one irreducible to movement. The distinction between action and movement is more like that between cows and sheep, than it is like that, say, between a wheel's being turned by hand and its being turned by machine. To say that action is irreducible to movement is to say that the statement that an action has been done is never equivalent to a set of statements describing only movements. This is so even if these statements characterize the movements in terms of the conditions they result in; for a movement which brought about a given result is still not the same thing as an action which was directed towards this result. And this is bound to be so as long as we characterize action by the goal towards which it is directed.[1]

---

[1] This logical barrier is not in any way lowered by the fact that we often characterize actions by the style of movement involved, or the type of instrument used (e.g. 'biting', 'grasping', 'jumping') as well as simply by the end ('obtain', 'arrive'). For that this style of movement occur, or even that it occur in such a way as to end in a certain result or meet a certain criterion (as in the case of, e.g., dancing) is not the same thing as the action's occurring (cf. the epileptic fit).

As a matter of fact we cannot even speak of the movement, in the sense of pure movement, as a usual empirical criterion for saying that an action has

Now the distinction between action and movement carries along with it a distinction between the type of system of which action can be attributed, i.e., organisms, and those of which it cannot. For of the former it can be said that they direct their behaviour, or that part of it which is action, in a sense in which this is not true of the latter. In other words, systems of the former

---

occurred. For when we do use overt behaviour as evidence for intention and hence for action, we almost never speak of *movement* simply, as against action. If I claim that someone tried to hit me, and adduce his movements as evidence, I am not generally talking about the movements which his limbs in fact underwent, but rather about his *directed* movements, i.e., actions. I infer that these movements could have no other aim, given the circumstances, than striking me. If it is shown that the man was completely asleep, the *premiss* of the inference collapses. The gap between movement and action is of little interest to common sense because we rarely use pure movement terms to describe actions.

There is thus an ambiguity in the term 'movement' which can be extended to 'behaviour', for we can mean by it either 'pure movement' or action. This ambiguity is exploited by behaviourism which gains a certain plausibility by moving illicitly from the assertion that we learn about people through their behaviour to the conclusion that we learn about them through the (pure) movements they execute.

The thesis here is to be distinguished from the point about the logical irreducibility of action- to movement-terms made by R. S. Peters; cf. *The Concept of Motivation*, pp. 12–15; Peters speaks of the 'logical gulf between nature and convention'. He points out that it would be impossible to find a set of statements describing movements which were equivalent to a statement like, 'he signed the contract'. But this is not strictly a distinction between action and *movement*; the argument also goes to show the irreducibility of 'signing a contract' to other action terms. For as Peters points out, 'he moved the pen in such and such a way' could not be taken as an equivalence; for it to entail the original, we would have to add certain statements setting out the conventions in terms of which this constituted a signing of the contract; but this composite of statements could not be in turn entailed by the original, for 'he signed the contract' does not specify in any way the conventions in force, it is only that we cannot verify it unless we know these conventions. Thus the equivalence fails. But it fails just as much with the action statement 'he moved the pen so', as it does with the movement statement 'his hand underwent such and such movements'. The gap we are interested in, however, is precisely that between these last two statements, i.e., the gap between action and movements as such.

It should be noted that the type of irreducibility of which Peters speaks is not co-terminous with the 'logical gulf between nature and convention', but extends beyond it. In the above case the movement counts as the action only in virtue of the conventions regulating contract signing, and thus the

type can be considered agents, to whom responsibility can be attributed for their behaviour in a special sense. For the notion of 'direction' which is implicit in action implies that of a 'director'. For when we say that it is essential to something's being an action that it be directed toward a goal, this does not mean simply, as we have seen, that it must bring about a given result, described as the goal; nor does it mean, as in the case of our imaginary teleological physical system, that it must be accounted for by certain laws; its having the character of being directed or aimed at some goal hangs rather on its being true of some locus of responsibility or agent that it directed the behaviour towards this goal, that it emitted directed behaviour. Thus 'action' and 'agency' are inseparably linked, as the etymology of these terms suggests.

Thus systems to whom action can be attributed have a special status, in that they are considered loci of responsibility, centres from which behaviour is directed. The notion 'centre' seems very strongly rooted in our ordinary view of such systems, and it gives rise to a deep-seated and pervasive metaphor, that of the 'inside'. Beings who can act are thought of as having an inner core from which their overt action flows. This metaphor has been taken up and interpreted by certain philosophical doctrines in such a way that the 'inner' is held to be another substance, different in kind to the observable 'outer' body and behaviour. The difference between those beings which are capable and those which are incapable of action thus lies in the former having an additional entity over and above their corporeal nature which the latter do not possess. But the metaphor of an 'inside' has a wider currency than these philosophical doctrines, springing as it does from the notion of a centre of responsibility which is inseparable from the notion of action.

---

two statements are not equivalent. But there are other cases where the movement (done, not suffered) will count as the action not in virtue of convention but of some natural fact, and in such cases, too, the two descriptions are not equivalent. Thus 'he closed the door with his foot' is not equivalent to 'he moved his foot in such and such a way'. For the second only amounts to the first in virtue of the fact that his movement in fact resulted in the door's closing on this occasion, and what movement would do this is not specified in the first statement. But the gap here is not that between nature and convention.

What is essential to this notion of an 'inside', however, is the notion of consciousness in the sense of intentionality. To speak of an 'intentional description' of something is to speak not just of any description which this thing bears, but of the description which it bears for a certain person, the description under which it is subsumed by him. Now the notion of an action as directed behaviour involves that of an intentional description. For an essential element involved in the classification of an action as an action of a certain type, i.e., as directed to a certain goal, is the goal to which it is directed by the agent, i.e., the description it has *qua* action for the agent. For, as we have seen, we can never unqualifiedly characterize an action as one with direction X unless X is the direction given it by the agent, and we can only characterize it as X even in a qualified way, if there is some connexion between 'X' and 'Y', the description which it has for the agent.[1]

Thus 'action' is a notion involving that of intentionality, and the types of system to which action can be attributed are those to which consciousness or intentionality can be attributed, beings of which we can say that things have a certain nature or description 'for' them. And this gives the force to the metaphor of an 'inside'; for aside from the many descriptions which a thing can bear 'externally', it also bears an intentional or 'inner' description which is essential to our understanding of its nature. Thus the locus of responsibility tends naturally to be thought of as an 'inner' locus.

An analogous point can be made about 'desire'. For if we are able to identify our feelings and behaviour as desire directly, that is, not as signs but as direct expressions of desire, then there is

[1] By 'intentional description' we cannot simply mean what the agent would say, even sincerely. For a man may vigorously disclaim an action correctly attributed to him. But as we pointed out above (note, p. 32), it is essential to this claim that it be true of the man that, in some unconscious way, he meant to do it. Thus it is essential to the claim that the gap between action and avowal be attributed to self-deception or lack of self-knowledge. But this means not knowledge about what results his action actually brings about, or about what description holds of his action *qua* event in the world—if this were all that was involved the question could be more easily settled—but knowledge about his purposes, i.e., the description the action really has for him. In a similar way it is possible for us to be deceived about other 'intentional descriptions', about our likes and dislikes, for instance, or our desires and aversions. Cf. below.

some sense in which the notion of desire involves that of consciousness or intentionality. For there must be some sense in which the state of desire contains the idea of what is desired, in which wanting something involves having the idea of that something; there must be some way in which a desire refers to or 'intends' its object, if we are to be able to identify the desire directly by what it is a desire for. Thus the notion of desire seems to be closely connected with that of 'having the idea of', in this sense, that is, to say of someone that something is a goal desired by him is to say that this goal has an intentional description for him, is an 'intentional object'.

Now this is clear enough in the large number of ordinary cases where wanting is knowing what one wants. But there is also a clear sense in which a man may be in error about what he wants—and this in a non-trivial way. That is, we are not simply speaking of the case where a man doesn't know the right word for an object, but could pick it out ostensively, or where a man is mistaken in thinking that A is a means to B, and wanting B wants A; for here the man is still right in knowing the description under which he wants A, even if this description does not apply, viz., as 'a means to B'. Nor are we speaking about cases where a man 'doesn't know what he wants' in the sense of not being able to make up his mind. The cases in question here are rather cases of unconscious desire, where a man doesn't recognize that he wants something or that he wants it under a certain description which is in fact the description under which he wants it.

But here, too, intentionality enters into our account. Thus, we can say that someone is in error about what he wants when he is unaware of the real motivation of actions of his which are in effect actions towards the goal 'really' desired. But in this case we can say that a man's being in error about what he wants is his being in error about the nature of his action, that is, there is a description true of his action which he would not accept as true. But to say that this description holds of his action cannot, in this case, be to say that it holds of it *qua* event in the world. This would be acceptable in the cases described above (pp. 27 et seq.) where we were speaking of actions attributable with the qualifications 'by accident', 'by mistake', 'inadvertently', and so on. With these it is often enough that the result be in fact brought about by the man's behaviour for the attribution to stick. But in these cases there is no implication that the result concerned was desired by the agent. Indeed, the opposite is usually the case. On the other hand, to amend the description of his action on the grounds of his real unavowed desire must be to amend its description *qua* intended action; that is, the new description must be in some way a description that the action has for him, an 'intentional description'. Thus to say that it is one thing and not another which moves a man to action is to say that his action really is directed in one way and not in another, and an account of what this means involves the notion of intentionality; for the goal concerned has an intentional description for him, as the goal of his action.

Then there are cases where we can say that a man wants something unconsciously, when he is doing nothing which tends in that direction, and may even be acting in a contrary sense, e.g., in the case where we can speak in a Freudian sense of a repressed desire. 'Repression' of course is a notion involving intentionality since it involves that of a desire once known and then put out of sight, as well as that of a characteristic attitude to the idea. Now the Freudian concept of repression may not be adequate, in some or in all cases, but any account of unconscious desire not acted upon must have some similar features. Thus, if we are speaking of a *desire*, there must be some factor which will explain why it is not acted upon, why the disposition is resisted. We cannot speak here simply of external obstacles, for these would not account for there not being any *attempt* to achieve the end desired, unless of course they were *recognized* as obstacles, which could only happen if the end was in some sense recognized as the end desired. In other words, the *resistance* must be itself motivated in some way, even if the *ignorance* may not be, as Freud believed. But then there must be some sense in which the man is refraining from, as against simply not doing, what he is unconsciously disposed to do. But the distinction between 'refraining from doing' and 'not doing' cannot lie simply in a description of a man's behaviour *qua* event in the world, for on this level the two may be indistinguishable, but must lie in the way the behaviour is directed, in the intentional description which holds of it even unconsciously. Now the intentional description by which the behaviour is identified is that of 'holding off from seeking X', where X is the end desired, and thus the 'idea of X' must enter into our account

60

of 'desiring X', even if this desire is unconscious and not acted upon. That is, X must have an intentional description for the agent.

If there were no motivated resistance it is difficult to see how we could speak of 'desire'. Thus it may be that a man wants to do something which it is completely out of the question for him even to attempt, such as seeking an interview with Khruschov, or dating Brigitte Bardot. And this desire may be completely unconscious so that it does not even present itself to him in a recognizable form in fantasy. But then we could not speak here of 'desire' at all unless there were some sense in which he was *deterred* by the thought that this was completely out of the question for him, even if he sincerely expressed ignorance of both desire and deterrence. If, as is more likely, its being out of the question was something he fully accepted, so that the 'thought never even crossed his mind' of attempting such a thing, then the notion of desire is no longer appropriate and we speak simply of 'wish'.[1]

Thus 'desire', like 'action', is a concept involving intentionality, and can only be attributed to beings to whom consciousness or intentionality can be attributed. The notions of agency, or of a locus of responsibility, and of intentionality are therefore deeply rooted in our ordinary language. This can be seen with other key notions besides those of action and desire. Thus the idea of agency is essential to the notion of a person, as that of a being to whom one can attribute purposes, who can be characterized partly by the goals he pursues and the way he treats the world around him. Similarly the notion of wanting in the sense we have outlined is essential to the notion of freedom because the distinction between what is free and what is unfree is founded on that between actions arising out of the purposes of the being concerned and what is imposed on him, what comes from 'inside' and what is imposed from without. And there are many other similar notions.

Thus explanation by purpose, as it appears in the paradigm case, viz., the form of explanation implicit in ordinary language,

---

[1] And this, too, of course, is a concept involving intentionality, although wishes may be unconscious. We couldn't speak of a wish at all unless, in some sense, the man had thought about what he would like, even in a way disguised to himself, e.g., in fantasy.

has certain important features which are not those of teleological explanation in general. For if the behaviour of a system to which 'action' and 'desire' can be attributed cannot be accounted for by non-teleological laws, it cannot be accounted for by the ordinary form of teleological explanation either. To speak of 'action' is to say not only that the laws governing the behaviour so described are teleological, but also that this behaviour can only be accounted for as action, i.e., in terms of intentionality.

This has as consequence another important difference from ordinary teleological explanation, which has been briefly mentioned before. This is the fact that when accounting for behaviour in terms of the goal to which it is directed, the situation in relation to which the action must be adequate to the goal is the situation as seen by the agent. In an ordinary teleological system with goal G, B will occur in the condition where B is required for G; (let us call this condition 'T'). But in an 'intentional system' with goal G, T is not sufficient for B. In this latter case, however, B will occur when T is *seen* to hold by the 'system' (in the absence of deterring factors), for otherwise we could not ascribe goal G to it. In other words, the condition of an action occurring is that it be believed to be adequate to the goal, and not simply that it is in fact adequate. And the two may not go together. The situation as it really is may differ from the situation under its intentional description for the agent, that is, the intentional description may not in fact hold of it.

We can thus see the full extent of the difference between explanation by purpose and the type of teleological explanation which would apply to our imaginary physical system. For in the former case the teleological account holds not of the organism in its 'geographical' environment, but of the agent in his 'intentional environment', the environment as it is for him.[1] Thus the notion of a centre of responsibility is integral to our account.

[1] Something analogous to this distinction between 'geographical' and 'intentional' environment must be introduced for any teleological account of the behaviour, at least, of the higher animals, even if notions involving intentionality are eschewed. Thus all organisms above a very low phylogenetic level can learn about their environment, that is, their behaviour alters over time in one and the same 'geographical' environment, after experience in that environment, and usually in the direction of greater adaptation. But then, if we are to account for the behaviour by teleological laws, the only way we can account for the change, granted the same goals, is in terms of a change

2. THE CONSCIOUSNESS OF ANIMALS

What, then, is the form of explanation which we have tried to outline in these chapters under the term 'explanation by purpose'? As it emerges from a study of the notions used in our everyday account of behaviour, it can be described as an account of behaviour as action; and this means necessarily, as we have seen, an account in terms of laws governing action. This defines explanation by purpose at once as a teleological account and as an account with special features of its own.

For the basic-level laws must be laws governing action, laws which set out the kinds of action the organisms will engage in, and the conditions, if any, for them. In characterizing the kinds of action, they will be characterizing the kinds of directed behaviour, that is, the goals or purposes action is directed towards. They will thus set out, since these are the basic laws, the natural or fundamental tendencies by which behaviour is to be explained, the basic purposes the organism pursues.

Thus the explanation will be teleological in kind. The laws will incorporate a principle of asymmetry. But—and this is the special feature—the tendencies concerned will not be tendencies to pure movement towards a given constellation, but tendencies to action. And this is why we can speak here of basic 'purposes' of the organism, in the sense of 'purpose' which can only be applied to the goal of an action. And this is also why we speak of 'explanation by purpose'.

The claim that animate organisms are purposive can thus be interpreted as the claim that their behaviour, or some range of it, can only be accounted for as action.

But before we proceed any further, there is an important question which must be raised, even if we cannot answer it very satisfactorily. Our outline of the features of explanation by purpose has been drawn from the concepts we use to talk about our own and others' behaviour in everyday speech. As such it

---

in the situation. But since the geographical environment has remained the same, we have to introduce a distinction between this and the situation as it affects the behaviour of the animal. And this is so whether or not we want to use the notion of intentionality. Hence the Gestalt concept of 'behavioural' environment which is contrasted with 'geographical' environment.

probably represents adequately the type of difference which is believed to hold between human beings and inanimate nature. But is there any sense in entertaining the hypothesis that this is the basis of the distinction between animate and inanimate nature in general? I do not believe that there can be an *a priori* answer to this question, that is, one which does not sift the evidence of animal behaviour to see if in fact this type of explanation holds in this region. But I think some of the motives which have led people to answer this in the negative have been based, at least to some extent, on a misunderstanding. In effect, to answer this in the negative is to assert that human beings are fundamentally different from animals in this respect. Now some philosophers have believed that this was the case in that animals were simply more or less complex machines; but, if one rejects this doctrine, then it is less easy to justify drawing a hard line between the human and the non-human in this respect. As a matter of fact, we commonly do speak of animals as emitting actions, and even as desiring, and it is hard to see what is wrong with this procedure.

A common ground for holding that it is wrong is one connected with the notion of consciousness or mind. For if we can only attribute 'action' and 'desire' to beings of whom we can speak in terms of consciousness or intentionality, then whether or not we can attribute action and desire to animals depends on whether we can attribute consciousness, in some sense, to them. Now there are many difficult questions here, not the least of which concerns what is meant by 'consciousness'. For it is clear that, if we define the term to mean 'human consciousness', then we must return a negative answer. But this is what we are easily tempted to do. Thus to take the notion of 'awareness of an end' in the sense in which this is required for 'wanting': We can only attribute this to an animal when he is actually trying to encompass the end, or, in the case of some higher animals, when the context and their behaviour shows visibly that they are inhibiting this action, e.g., when held at a distance by some danger, or told to wait by a master. Now, if we think of consciousness of ends as something essentially separate from and preceding action, then we have no grounds for attributing this to animals, and hence for attributing to them action and desire. But what is the reason for doing this? To do it is in fact to screw up the criteria for 'consciousness' so that only human beings can qualify for the term. For human beings as language-users can become aware of the ends they wish to pursue through self-avowal before they undertake any action towards these ends, and even if they never undertake such action. But consciousness of this kind cannot be attributed to non-language-users, for, of those who cannot avow to others, we cannot have grounds for saying that they avow to themselves. Thus animals are excluded by definition.

But the question is whether anything will have been gained by this re-definition. Does it show that the consciousness required for action is of this kind? If it does not, then the question whether we can attribute 'action' to animals remains unanswered. What then is the evidence that 'consciousness' in the sense which implies the possibility of self-avowal is essential to 'action'?

The facts which may incline us to this conclusion are these: Supposing an animal flees an object which I hold out to it; how do I discover what exactly it is afraid of, that is, under what description the object is frightening to it? I can only do this by experiment, by varying the conditions, in this case the object in my hand, trying out different sorts of object which each resemble the original one in some respect, and seeing whether the animal flees or not. The same procedure is necessary in many other cases, and we shall see animal experiments later on in which this procedure is used, e.g., to determine what an animal has learned during an experiment. The verification, then, of the proposition 'the animal is fleeing (or running towards, or attacking) the red object', when this is meant as a description of the action *qua* action, and not just of his movements, must lie in a set of experiments in which the animal's reactions are studied under different conditions. And this must be the case for beings who cannot state their purposes in language. But then, we might say, what we mean when we attribute 'fleeing the red object' (as against the 'square object' or the 'large object', or any other description which the object in my hand in fact has) is simply that when confronted with red objects the animal flees. But then, surely, to attribute this action to him, to identify his behaviour as this action, is simply to state the antecedent condition (the presentation of a red object) which conditions this behaviour, to subsume this behaviour under a law ('he always flees from red objects'). But if this is what is meant by attributing an action to him, then, as we have seen, the notion of action is not being used in its normal sense.

But the conclusion doesn't follow. It is certainly true that our only grounds for saying that the animal's action has *this* description is that he responds in the way he does in the different conditions. But this doesn't mean that *all* attributions of actions to animals are of this kind, that is, are simply subsumptions of the behaviour under a law. When I say that the animal is fleeing, for instance, or that the dog is leaping the fence or that the lion is stalking its prey, I am not subsuming the behaviour of these animals under any law or stating the antecedent conditions on which it depends. To put the point in another way: The fact that we can only determine whether an animal's behaviour bears *some* descriptions by discovering the correlation of which this behaviour is an instance does not show that we cannot characterize their behaviour as action in the normal sense. For the question can still arise whether the law or correlation concerned is a law governing action or a law governing movement. That is, the question still arises whether the behaviour governed by the law is action or movement. For it is still possible that we shall want to call it action because it can be identified as such under *another* description; because, e.g., we shall want to say that the animal *flees* whenever the red object is presented, and not just that his limbs move in such and such a way when this happens.[1]

Thus the absence of self-avowal in animals, and the consequent impossibility of attributing some action terms to them without discovering the law concerned, does not mean that we cannot ascribe action to them and distinguish, in their behaviour, between action and movement.

And we generally want to do this, and to distinguish in animal behaviour between action and movement. We seem to have good

---

[1] Of course, with human beings as well we can use the evidence of a law governing their action to over-rule their own avowal or self-avowal in assessing the nature of their action. Thus we may use our knowledge of what a man fears in general to call in question his claim about what he was avoiding on a given occasion. In fact, what we are saying here, against his protest, is that his behaviour actually fell under this law. But this does not mean that subsuming the behaviour under this or any other law is what we usually mean by attributing this action to someone. Here we are in fact inferring to the nature of the act from a plausible explanation of it, but this does not mean that the nature of the act is identified by this explanation.

physiognomic grounds for distinguishing between, e.g., a dog's salivating or the flexion of his forelimb under cortical stimulation, on one hand, and his chasing a cat or seeking food, on the other. We seem to have equally good grounds for attributing desire, frustration, pain, fear, and so on, to at least many higher animals. In short, we have at least *prima facie* grounds for classing them as agents in the sense in which we used this term above (p. 57). That is to say, we want to class them as beings who direct their behaviour, such that attributing a given direction to a given segment of an animal's behaviour is not simply saying that this segment has a certain end-product, or that it is to be explained by certain laws, but rather that, whatever the explanation, and whether it achieves its end or not, it is given this direction by the animal.

The absence of self-avowal, therefore, does not seem to debar us from applying something very like our notion of action to much of animal behaviour. It is necessary, however, to say 'something very like action', because we cannot deny that self-avowal makes an enormous difference. And the examples above help to show it. For we can often only determine the precise descriptions of an animal's action by experiment. Thus, as we have seen, we can only tell what an animal is reacting to by testing in different conditions, whereas with a human being we can ask. But this does not mean simply that we are fortunate enough to have a second and more direct mode of access in the second case. It means that human beings are conscious of what they are reacting to in the way that animals are not. Thus when I say of a man that it is under this description, X, that he is afraid of or hopes for a certain contingency I am not saying the same thing as in the above case, where I discover that the dog is afraid of the object that is in my hand because it is a red object. For it makes sense to say of a man that he is thinking of or considering this contingency under description X, while it does not make sense to say of a dog that he is thinking of this object as a red object. For a human being, a language user, thinking of something under a description X usually involves applying that description to it. Now it is a feature of our language that, in applying a description to something, in picking something out under a concept, we are picking out something to which other descriptions also apply, which falls under other concepts as well. This feature is implicit in a

67

common form of proposition where to a thing picked out under one description another description is ascribed ('this heap of stones is a tomb'). Thus for a human being, who is able to understand a proposition of this kind, thinking of something as a heap of stones is thinking of this as something which, he is able to recognize, can also bear other descriptions. Thus for language users the expression 'thinking of something *as* an X' has a specific force, for of these it is true that they could also think of (what they recognize as) the same thing under some other description. And 'wanting or fearing something as a so-and-so' is given a sense because this description is one among many under which the man now, or at some other time, could think of this object.

But for an animal thinking of or fearing something 'as a so-and-so' cannot be given this sense. For of an animal we could never say that he was conscious of this same thing (that is, what to him is the same thing) under two different descriptions, either at one time or on different occasions. Thus the dog who is fleeing the red object cannot be said to be conscious of this *as* a red object.

This means that the only type of consciousness of the objects around them that we can attribute to animals is a consciousness of their immediate relevance to their behaviour.[1] The red object is something to fly from, the meat something to be eaten, and so on, but the animal is not aware of the object *as* something he must fly from, or of the meat *as* something to be eaten. And correlatively, the only consciousness of their action, of the goals they are pursuing, that can be attributed to animals is that which accompanies the action itself, the attempt to achieve the goal.

Our question, then, is this: would we be justified in denying this the name 'consciousness', and hence in denying the behaviour the title 'action'? It would seem arbitrary to do so. For although

---

[1] Cf. the discussion in M. Merleau-Ponty's *Structure du Comportement*, pp. 123–30. Merleau-Ponty uses the term 'functional value' to describe the relevance of the object to the animal. Objects appear, as it were, 'invested with a functional value'. This is used to throw light on some of the findings of Köhler, reported in *The Mentality of Apes*, about the limits in the capacity of animals in solving problems requiring the use of instruments. Thus an ape who has had experience with the use of boxes to obtain food that was out of normal reach nevertheless doesn't try to use one on which another ape is sitting. The box is given the relevance of a 'seat', and cannot be seen at this moment to have that of a 'stool'.

this 'consciousness' differs from the human in that it contains no analogue of verbal human thought, it resembles the human in that it justifies our speaking of the animal's behaviour as directed in the strong sense outlined above,

If we language-users find it hard to conceive of a reduced form of consciousness of this kind (which perhaps we shouldn't because there is a wide range of routine human action which seems to be on the same level), we cannot make of this an *a priori* ground for rejecting it out of hand. For whether or not such a form exists must surely be considered an empirical question, to be decided, presumably, in this way: we must discover ultimately whether animal behaviour can only be accounted for by laws governing action, or whether it is amenable to explanation of a more mechanistic type. This is the question which we shall be dealing with in the second part.

But it should be clear that in speaking of 'intentionality' in this context, we are using the word in an extended sense.[1] For when we talk of the 'intentional description' of something, an action, or object, in the case of human beings, we often mean the 'privileged description', i.e., what among its many intentional descriptions the object is desired or feared *as*, or what description of the action incorporates our reason for doing it. But we cannot speak of 'privileged description' in the case of animals. And this makes a crucial difference for any science of behaviour. For men and only men can be said to be conscious of the reasons for their action, in the sense that they can describe them to themselves and to each other. Thus whereas the behaviour of animals can be accounted for simply by a set of species laws, a number of natural tendencies towards certain types of activity—seeking food and

---

[1] The notion in the senses used here resembles that which figures in the work of philosophers of the school of Phenomenology. Cf. the notion 'Sinn' or 'sens' in phenomenological writings, notably M. Merleau-Ponty, *Phenomenologie de la Perception*. The thesis of intentionality is interpreted in this latter work as the thesis that things have a 'sense' or meaning for conscious beings. But this notion goes beyond that of 'international description' in the sense in which this can be attributed to language users. For the objects which are relevant to an animal's behaviour can also be said to have a 'meaning' for him. In the chapters which follow 'intentionality' and 'intentional description' will be used in this extended sense so that we can apply this latter term to the relevance to the animal's behaviour of an environmental object or to his purpose in emitting some action.

drink, mating, etc.—which operate monotonously and in the same way in all members and from generation to generation, with men a factor of variance is introduced by the fact of convention. For the way the 'species laws' operate, the way men go about seeking the goals which are common to them, is dependent on the idea they have of these goals, the way they describe them to themselves. And thus the human species shows an immense variation from society to society, and even, with exceptional people, from individual to individual, in the goals they accept and the way they seek them. Moreover, these fundamental ideas are transmitted with language and custom from generation to generation and are received or altered in each generation, so that human behaviour is, in part, a function of human history, of what men have made themselves over the centuries. In this sense only man can be said to have a history.

But this important field of study lies outside the scope of the present work. The question we are dealing with, concerning the validity of explanation by purpose, touches that aspect in which human and animal behaviour is alike; or so we generally and unreflectingly believe. And thus, although what can and what cannot be proved in this area is not entirely clear, it would seem best to proceed on the assumption that it makes sense to speak of 'action' and 'desire' in the case of at least some animals and try to put to the test the thesis that these differ from inanimate nature in the radical way outlined.

But, in doing so, we will be losing one advantage of the other view, which is the clearly demarcated line between the different types of being contrasted. For the line between the human and the non-human (leaving aside hypothetical and now fortunately extinct 'missing links') is much clearer and sharper than that between the animate and the inanimate. But the indefiniteness of the watershed is not the only difficulty. There is also the fact that, as we approach the lower ends of the phylogenetic scale, such concepts as 'action', and even more, 'desire', in any sense stronger than that which is involved in any non-constrained action, seem less and less appropriate. Thus while we can speak of dogs as 'wanting', this becomes difficult with crocodiles, and totally impossible with beetles. The concept 'action' seems still to have some use at greater depths than 'desire' in this stronger sense, but it, too, becomes progressively emptied of content as we approach the bottom. Now this fact certainly poses a problem for those who would hold that animate and inanimate are different, but it does not constitute an objection. For the decisive evidence for this thesis will have to be whether or not the type of explanation which in fact holds of certain ranges of animals, particularly man and the higher animals, is the type we have called explanation by purpose. If this is in fact the case, then the problem will remain of accounting for the growth of this type of being in evolution through a number of stages, an evolution which has left behind a phylogenetic trail in which there are no sharp breaks. It is quite possible that a continuous progression will be found, leading from inanimate non-teleological systems, through animate teleological systems to those which are not only teleological but purposive in character. Thus, it may be that those lower species to which the concept 'action' has no application (as well as those relatively integrated sub-systems in higher organisms which are studied by biologists) are nevertheless such that their behaviour can only be accounted for by teleological, although non-purposive, laws.

But this is speculation. It would seem that our best manner of proceeding would be to examine the behaviour of higher organisms in order to test the claim.[1] But in doing so we have to be conscious that we are not dealing with a sharply demarcated class of beings, but one which shades off at the edges. We will have, in fact, to deal with those members of the class to whom we have little hesitation in ascribing the notion 'action'.

[1] In fact, since, as we shall see later, we shall mainly be discussing a range of theories which have been elaborated primarily for animal behaviour, the bulk of our examples will be taken from the behaviour of the higher animals. But the behaviour we shall be examining has obvious analogues in human action, and to the extent that this tends to point to the validity of explanation by purpose for these animals, it will *a fortiori* strengthen the case as far as human beings are concerned.

IV

THE DATA LANGUAGE

I. SCIENTIFIC NEUTRALITY

IN the last chapters we have attempted to outline what is meant by explanation in terms of purpose, and thereby what is meant by the claim that animate beings differ from inanimate nature in being 'purposive'. The next step, then, should be to try to discover how this thesis can be established or refuted. But before examining this question in any detail, we must consider another claim put forward by those who reject explanation by purpose, to the effect that the issue can be settled *a priori*, that is, without having to examine the type of explanation which actually applies to living things. This claim takes the usual form, viz., that explanations in terms of purpose are non-empirical, that they involve us in propositions which are not amenable to empirical test.

Now we have already examined claims of this kind in connexion with teleological explanations, which turned out to be unfounded. But this objection concerns the other aspect of explanation by purpose, namely the use of notions involving consciousness or intentionality. For it is held that the 'data language' of any science cannot include concepts of this range.

By 'data language' here is meant the language used to describe the evidence which is adduced in support of any theory or law. Now it is obvious that the concepts so used must be such that they can receive an unambiguous and commonly agreed application. Otherwise any theoretical conclusion would be uncertain, and above all, could never find common acceptance. Science is essentially an enterprise carried on by many people. It is essentially public, in the sense that any result achieved by one man must be capable of check by others, and this is impossible if our terms are unclear and have no agreed usage. This, of course, applies to the data language. Thinkers may have certain theoretical terms which are not commonly accepted, but as long as these are clearly interpreted in terms of the expressions of the data language, others will understand what is being said and can verify it.

Now this approach to the problem, the distinction between data language and language of theory, is very common among behaviour scientists. And almost equally widespread is the view that concepts which involve consciousness or intentionality, those referring to knowledge, belief, expectancy, wanting, and action, in the sense of directed behaviour, cannot belong to a satisfactory data language. It is assumed that the data language must contain only concepts which are part of what was called by Logical Empiricists the 'physical thing language'. For it is held that terms involving consciousness, or psychological terms, as we might call them, are such that propositions containing them are, without special interpretation, untestable. This is believed to be virtually a self-evident truth by many thinkers. Thus Estes, in his discussion of Lewin's theory, can exclaim in surprise,

> . . . surely no one of Lewin's theoretical sophistication would maintain that any proposition that can be formulated in the conventional psychological vocabulary can be assumed uncritically to be confirmable by observation.[1]

Of course, some theorists do use these concepts, but their application inevitably involves a certain arbitrariness, a certain reading into the phenomena of the observer's own biases and interests, as, say, concepts designating physiognomic properties sometimes do. This seems to be the point made by Hull, again in connexion with Lewin.

> The main reason why I believe the methodology favoured by Lewin cannot yield a satisfactory natural-science theory of behaviour, . . . is that his field when secured is primarily subjective and his preferred method of securing it is primarily introspective. As I read him, experimental extinction occurs because 'the individual catches on', conditioned reactions are evoked in part

[1] In Estes et al., *Modern Learning Theory*, p. 325.

because of a concurrent 'expectation' and so on. Moreover, when attributed to inarticulate organisms, subjective entities such as 'expectancy', 'catching on', 'life space', 'subjective probability', and the like, would seem to degenerate to sheer anthropomorphism; the investigator in effect projects himself into the rat, the cat, the dog, the monkey, the ape, or the young child, and says 'If I were in that situation, I would perceive, cognize, feel, think or hypothesize so and so.'[1]

Thus, for Hull, the application of psychological concepts to animals seems wholly arbitrary, the result simply of the observer imagining how he would think or feel. Naturally, intersubjective test for statements involving terms used in this way is impossible. But the use of such terms in a science of human behaviour is equally to be eschewed.[2] Not least among the disadvantages of this procedure is that it makes impossible a mathematical science of behaviour:

> The main trouble with the subjective and anthropomorphic methodology ... is that the entities which it yields are not really measurable, whereas the satisfactory verifiability of natural-science theory requires rather precise quantification: in so far as a theory or hypothesis is incapable of verification, it falls short of the scientific ideal. For example, the trouble with such a concept as expectancy, ... is that when we attempt to verify the hypothesis in which it appears we cannot tell how much expectancy to expect; neither do we know the magnitude of the reaction which the expectancy is expected to mediate.[3]

Thus it would seem to follow from the nature of science itself, as a form of enquiry requiring intersubjective verification, that a science of behaviour cannot make use of psychological concepts in this sense, i.e., concepts involving consciousness or intentionality. And thus the claim that animate organisms differ just in this, that an account of their behaviour must use concepts of this range, is ruled out from the start. But, it might be objected, this drastic consequence doesn't necessarily follow. All that has

---

[1] 'The Problem of Intervening Variables in Molar Behaviour Theory,' *Psychological Review*, 1943, p. 287.

[2] Cf. 'Mind, Mechanism and Adaptive Behaviour,' *Psychological Review*, 1937.

[3] *Psychological Review*, 1943, loc. cit.

been shown is that such terms mustn't appear in the data language. But this does not necessarily mean that they cannot be used as theoretical terms, provided they are interpreted clearly enough in terms of the expressions of the data language. Most behaviour theorists, indeed, hold that there is little use for these concepts, but this is to go beyond the demand simply that their use be clear and unambiguous. This argument would only weigh against their use in an illicit way, to smuggle in hidden and unclear theoretical assumptions, which, moreover, are private to the theorist who uses them; and although this would follow from their use as uninterpreted concepts in the data language, to their use as theoretical terms there would be no objection.

Thus, on this more lenient view, all that is required is a theoretically neutral data language. This is the prerequisite of communication among scientists. This will allow us to use psychological concepts, but it rules out their inclusion in the data language. For, as theoretical notions, they are the property of one particular group of theorists, whereas the terms of the data language must be neutral between all theories. This requirement is stated by Estes:

> In so far as a theory is intended to be communicable and susceptible of general acceptance among researchers, it is necessary that the data language be limited to terms for which agreement upon usage can be obtained among qualified investigators regardless of theoretical orientation. As Skinner has pointed out, some terms from ordinary English are appropriate for inclusion in the data language of a science of behaviour; others are not. In the description of animal behaviour, for instance, agreement can be reached upon the use of terms referring to movements of the animal or its parts (e.g., walk, run, forelimb flexion), but not upon terms with hidden theoretical implications (e.g., 'attempt, belief, search').[1]

But this concession to the opposition amounts to very little. In fact, it already looks suspicious. For the position amounts to this, that statements attributing beliefs, expectancies, desires, actions, and so on, in short statements using psychological terms, cannot be given an unambiguous and clear empirical sense unless they are interpreted by means of statements using only concepts

[1] In Estes, et al., *Modern Learning Theory*, p. 321.

which belong to the physical thing language. Hence Verplanck interprets Skinner as saying that

> 'hear', 'feel', 'try', 'need', 'in order to', and 'intention' cannot be included in the data language of a science of behaviour, although in many cases it might be possible, by a Watsonian process of translation or by the recently fashionable and perhaps overworked 'operational definition', to give these terms a sharply restricted meaning within the data language, and so to introduce them in-to it.[1]

The question arises then whether these terms so 'translated' will be recognizably like the concepts in their ordinary use, whether they will be enough like them to allow protagonists of purposive explanation to state their case, and still be within the bounds of meaningful, testable utterance.

2. OPERATIONAL DEFINITION

What is meant by 'translation' here? The most common way of putting this requirement these days, as Verplanck indicates, is in terms of 'operational definition'. This term has by now a long and fairly troubled history. Introduced by Bridgman,[2] it has gained great currency among those thinkers who have been influenced by Logical Empiricism, and resembles closely its stablemate, the verification theory of meaning. As with this latter, there has been a running dispute through the years as to its exact meaning, and earlier, cruder versions have been replaced by later more refined ones. In Bridgman's first form, the requirement seemed impossibly stringent. A concept was held to be equivalent to the operations by which it was introduced.[3] This seemed to mean that any statement using a theoretical concept was logically equivalent to the statement or statements describing the results

---

[1] In Estes, et al., *Modern Learning Theory*, p. 278; Verplanck speaks here of 'introducing' these terms to the data language, as against introducing them as theoretical terms. But this must be a slip on his part. For if data language is to mean 'language of immediate observation', then we cannot speak of introducing terms into it by operational definition, but rather of giving these terms meaning by definition in terms of the expressions it contains.

[2] *The Logic of Modern Physics.*   [3] Cf. Bridgman, op. cit., p. 5.

of the operations of measurement or tests by which one determined its truth value. This would amount to the thesis that theoretical terms were logical constructions out of terms for observables, or the terms used in describing the results of the operations of measurement.

But this requirement was visibly too strong. For instance it would make it nonsense (self-contradictory) for anyone to say that a given test resulted in so-and-so, but that this didn't mean that the corresponding theoretical property had the value that was usually indicated by this test result. Now we not only frequently say things of this kind, but we also have good grounds to, e.g., if something has gone wrong with the apparatus.[1] Similarly, a convention of this kind would prevent us saying that two tests were tests for the same property, for the statements relating the results of two different tests which were both indications of T, the statement that a theoretical variable had a certain value, would both be logically equivalent to T, and hence logically equivalent to each other, which is absurd.

Thus a new and more sophisticated interpretation of operational definition was devised, using the notion of 'partial interpretation'. Carnap was one of the pioneers in developing this new form, and it would be best to expound it in his terms.[2] The total language of a science can be considered as consisting of two parts, the observation language and the theoretical language. The theoretical language can be considered as a logico-mathematical system, with its formation and transformation rules, its primitive non-logical vocabulary and its postulates, which permit the derivation of non-primitive non-logical terms. Then between the theoretical and the observation languages certain 'correspondence rules' are established linking sentences using theoretical terms with those using observation terms. In this way the theoretical terms are partly interpreted, i.e., given empirical meaning, but they are only interpreted by means of the observable predicates, since the

---

[1] Of course, we could build it into the notion of 'the test has such and such a result' that the test should not deceive us in this way, but then we could not be sure what the result was until we knew what value the property had, so that the test would cease to be a test for that property.

[2] Cf. 'Testability and Meaning', *Philosophy of Science*, 1936 and 1937, and 'The Methodological Character of Theoretical Concepts', in *Minnesota Studies in the Philosophy of Science*, Editors H. Feigl and M. Scriven, Vol. I.

extent of their interpretation depends on the correspondence rules. As Carnap puts it:

> All the interpretation (in the strict sense of this term, i.e., observational interpretation) that can be given for [the theoretical language] is given in the correspondence rules, and their function is essentially the interpretation of certain sentences containing descriptive terms, and thereby indirectly the interpretation of the descriptive terms of [the theoretical vocabulary].[1]

Now the notion of a 'correspondence rule' does away with the disadvantages of the old logical construction view, for terms operationally defined by the expressions of the data language are no longer logical constructions out of these expressions, that is, theoretical statements are no longer held to be logically equivalent to statements using only terms from the observation or data language. But, at the same time, all the empirical interpretation which can be given to these terms can be given in statements of this latter kind, for, for any theoretical statement, there must be a finite list of statements in the observation language which give its entire empirical meaning, those which are linked with it by the correspondence rules. What, then, is the force of the notion of partial interpretation? The idea is that, at some future date, we may wish to add to the empirical meaning of this term by linking sentences containing it by means of new correspondence rules to sentences containing observables. We do not therefore claim at any one time to have exhausted the possible interpretations of the term, as the 'logical construction' view did.

Carnap had physics mainly in mind, of course, and he could thus speak of the theoretical language as a 'logico-mathematical system'. This term is a little too ambitious for psychology, at least at the present time.[2] But the notions of 'correspondence rule' and 'partial interpretation' can be applied to the problems we are discussing as well. For these purposes, the theoretical terms are psychological terms, and their operational definition is to be effected in the physical thing language. Thus for any statement using a psychological term, there should be a set of

---

[1] *Minnesota Studies*, p. 46.

[2] Although not all psychologists think so, as one can see from reading Hull's works. But the word 'system' applied to Hull's theory is a little pretentious, to say the least.

statements using only terms in the 'thing language'[1] which give
its entire empirical meaning. Thus, to give an example, Tolman[2]
tries to define 'the rat expects food at location L' in the following
way:

> When we assert that a rat expects food at location L, what we assert
> is that *if* (1) he is deprived of food, (2) he has been trained on path
> P, (3) he is now put on path P, (4) path P is now blocked, and
> (5) there are other paths which lead away from path P, one of
> which points directly to location L, *then* he will run down the path
> which points directly to location L.
>
> When we assert that he does *not* expect food at location L, what
> we assert is that, under the same conditions, he will *not* run down
> the path which points directly to location L.[3]

In a similar way all other statements using psychological terms
can be 'translated', so that we can obtain an 'operational definition' of these terms using only expressions of the data language.[4]

But now we can see that psychological concepts, so defined, are
hardly equivalent to their counterparts in ordinary speech. Thus
Tolman's definition hardly gives the empirical sense which we
would ordinarily attach to 'the rat expects food at location L'.
We can well see that in certain conditions this could be the
description of a test for the truth of the proposition defined. But

---

[1] A question arises, of course, whether there is a 'thing-language', i.e.,
a stratum of descriptive discourse, separable from the rest, which deals with
'things' in some paradigmatically observable sense. But we leave this aside
for the moment to return to it below, pp. 87 et. seq.

[2] Tolman, E. C., Ritchie, B. F., and Kalish, D., 'Studies in Spatial Learning,
I, Orientation and the Shortcut', *J. exp. Psychol.*, 1946.

[3] Op. cit., p. 15. The stress is Tolman's. It should be noticed that 'operational definition' has got away from any necessary connexion with operations
of measurement. The name is retained, derived from Bridgman's original
pre-occupation with operations of measurement in physics. But in psychological theory, the requirement is simply that we express the empirical content of the theoretical statement in a set of empirical conditionals using only
the terms of the data language. Cf. the 'bi-conditionals', and 'conditional
reduction pairs' of Carnap, 'Testability and Meaning', *Philosophy of Science*,
1936 and 1937.

[4] Of course, one might cavil at the terms used in Tolman's definiens. But
all these should themselves be open to operational definition, if not themselves
expressions in the data language. Thus 'deprived of food' would be defined
in terms of feeding schedule, as would 'trained on path P' in terms of training history, and 'run' must be interpreted as referring to movement as
against action.

there are other conditions in which it would not be. Thus, if there were a cat astride the path leading to L, we would not take the immobility or even retreat of the rat as evidence that he did not expect food at L. Or, take the example used by MacCorquodale and Meehl in their discussion of this example,[1] if path P were white, and the path leading to location L were also white, the other paths being of some other colour, we might not take the rat's running up this path as evidence for his expecting food at L. Well, one might say, these are just the conditions in which the test would break down. But the point is surely this: that these are conditions of break-down of the test has just as much right to be called part of the empirical sense of 'the rat expects food at L' as has Tolman's definitional test itself. That is, anyone who understood what we mean by this expression, and therefore who understood why Tolman's conditions can provide a test for its truth, would also have to agree, once he was told about the fear-inducing properties of cats, that the cat was a disturbing factor which might invalidate the test, or, in the case where both paths are white, would have to agree that, if the rat was simply trained to take the white path, this would not constitute expecting food at L, just as Tolman himself knew that placing a satiated rat at the opening wouldn't show anything one way or the other.

Thus, if Tolman's definition is held to give the entire empirical interpretation of 'the rat expects food at L', then we must conclude that he is using 'expect' in a way which differs sharply from its use in ordinary language. For, in any sense in which a test can be held to give an empirical interpretation to a statement of this kind, it cannot be said to give the entire empirical interpretation. Now there certainly is a sense in which the description of a test for a statement's holding can give the empirical sense of that statement. For it hangs on that statement's asserting what it does about the world, that this is a test for it. That is, if we alter what is meant by the statement, then the test may no longer be valid. And thus we can often help someone to understand what is meant by a statement by describing to him a test for its validity. But if the test is to be an empirical test, then it must describe an event which will happen in certain conditions and which is empirically or contingently linked with what is described in the statement. But if the link between test and what the statement

---

[1] In Estes, et al., *Modern Language Theory*, p. 184.

asserts is contingent, then it hangs on certain conditions. But that these conditions are the conditions in which the test holds also hangs on the statement's asserting what it does, in exactly the same way. Thus if we can say that part of what we mean by a statement is that a certain test will have a certain result,[1] we can just as easily say that the conditions for the test holding being of a certain kind is part of what we mean.[2]

Might it not be said, then, that Tolman's definition is just incomplete, that it requires to have added the conditions of its holding? But the point is that the conditions of its holding are not finite in number. There is no limit to the number of conditions in which the Tolmanian test for an expectancy would be invalid. Thus as the example of the cat showed, as well as Tolman's own condition that the rat must be hungry, it must be the case that the rat is not motivated by anything else than the desire for food. Then, as the hypothesis about the white path showed, it must be the case that the rat's behaviour can actually be described as 'going down the path to L', and not 'taking the white path'. *A fortiori*, it is necessary that the rat's behaviour qualify as action, i.e., that this not be some reflex behaviour, or effect of drugs or whatever. Now there are an indefinite number of ways in which any one of these conditions could be falsified, e.g., the rat must not also be thirsty and expect water at M, or sexually aroused and expect a mate at N, or suffering from intense fatigue, or experimental neurosis, and so on and so on. The job of giving all the conditions in detail is endless, as is therefore the job of giving an operational definition. That is, the job is endless unless we can give the general formula for an adequate test. But the only way to give the general formula for O's being an adequate test for p is to say something like 'the conditions must be such that the connexion $O - p$ holds', i.e., a statement of the conditions from which it follows logically that $O - p$. For if we name any conditions of $O - p$ such that it is a contingent fact that $O - p$ holds in these conditions, then $O - p$'s holding in these conditions will

---

[1] We often do: Thus if I say 'p', someone could reply 'do you mean that if I X, then Y?.' This is a perfectly good sense of 'mean' in which it is equivalent to 'give (part of) the empirical content of'.

[2] Of course, in one sense of 'mean' this may not be the case, that in which we have to know a consequence of what we assert to be said to mean it. But we are using the term in the other sense here, that in which a person can be made to abandon a belief for instance by being shown 'what it means'.

itself depend on further conditions, and we shall not have succeeded in naming all the conditions. Thus, in this case in hand,
the only formula in general for the test holding is that the conditions be such that the animal's running down the path actually is a
case of his acting on the expectation that there is food at L.

Thus an operational definition can only be said to give the
entire empirical meaning of a given statement if it specifies the
conditions which must hold in some such circular way. But this
is not all. We have spoken up to now as though there were only
one test for a given statement. But, of course, there is no definite
number of such tests which can 'give the meaning' of a statement
in the above sense, and therefore, to give the entire empirical
meaning of a statement in terms of the tests for its truth would
be a doubly endless task, which could only be accomplished by
some such circular and cumbrous locution as, 'when we assert p,
what we assert is that any test for p will be positive provided the
conditions hold under which it is an adequate test for p'. In
other words, we can only give the 'entire empirical meaning' of
any statement by repeating the statement (or what it entails);
which is what one would expect.

3. NON-PSYCHOLOGICAL PSYCHOLOGY

Enough has been said to show that any recognizable operational
definition of a psychological term, as this is understood in ordinary
speech, would be relatively useless, and could hardly meet the
criterion of the operationists, that the term must be defined by
the expressions of the data language, for the 'definition' would
require the use of the term it was meant to define. Thus, if we
take operational definition as our standard, the 'translation'
offered by some theorists of psychological concepts amounts to
a 'transformation' beyond recognition. And this of necessity.
For any finite operational definition of a psychological concept in
the thing language has, as it were, to cut off the empirical implications of the concept at a certain point, and thus to alter its meaning.
Thus if all Tolman means by 'the rat expects food at L' is that the
rat takes the path to L in the conditions he describes, then he is
not using anything remotely like the ordinary concept 'expect'.

As a matter of fact, it is not even a psychological concept, if
we mean by this an empirical concept which can be used to

describe events of a certain range, known as psychological. For the status of empirical concept, in this sense, is not given to theoretical terms by the operationist interpretation. In fact the status of the statements of a theoretical language is a very odd one which it is not easy to define.

It is clear that theoretical statements, on this operationist interpretation, are not held to be equivalent to the statements which interpret them (which are linked with them by the correspondence rules). That is, it is supposedly a merely contingent fact that the state of affairs they describe is linked with those described by the statements phrased in the data language. This seems to be what Carnap wanted, since he wanted to cater for the case where the test is negative, say, and we nevertheless want to say that the property holds.

But this supposed status is undermined by the procedure for validating these theoretical statements. For the observable states of affairs which count as 'evidence' for them do so by stipulation, and this is incompatible with their being independent statements of empirical fact, merely contingently linked with the observable facts we test for, as Carnap would have them be.

The confusion about the status of theoretical states of affairs on the operationist interpretation can be put in this way: their links with observable states of affairs are supposed to be contingent, and yet the connexions between the statements of the two ranges turn out to be purely stipulative. But these two relationships are incompatible. According to the first, it is an empirical fact that a given theoretical state of affairs, T, is linked with a given observable state of affairs, O, such that O provides evidence for asserting that T holds. But then O's providing evidence for T cannot be the subject of a decision on our part, but either holds or doesn't hold independent of us; and thus the connexion between the corresponding statements 'that O' and 'that T' cannot be a stipulative one. But this, by the second relationship, it is held to be.

That the relationship between the statements of the two ranges must be a stipulative one according to operationism may not be immediately evident, but can be shown. An empirical fact must be such that it can in principle be established or refuted by empirical evidence. And to say that it can be established by evidence is to say that there are grounds for holding it to be true which weigh as grounds independent of our decision; indeed, it is an essential part of what we mean by 'evidence' that it be a sign of something's being true which holds as such independent of us, and whose weight can itself be established empirically.

Now it is the thesis of operationism that the entire empirical sense of a theoretical statement is given in a certain finite set of correspondence rules which link it to statements about observables. The list may be long or short, but the number of rules matters little to the argument, so long as it be finite. Let us suppose, then, a theoretical state, T, linked by correspondence rules to the test results O_1, O_2, O_3. T is said to hold ('that T' is true) whenever O_1, O_2 and O_3 occur ('that O_1', 'that O_2' and 'that O_3' are true). But then supposing that we ask whether O_1, O_2 and O_3 are really adequate tests for T, whether they constitute valid evidence for it? If this were an empirical question it should be possible to establish or refute it by the evidence. But the only evidence which would serve us here would be of the kind which, in the presence of O_1, O_2 and O_3, would help to determine whether T held or not, or vice versa. In other words, to have evidence relevant to the question we must have an independent test for T, independent, that is, of the tests which produce results O_1, O_2 and O_3. But this, by hypothesis, we cannot have, since the entire empirical sense of 'that T' is given in 'that O_1', 'that O_2' and 'that O_3'. It is therefore in principle impossible to decide this question one way or the other by evidence, and it is thus not an empirical question; it is a stipulative one.

Of course, it is in the nature of 'partial interpretation' that we can increase the range of tests for T by extending the interpretation of the term and adding new correspondence rules. But this process of addition, involving as it does an alteration in the empirical meaning of the term, will itself be effected by stipulation. The new tests could not, therefore, be held to give us 'independent evidence' for T, since it is open to us to give or withhold this status from them, and it is, as we have seen, in the nature of evidence that it provides grounds for asserting something which hold as such independent of our decisions.

Nor will it help to invoke another theoretical state, S, with which T is supposedly linked, and to bring into operation the empirical tests for S, N_a, N_b and N_c. These will extend the list of tests for T without altering the basic difficulty, the fact that the number of correspondence rules defining the meaning of the term is finite, and the question whether they are all valid tests for T must be a stipulative one.

Nor will we be better off if we ask this question of each test severally. How would we establish that O_1 was evidence for T? By seeing that when O_1 occurs, O_2 and O_3 also occur? But this will only give us what we want if we can establish that O_2 and O_3 constitute evidence for T. And how could we do this? Certainly not by seeing if O_1 occurs. At some point we will have to break the chain of questions by a decision. We can break it at any point, but let us stipulate that O_1 provides evidence for T. Then it will be an empirical question whether O_2 and O_3 provide evidence, but the evidence for this will simply be that the three test results occur together, and never occur separately. It is purely by stipulation that we call this case the case where O_2 and O_3 constitute evidence for T. We are in the same position as was described above, where, in the face of the joint occurrence of O_1, O_2 and O_3, we searched in vain for an independent test for T. Only we have chosen to call it by a different name.

Thus although the connexions between the different observable states of affairs are contingent, that any of these is held to count as a connexion between an observable state and a theoretical state is established by stipulation. Despite the claim that the states of affairs described in theoretical statements are only contingently linked with observable states of affairs, that the latter serve as evidence for the former, the actual logic of operational definition shows that the connexions between the two types of statements are really of a stipulative character. An operational definition is thus a stipulative truth.

Thus the theoretical statements of operationism have, as it were, no empirically independent existence. For as empirical statements, the evidence for them is identical with the evidence for the observable statements with which they are linked by correspondence rules. They carry no extra information not already given by the observable statements. They are in effect eliminable without loss. And we could on the basis of the same observable facts raise an entirely different structure of theoretical statements.

The theoretical terms of operationism are, therefore, theoretical only in a weak sense of the word. For *qua* empirical concepts they are totally eliminable, they have the status of paraphrases or shorthand notation for observables; but considered as theoretical concepts, i.e., concepts which can be used in statements about specifically theoretical, as against observable, states of affairs, they are totally non-empirical since the statements in which they figure can have no verification other than that which is determined by stipulative definitions in terms of observables. Properly speaking, operationism has no place for theoretical concepts, if we mean by this *empirical* concepts which can figure in statements about a certain range of things called theoretical.[1]

And by the same token, operationism doesn't allow for any psychological concepts. For as 'translated' into the thing language psychological statements are in the same case: To the extent that they are empirical they deal with non-psychological events, and to the extent that they deal with psychological events, they are inadequately 'interpreted' and therefore non-empirical.[2]

[1] This is clearly recognized by Braithwaite, *Scientific Explanation*, who wishes to avoid the expression 'theoretical concept' and substitute that of 'theoretical term'. Indeed, the whole positivist notion of interpretation, as represented by Carnap, op cit., Hempel, cf. 'Problems and Changes in the Empiricist Criterion of Meaning', in Linsky, Ed., *Semantics and the Philosophy of Language*. and Braithwaite, op. cit., is confused and inconsistent. For the aim was to construe the link between a theoretical state of affairs and the test for it as a contingent one, i.e., empirical one, which could break down if the conditions were not right, and yet at the same time to deny to the theoretical terms any empirical meaning which could not be clearly derived in some way from observables. But the second aim defeats the first, for it results in the doctrine of partial interpretation which makes the link between a theoretical state and the test for it stipulative. Of course, some extreme positivists would be happy to accept the notion that the entire structure of theory was stipulatively true, but it is very much to be doubted whether this is really a correct analysis of scientific theory and therefore whether partial interpretation is a correct analysis of the empirical meaning of theoretical terms.

[2] The view of theory as entirely stipulative because the entire empirical meaning touches only observables has led to the 'Theoretician's Dilemma'. Thus, as exposed by Hempel, cf. *Minnesota Studies in the Philosophy of Science*, Vol. II: the paradox of theorizing 'asserts that if the terms and the general principles of a scientific theory serve their purpose, i.e., if they establish definite connexions among observable phenomena, then they can be dispensed with since any chain of laws and interpretative statements establishing such a connexion should then be replaceable by a law which directly links observational antecedents to observational consequents'.

Hempel's defence of theory which is exclusively on pragmatic lines shows

Thus the concession that psychological terms can be introduced provided that they are interpreted by the terms of the data language turns out to be an empty one, for these terms are not like the psychological concepts of ordinary speech, and, in an important sense, are not psychological concepts at all. But if this is so then the view that animate organisms are distinct precisely in that the laws governing their behaviour must be stated in concepts involving consciousness or intentionality, that is psychological concepts, cannot be meaningfully stated. That is, any theory which used such concepts cannot meet the requirements for intersubjective validation of a scientific theory. Thus once more the question seems to be decided *a priori*, and one view rejected as meaningless.

4. EMPIRICAL ASSUMPTIONS

If we are to make any progress, therefore, we must examine the premisses of this argument, that psychological terms can only be introduced if they are 'interpreted' by operational definition. Why does this follow from the nature of science? The crucial premiss seems to be that the events described by psychological statements are, if they occur at all, unobservable, that only the events which can be described by predicates in the physical thing language can properly be said to be observable, and that therefore statements using psychological terms can be said to designate observable events only to the extent that their empirical content can be expressed in statements using only terms of the physical

---

that he fundamentally accepts the stipulative view which gives rise to the paradox. But if theory is to be defended on pragmatic grounds, can it not be attacked on those grounds, as, e.g., Skinner does, when he claims that theoretical terms are constantly likely to inveigle us into accepting non-empirical entities and verbal explanations? In positivist hearts this appeal for radical purity will always raise an echo. But see M. Scriven, 'A Study of Radical Behaviourism' in H. Feigl and M. Scriven (Eds.), *Minnesota Studies in the Philosophy of Science*, Vol. I, for a more fundamental logical critique of Skinner.

For a discussion among behaviour theorists of the role of theoretical terms, see also the Symposium on Operationism, *Psychological Review*, 1945, and the discussion on hypothetical constructs and intervening variables in *Psychological Review*, opened by MacCorquodale and Meehl, loc. cit., *Psychological Review*, 1948.

thing language. In other words, the criterion for belonging to the data language for any term is that it can be used to make statements which describe observable events without any further interpretations or operational definitions. The data language consists of 'a set of terms which are taken as undefined within the theory but which can be set in correspondence with observables'.[1] Now psychological terms do not qualify in this way, and therefore they do not belong to the data language. But then they can be used only to the extent that statements made with them can be given an empirical sense in terms of observables. Thus if what a psychological statement describes is to be observable, and therefore if the statement is to be verifiable, it is necessary that the entire empirical content of the statement be given in statements using only terms of the data language; in other words, it is necessary that they be operationally defined. But then these terms will no longer be psychological concepts. So that it follows from the nature of scientific theory as a body of verifiable statements that no place for psychological concepts can be found in it. The crucial premiss thus concerns the nature or 'ontological status' of psychological events. But how is this established?

It can be seen how operationism in psychology belongs to the positivist tradition, and how the attempt on epistemological grounds to eliminate psychological concepts resembles the attempts to eliminate concepts designating human collectivities (e.g., nations) and even concepts designating material objects in favour of some alleged language of 'immediate observation'. But it is hard to see how this attempt is any better founded than those which have gone before. For it is a fact that we do make and verify statements using psychological concepts in ordinary speech. Nor can it be said that we do so only because these terms are operationally defined, for we have seen that an operationally defined psychological term differs from the concept as it is ordinarily used. Operationists themselves sometimes realize this: Thus MacCorquodale and Meehl accept that psychological statements as these are ordinarily understood cannot be truth-functions of statements using only data language terms.[2] But, if

[1] Estes, op cit., p. 321.
[2] In Estes, et al., *Modern Learning Theory*, p. 185; a statement is a truth-function of some others, if its value as true or false is necessarily determined once the values of these others are determined.

the term were operationally defined, and if the entire empirical interpretation of the statements were given in the data language, then they would be truth-functions of data-language statements. Thus there is a tacit admission that operationally defined terms differ from the corresponding concepts. But then, if operationally defined terms alone can figure in verifiable statements, how can we verify the psychological statements of ordinary speech?

Psychologists who hold to operationism have never adequately resolved this inconsistency in their position. On one hand they feel bound to accept the meaningfulness of ordinary speech in ordinary contexts; on the other, when it comes to science, they feel bound to reject large parts of it, not just on the grounds of its inexactness or on grounds of its not designating the crucial variables, which would be perfectly comprehensible, but because it cannot be used to make verifiable statements. Thus Hull tells us that his approach

> doesn't deny the molar reality of purposive acts (as opposed to movement), of intelligence, of insight, of goals, of intents, of strivings or of value; on the contrary, we insist on the genuineness of these forms of behaviour.

But then he goes on to say,

> We hope ultimately to show the *logical right* to the use of such concepts by *deducing* them as secondary principles from more elementary objective primary principles.[1]

But since Hull has already told us in the previous sentence that his primary principles will be couched only in terms of the physical thing language ('colourless movement and mere receptor impulses as such'), we can readily see that the 'concepts' of action, value, intelligence, etc., to which we shall soon have a 'logical right', are not those of ordinary speech. For the statements made with these 'concepts' will be deduced from statements of the physical thing language, that is, we shall be able to give sufficient conditions for the application of any such concepts in the physical thing language; and, if this is the case, then we are no longer dealing with our ordinary concepts, nor even with psychological concepts at all. But then the 'reality' of purposive acts, goals, insight, etc., which is conceded is a very Pickwickian one.

---

[1] *Principles of Behaviour*, pp. 25-6. My emphasis.

In fact theorists of this persuasion seem to take the premiss that psychological events are not observable on faith. But we certainly cannot accept a premiss of this kind without some proof. This would have to show that our ordinary notion of observation was inadequate. For in the ordinary sense of the term I can observe that Jones is shaking hands with Smith (meaning action, not movement only) or that my dog wants the meat in my hand just as I can that the cat is on the mat or that the needle points to 3·5°. We might say that I infer that the dog wants the meat from his behaviour. But this doesn't mean I infer it from his movements. I know he wants the meat because he is not only drooling, but snapping at it, or begging me for it. In other words, his behaviour in the sense of *action* is that of a dog wanting food. And this *action* is observable, just as observable as the salivation or the movements of the hands of a clock. The confusion of action with movement can often be used to lend credence to behaviourism. It is true that we learn about people through their behaviour. This becomes even more true if we include speech in 'behaviour'. But it does not follow that we learn about them through their movements or through their autonomic reactions, or through the chemical processes which their bodies undergo. For the behaviour which we mainly learn from is action, and it is only *qua* action that it is revelatory, just as speech tells us little or nothing as a stream of sound, but much as meaningful language. Thus, if we can say that some psychological events are 'inferred' as against 'observed', they are inferred from other psychological events; just as some physical events may be inferred from others. So that even if we use 'observed' in the sense of 'not inferred', we cannot say that psychological events are not observed.

Unless we can show that the ordinary sense of the term 'observe' is wrong, then the premiss on which psychological concepts were excluded from scientific discourse must fall. Now, as a matter of fact, there is a philosophical view which underlies this re-definition of observation, although rarely avowed, and this is traditional empiricism. By this is meant the original empiricist doctrine concerning the nature of experience. This notion was of experience as passive, as consisting in the reception of impressions into the mind from the 'external world'. But this had ramifications in epistemology. For, if experience was the receiving of impressions, then any belief about the world must find its evidence in impressions received on the mind. Every 'idea' which was empirically founded must have a corresponding 'impression'. And if a distinction between two ideas was to be empirically founded, there must be a corresponding distinction between the impressions. But on this view the empirical foundation for psychological concepts must be shaky. We can see this with the concept of action, which in many ways is a key concept, since so much of the evidence for the attribution of other psychological properties and the verification of psychological events is found in action. What is the impression from which the 'idea' of action comes? It is clear that in the impression which it makes the execution of an action cannot differ in any way from the occurrence of the corresponding movements. Thus *qua* impressions, the evidence for a statement attributing an action to someone will be the same as that for a statement to the effect that his limbs underwent certain movements. But then the idea of action as distinct from mere movement cannot be an empirically founded idea. In other words, if to observe X is to receive impressions of kind x, then we can never be said to observe actions as distinct from movements; we cannot be said to observe Jones shaking hands with Smith, if we mean more by this than that we observed certain movements of Jones' and Smith's hands, heads, etc. But to say that Jones and Smith shook hands is to say something other than that their hands, heads, etc., moved in a certain way, and we cannot be said to observe that an event of this description took place. This therefore must be inferred. But, and this is the point, we can never have adequate evidence for this inference, for as far as our observations go, they never yield anything but movements. Thus, in this sense, actions are unobservable, and with them all other psychological events. But then statements describing psychological events are unverifiable unless translated into the language of immediate observation which does not include psychological concepts.

This philosophical view, or something like it, seems to underlie operationism in psychology and the naïvely accepted belief that psychological concepts are not empirical concepts.[1] And, indeed, this also seems to be the philosophical underpinning for the whole positivist notion of the 'data language', the view that

[1] Cf. the quotation from Estes above, p. 73.

91

only certain ranges of concepts designate observables, and that all others must be given an empirical meaning by definition in terms of these concepts. This privileged stratum has at various times been held to consist only of those terms which are used to describe the impressions themselves (the sense-datum language), or, at other times, it has been held to consist of terms which characterized things by the impressions they made or would make (the language of observable things). And reduction into both of these has been tried.

The choice of the different privileged strata has been partly a function of differing preoccupations among the modern heirs of empiricism. Those whose primary interest was epistemological have tended to attempt the reduction to sense-data; those who were primarily philosophers of science have been mainly interested in discovering a language of observable things. Philosophers of the Vienna Circle, who had a foot in both camps, alternated between the two (and some, in a later development, even attempted a third—physicalism). What the two attempts have in common, however, is the basic thesis of traditional empiricism, that perception is passive, and that our experience is the effect produced by external reality on the mind or 'receptors'. This underlies both the view of the epistemologists that the basis of all knowledge must reside in the effect (the sense-data), and the view of philosophers of science that the objects of experience impose on us a certain epistemologically privileged mode of classifying them (exhibited in the language of observable things). The interest of the behaviourist thinkers with whom we are dealing in this book is focused, of course, on the second approach.

Thus the epistemology of traditional empiricism seems to lie behind operationism. But so does what one could call its philosophical anthropology, which it shares with Cartesianism. This, too, is connected with the notion of experience. For if we see this as the imprinting of impressions on the mind from the external world, then we see the mind as something in causal interaction with this world, that is, something events in which are causally related to events in the outside world. But if we wish to interpret all experience on this model, we shall have to speak of proprioception also as the reception of 'external' impressions. For these purposes, then, the body is part of the external world and events in it are the causal antecedents for events in the mind.

But like all causal connexions the link between these is contingent (hence the doubts which have always arisen within empiricism as to whether someone else really sees the world as I do, i.e., whether the outer events produce similar events in him as in me). And therefore the connexions between bodily and mental events are contingent (hence the doubts about whether other people really have minds). But the causal interaction between mind and body is two-way, the mind affecting the body as well; and here too the connexions are contingent. But then the mind comes to be seen as separate from the body, that is the events in it are only contingently linked with bodily events, are therefore separately identifiable from bodily events. But we cannot observe, except perhaps in our own case, a set of mental events separately identifiable from their bodily accompaniments, and therefore mental events are held to go on somehow 'behind' the physical events. They are therefore unobservable in principle, and must be inferred from overt bodily behaviour. But then it is just a step to the behaviourist conclusion that they need not be taken into account at all.

In other words, if an action is a piece of behaviour directed by the agent, its being directed by the agent (mental event) is only contingently linked with the corresponding movement's occurring (physical event). The directing of an event must therefore be separately identifiable from the movements' occurrence. But the only criterion we have for saying that an event which could be described as the agent's directing his behaviour has occurred is that a piece of directed behaviour, i.e., an action, occurs. Therefore the directing of behaviour must be a hidden 'inner' event, going on behind the overt movement, which we can never witness. But if we cannot witness it, then we cannot verify propositions about it, and so events of this class cannot be the subject matter of science.

Now the empiricist (and Cartesian) notion of the mental as something 'inner' and unobservable in interaction with the body also underlies the behaviourist rejection of psychological concepts. Thus Hebb[1] speaks of 'animism' as a doctrine which inevitably involved 'interactionism' between mind and body, a doctrine which was bound to be non-empirical since one term of the interaction was unobservable. This is also evident in the

[1] *The Organization of Behaviour.*

awe-inspiring crudity of Hull's account of the origin of the belief in consciousness.[1] The notion originated in the Middle Ages, when it was necessary in order to affect 'social and moral control' to hold out the prospect of reward and punishment after death. Thus the need was for something non-physical which was nevertheless 'an essentially causal element in the determination of moral conduct or behaviour'.[2] Thus consciousness was invented.

We can thus see the origin of the belief that explanation by purpose must involve the invocation of an unobservable entity. As we saw in the first chapter, this is partly a consequence of atomism, the requirement that it not be a condition for the identification of any term that it be linked to any other. But, even more important in the make-up of this view is the set of epistemological and 'anthropological' beliefs of traditional empiricism. For if the mental is something separate, and mental events are unobservable, then any explanation which uses psychological concepts, as explanation by purpose does, must invoke unobservable entities. And in so far as the notion 'purpose' involves that of direction by the agent, it must refer to an unobservable antecedent of action, the inner event of willing or purposing.

But unless one accepts these special doctrines of empiricism there seems little reason to accept the premiss that psychological events are unobservable, and that our ordinary notion of observation is somehow misleading, and therefore little reason to accept the view that explanation by purpose is inherently non-empirical. And, to put it mildly, compelling reasons have yet to be given for accepting these doctrines. We have yet to make sense of the notion that our experience consists in the reception of impressions, (or 'sense-data' as they have most recently been called) or that it is fixed, as it were, in a certain conceptual shape by the things we observe; and we have yet to find a data language to which all other concepts which we in fact use for successful description can be 'reduced'. We might perhaps with more justice assume that 'primitive experience', or our ordinary perception of the world, is not a passive reception of impressions but is always accompanied by classification, a subsumption of the things and events seen under some description. There would thus be many ways of seeing a given set of things or events, many

[1] 'Mind, Mechanism and Adaptive Behaviour,' *Psychological Review*, 1937.
[2] Op. cit., p. 31.

descriptions under which the seer could subsume them, depending on his interests, background, training, etc., none of which would be the basic way. That is, the division between 'seeing' and 'interpreting', between 'observation' and 'inference' would not be clear cut, for there would be no way of seeing which could be considered, relative to the others, as pure seeing, without interpretation. Thus the notion of a specially privileged stratum of expressions, the data language, would have no basis; for seeing something under the description of an action would involve no more inference or interpretation than seeing it under the description of a movement.[1]

Similarly, cogent reasons have yet to be given for considering the mind as an inaccessible inner locus of events. But until these are produced, there is no reason to accept the operationist premiss that psychological statements are unverifiable unless interpreted in non-psychological terms. The epistemological ruling to this effect, then, seems to be simply another attempt to legislate *a priori* on the question whether explanation by purpose is the mode which obtains with animate organisms. The supposed neutrality of these epistemological requirements is a sham one. The claim of Estes[2] that the data language must be 'limited to terms for which agreement upon usage can be obtained among qualified investigators regardless of theoretic orientation' sounds reasonable enough. But this is taken as excluding the case where different 'investigators' will want to use different types of mutually irreducible concept in their 'data language', that is in the language in which they express their observations.

[1] As a matter of fact, the issue here between the empiricist and non-empiricist view raises in another form one of the principal issues of this book, that surrounding the notion of intentionality. For what is at stake here is whether the idea of an 'intentional description' is essential to an account of seeing. Can seeing be understood as the impress of a thing seen on the seer only, or must we also take account of the description under which it is seen? In other words, is there a valid sense of 'see' in which we can say that a person saw the X but not the Y where 'the X' and 'the Y' refer to the same thing? Or is this a question of interpretation? On the former view, the notion 'see' in this sense involves that of 'seeing under a certain description'. We can thus speak not only of the object seen which can be identified indiscriminately as X or Y, but also of the 'intentional object' which can only be identified as X. Cf. the thesis of Maurice Merleau-Ponty, *Phenomenologie de la Perception*, that all perceived objects have a 'sens'.

[2] See quote above, p. 75.

But there is no reason why students shouldn't be able to reach agreement on each other's usage even if they prefer not to use each other's terms. We can certainly agree with Hull on what 'stimulus' means in his theory, even if we don't believe he will get very far with it. This case is only excluded if we assume that there is only *one* data language, one which is common to and neutral between all theories. Then, in the case presented here, it must be that either one side or the other is talking nonsense. Now this assumption follows from empiricist epistemology where the basic evidence for all beliefs is given in the impressions of primitive experience which sets the form of the basic data language. But otherwise there is no need to make it. If this is not the case, then the assumption that a certain language is *the* data language is precisely the assumption that one theory must necessarily be the correct one, for the other one isn't a theory at all. The invitation to protagonists of explanation by purpose that they express their observations in the data language recommended by the operationists is an invitation to abandon their theory, and for no good reason.

An excellent example of this is afforded by Skinner's amendment of Freud.[1] Skinner starts off by regretting that Freud had not quite freed himself of the 'traditional pattern of looking for a cause of human behaviour inside the organism'.[2] This pattern is exemplified in 'animism', which is defined in the usual dualist way as the postulation of an 'inner determiner'. This, of course, cannot account for behaviour, for the antecedent conditions of the inner determiner must be laid bare as well. This Freud attempted to do, says Skinner, but he still remained too much a prisoner of his past in using terms which applied to the mental life at all. The implication is that all that is valuable in Freud's theory could survive the purging of all psychological concepts, which would simply rid it of some confusing connotations and unprofitable philosophical puzzles. But it is sufficient to look at some of Skinner's examples to see that such a purge would utterly destroy the theory. Thus, it is seriously suggested that terms like 'aggression', 'guilt', etc., be done away with, and that the theory should be expressed instead in terms of the 'explicit

[1] Critique of Psycho-analytic Concepts and Theories,' in *Minnesota Studies in the Philosophy of Science*, Vol. I.
[2] Op. cit., p. 79.

shaping of behavioural repertoires'.[1] 'What has survived through the years is not aggression and guilt, later to be manifested in behaviour, but rather patterns of behaviour themselves.' At one level the proposal seems totally confused. For the point of Freudian theory is that we can identify the 'patterns of behaviour' (that is, actions) in terms of 'aggression' and 'guilt': Some act is an act of aggression, the point of some other act is to alleviate guilt for aggression, and so on. It is only *qua* characterized in this way that these actions can be linked to their antecedents in the person's development, or perhaps predicted from this early development. To discover the 'latent meaning' of, say, a neurotic ritual is not to indulge in a flight of fancy which could be inhibited without damage to the theory; it is to identify the action by the description under which it is linked to its antecedent conditions, by the part it plays in the psychic economy. Thus it seems nonsense to speak of the 'patterns of behaviour' *as against* guilt, aggression, etc. But on another level, Skinner's proposal is not confused but totally destructive of the theory. For we might interpret 'patterns of behaviour' as 'patterns of movement' (as against action), in keeping with the type of data language which Skinner himself uses and enjoins. But then nothing remains. For it is only as actions, and as actions with a certain meaning that these patterns can be linked in the theory with their antecedents. What is important is not that water is passing over my hands, but that I am washing my hands, that I am trying to cleanse them. The notions of action, desire, and so on are essential to Freud's theory: They form part of his 'data language'. To try to 'translate' the theory into the data language considered adequate by those who do not share the same fundamental assumptions is to make nonsense of it. There is no such thing as Freud without psychology.

[1] Op. cit., p. 84.

V

THE PROBLEM OF
VERIFICATION

1. EMPIRICAL OR CONCEPTUAL?

AT the beginning of the last chapter we raised the question of
how the thesis that animate beings are purposive could be tested,
only to set it aside in favour of an examination of the positivist
theory of scientific language. This latter question had to be
tackled first, since if the positivist theory were correct, the former
question would never arise: the thesis that animate beings are
purposive would be simply a lot of confused nonsense, unworthy
of consideration in a scientific age. But we have seen that this
short way with the question will not do.

In fact, in the foregoing chapters, we have considered two
basic objections of positivist theory to explanation by purpose,
and found them wanting. The first, which was dealt with in
Chapter I, focused on the teleological form of explanation implicit
in any account in terms of purpose. This form was held to be
inherently verbal and empty, since it was supposed to involve
the invocation of vague 'purposes' or 'powers', whose operation
could never be predicted *ex ante*. But we have seen that a teleological explanation is marked out as such by the form of its laws
and not by reliance on some special type of antecedent variable.
This objection, therefore, falls to the ground.

The second objection, which we considered in the last chapter,
also levelled the charge of empirical emptiness or 'meaningless-
ness' against explanation by purpose, this time because of its use

of psychological concepts. But, to put it mildly, no proof has even been shown that the use of psychological concepts necessarily involves such disastrous results, and this objection could not be sustained either.

It would appear, therefore, that there is no short-cut to the solution of this problem. The belief that there is such a short-cut is, of course, very widespread among students of the sciences of behaviour, and particularly among the school in experimental psychology known as 'behaviourist'. The attractions of the positivist arguments for thinkers of this cast of thought are evident. Opponents of the view that living beings are purposive, they wish to approach the study of behaviour with a method as close to that of the natural sciences as possible, and this for them means explaining behaviour by laws linking physical events. But the whole weight of our common-sense understanding of and everyday language about our behaviour is against this approach. The temptation is therefore great to sweep all these obstacles aside with a simple and decisive argument which will show that the very notion of purposiveness is confused and non-empirical. But, if the arguments of the last chapters are right, then the question cannot be foreclosed in this way.

But can it not be foreclosed in some other way? The question naturally arises at this point. Granted that we cannot summarily decide the issue in favour of 'mechanism' by showing the notion of purposiveness to be non-empirical, can we not nevertheless turn the tables and decide in favour of the contrary thesis by showing this notion to be inescapable? An argument to this effect would start from the fact, which we discussed in the second chapter, that the logic of our ordinary language, and particularly of terms like 'action' and 'desire', contains implicitly the assumption that our behaviour is purposive. If this is so, how can we doubt that we are purposive beings without introducing the implicit hypothesis that we may have been talking nonsense all these centuries? But surely this latter hypothesis is untenable, since we have managed to communicate, to verify propositions, to reach inter-subjective agreement in a great number of cases.

But, strong as it appears, this argument, as we have seen in the second chapter, is not decisive. For the fact that the assumptions behind a given set of concepts are invalid does not imply that they cannot be used to make distinctions and formulate propositions which can be inter-subjectively agreed and verified. For, as with the case of the Aristotelian notions of 'natural' and 'violent' movement, what they distinguish may be really distinct, and what they pick out as a class of phenomena may really have a principle of unity beyond that it is so picked out; what is wrong may simply be that the criteria of this distinction or the principle of unity of the class are wrongly conceived. Thus to say that we may one day discover that our behaviour may be accounted for by a mechanistic theory is not to say that we may one day find that we have been talking nonsense all our lives. The former possibility thus remains open, even though the latter is inconceivable.

Thus the argument from ordinary language is no more fruitful than the positivist argument in yielding a short-cut to the solution of our problem. How then can we go about establishing or refuting the claim that animate organisms are purposive?

We might perhaps put the matter in this way. The preceding discussion seems to show that there is no *a priori* way of deciding the issue, that is, no way which does not involve examining the behaviour of animate organisms itself. Both the above arguments, in effect, purport to rule out one solution to the problem on the basis of more general considerations, leaving the other sole occupant of the field; for the argument from ordinary language, these considerations are logical: the thesis of mechanism is reduced to absurdity by being shown to imply that our language is nonsensical; for the positivist argument, the considerations are epistemological: the thesis of purposiveness is shown to be empirically empty. If both these are shown to be invalid, might we not conclude that the question can only be decided by examining the behaviour in question itself, that it is, in short, an empirical question?

But the word 'empirical' here may mislead. In fact what is at stake here is not an ordinary matter of fact, such as whether rabbits eat lettuce; it concerns the form of the laws to be used in explanation and the concepts in which these laws are to be cast. As we saw in the first chapter, to say that a being is purposive is to say that his behaviour can be accounted for in terms of purpose, and this in term implies that the basic level laws are teleological in form. Again, in the second chapter, we saw that the form of explanation implicit in our ordinary language was incompatible with a more basic level explanation of a non-teleo-logical type, so that, if this latter were shown to hold, we should have to undertake a far-reaching conceptual revision. Our ordinary notions of behaviour require that this be accounted for by laws governing action. Thus the thesis that living beings are purposive is the thesis that their behaviour is to be explained on the most basic level by that form of teleological laws which we have called laws governing action. And the thesis of mechanism, directly negating this, is to the effect that the most basic level laws are non-teleological laws governing movement. What is at issue, then, is the form of the laws and the concepts used in them.

Now this could be called an empirical question, but it could with equal justice be called a conceptual one. But in this case it would be a mistake to consider these two descriptions as mutually exclusive. In fact this issue can be called empirical in the same sense as the Principle of Inertia can be called empirical, and it can be called conceptual in the same sense in which the discovery of this principle can be said to have involved a conceptual shift.

In fact, the issue which we are discussing presents a close analogy with the issue about the explanation of motion in seven-teenth century physics. For, like the classical discussion, it touches the conceptual form of the laws, and thus on it depends the entire direction in which the science concerned will proceed. There is, of course, a closer analogy, and this has not been lost on behaviour theorists. Seizing on the similarity of purposive explanation to the form dominant in Aristotelian science, they have ventured to predict that the same fate awaits the former as befell the latter. For both Hull and Lewin, for instance, psycho-logy is about to enter a 'Galilean' age. But whether they will be resolved in the same way or not, these two issues are similar in that they concern the type of laws we should try to establish and therefore the way in which the enquiry should proceed.

Now these issues, touching as they do on the conceptual frame-work of enquiry, are nevertheless empirical in this sense, that whether or not a given principle, say that of mechanism, or that of purposiveness, is judged valid will depend ultimately on whether laws of the type it prescribes are found to hold of and account for the phenomena. The Principle of Inertia won universal acceptance because it was the foundation of the most fruitful set of explanatory laws discovered up to that time. It is only by discovering the type of laws which hold of behaviour that the claim that humans and animals are purposive beings can be established or refuted.

2. TESTING A THEORY

The issue, then, is, in this special sense, an empirical one. But this is not to say that it can be easily decided. It is one thing to establish whether a state of affairs obtains at a given place and time, another, and harder, thing to establish whether a given law holds; but it is even more difficult to discover whether the laws which hold in general of a given range of phenomena are of a certain type, and this is the kind of question we are dealing with. It is not easy to see how we should set about it to answer a question of this kind.

There is, moreover, a sense in which the issue we are concerned with here can never be conclusively decided, or, rather, can only be conclusively decided in one direction. For the claim we are discussing is to the effect that the most basic laws have a certain character, i.e., are laws governing action. And this would mean not only that a set of such laws be found to apply, but that no other laws can be found, from which these can be derived, which are of a different character. The claim, therefore, involves a negative existential statement, and as such there is a sense in which it can never be conclusively established, however strong the evidence may be for it. But it can, however, be conclusively refuted; for all that is required is for a set of laws of the type which it rules out to be found. Thus, while we may have evidence for the claim, in the sense that all attempts to account for behaviour on non-purposive principles are found to be inadequate, the possibility is always there that some other set of laws not yet considered will refute it. This is bound to be the position of any claim to the effect that the most basic laws in any region are of a certain type.

But, though the final conclusion evades our grasp, evidence can still be gathered in favour of the claim. For it is possible to examine rival views and find them wanting, and even if the question must remain open whether there are not other rival theories which are adequate, we can legitimately put more confidence in the thesis as a result. One way,[1] then, of testing, at least partially, the claim that living beings are purposive is by elimination. But, the question remains, how should we proceed?

Now in conceptual questions of the kind we are discussing here, the empirical substance of the conceptual thesis touches the type of laws which hold, the type of correlations we should seek. It is a thesis to the effect that independent and dependent variables are of a certain sort or should be picked out by concepts of a certain kind. Thus to decide a question of this kind what we have to discover is whether stable correlations or functions can be found to hold between variables so characterized.

This may sound impossibly long and difficult, but it is not always so. The major difficulty in these questions is often one of definition. Once we have left the level of high generality and have defined clearly the type of correlations which a given conceptual thesis calls for in a given range of phenomena, it is often possible to show that the kind of regularities posited cannot be found in the phenomena. If the thesis is incorrect, this will often become evident on examination by fairly reliable signs.

Thus, in the case we are considering, a rival view to explanation by purpose will mark itself off as such by the types of correlations it seeks to establish. These will be, as we have mentioned, laws governing movement, and will be non-teleological in form. We can call these general views, to the effect that the crucial correlations explanatory of behaviour hold between events of a certain sort or characterized in a certain way, theories and distinguish them from the particular correlations which are put up for examination and are usually called hypotheses. A rival theory, then, will be a view to the effect that the crucial correlations hold, e.g., between stimuli and responses, or between tensions and force-fields, or between cell-assemblies, and so on. Thus, for any given range of behaviour which is in dispute, it will be the claim of a rival theory that the phenomena of this range can be accounted for by correlating events of the particular type which it selects,

[1] There is obviously another, more positive way of strengthening this thesis and that is to elaborate satisfactory theories of the kind it prescribes, using laws governing action. But the state of our knowledge at present is such that this would be a less fruitful road than the negative one. In this field, it is still easier to destroy than to build. The consolation is that destruction, by eliminating false routes, can help to point the way. For this reason we shall concentrate here on the negative task of elimination.

that the regularities, in other words, are of a certain sort. And since these correlations will govern movement and the terms will not be picked out by concepts involving intentionality, this claim will conflict with that of explanation by purpose.

Now it should be possible to establish whether any regularities hold of the phenomena among events of this type, or whether all hypotheses linking terms of this kind are bound to encounter contrary instances. This may seem impossible to establish conclusively because it involves, too, a negative existential statement. But in fact the gamut of reasonable hypotheses open when we are trying to discover regularities of a certain type in phenomena of a certain definite range is often very limited; and, what is even more important, it is often limited to correlations of a certain specific form. In this case it will usually be possible to determine whether the regularities are such as to give a possible foundation to hypotheses of this form.

But, of course, where the hypotheses appear not to hold, it is possible that one could save them by making them more complex, by introducing special auxiliary hypotheses or adducing special factors. Until one has examined and rejected such special hypotheses one cannot abandon the theory. But these special hypotheses will generally themselves be limited in their form by the nature of the theory itself, and this will sometimes enable us to determine fairly unequivocally whether the theory can be saved by having recourse to them. And, moreover, these special hypotheses will have themselves to be verifiable, which means that the special factor must itself have antecedent conditions. If the theory is wrong, then such antecedents will be hard to find, and the number of such gratuitous hypotheses will multiply. Sometimes the only factor or special hypothesis that can be adduced to account for the deviant phenomena is one which itself violates the requirements of the theory in some way, so that introducing it leaves us with the same problem as we had before. Such hypotheses often turn out to be purely verbal 'solutions'.

If we find that factors of this kind tend to be adduced by supporters of a theory, then we have a serious sign that the theory is wrong. An example can be given from the disputes in physics prior to Galileo. The Aristotelian principle that all movement required a mover came up against the obstacle of the cannon ball, or thrown object. These were 'violent' movements, and hence the principles of movement would not be internal, in the nature of the things. But by external causes one could only account for the *initiation* of these movements and not for their continuation. This problem was, in effect, only ultimately solved by dropping the principle, no movement without a mover, in favour of the principle of inertia, for which the continuation of motion didn't need an explanation separate from its initiation. But in the meantime, all sorts of special hypotheses were put forward in order to account for the continued motion of the cannon-ball after it had left the cannon, or the spear after it had left the hand, such as, for instance, that the air rushed around the back of the projectile and pushed it forward. But these special factors, as was readily seen by critics, raised again the problems they were meant to solve; for the question arose, what moved the special factors? And if one tried to answer, in the example just cited, for instance, that the projectile itself displaced the air, then the whole phenomenon looked very much like a case of lifting oneself by one's own bootstraps. And, if not, then the question of accounting for continued movement remained entire.

Thus although, as we have remarked above, it may be thought in principle impossible to prove conclusively that no correlations among events of a given range can be established, in practice we shall often be able to gather fairly convincing evidence for this. If a theory is wrong, then it is very likely that no stable correlations of the type concerned can be found. And it can be taken as a fairly reliable sign that a theory is ill-founded, if the hypotheses that are put forward which satisfy it, i.e., link events of the type it indicates, are found not to hold, so that a great and constantly increasing number of special factors have to be adduced, whose operation cannot be verified, that is, the antecedent conditions for whose operation remains unclear; and the case will be even stronger if these special factors are of such a nature that they pose the question once again that their introduction was meant to solve.

3. THE SCOPE OF THE ENQUIRY

This, then, is what our procedure should be, if we are to test the thesis at issue in this book. We must examine the phenomena to see if hypotheses of the kind proposed by rival theories hold of them, or whether, on the other hand, these theories, once in contact with the facts, begin to display the symptoms mentioned in the last paragraph. In the latter case, we shall have good grounds for eliminating these rival theories, and the thesis of purposiveness will be correspondingly strengthened.

This procedure obviously has its limitations. It is clear that the validity of our conclusions will be relative to the state of our knowledge at any point. Thus we cannot criticize a given theory until something is known about the kinds of regularities which hold between events of the type it singles out for its hypotheses. The type of question we are trying to answer is a scientific one, one concerning the principles which should lie at the basis of a science of behaviour, and like all such questions, it cannot be answered prior to all scientific enquiry. But, as the area of fact gathered increases, it is possible, by the way outlined above, to eliminate certain theories, the search for certain kinds of laws, as unfruitful, and thus come closer to the correct theory which can be at the basis of a satisfactory science of behaviour.

We have constantly to bear in mind, of course, that to come closer may not be to come very close. For the elimination of some theories of a certain type doesn't show that all theories of that type are invalid; and the establishing of a theory of a certain type doesn't show that the phenomena cannot be accounted for by a theory of another type which has not yet been dealt with. But even to examine all the theories which have been propounded so far would be the task of several life-times, and when one thinks of the new theories and modifications of the old which will emerge with time, one can well believe that the question will not only not be decided conclusively, but will not even find a solution which achieves something like general acceptance.

But one can discuss fruitfully even inconclusive questions; and we shall try following the procedures outlined above to pursue the enquiry in the second part of this book. But to do so it is necessary to select a certain range of theories if the discussion is to have any value. The range which will be discussed here are drawn from the field of experimental psychology, the study of the behaviour of animals and men by experimental means. This is the field in which behaviourism has been the dominant approach for some decades, and the theories which will be particularly weighed are those of the 'neo-behaviourists', or stimulus-response theorists.

This means, in effect, that we shall be concentrating mainly on what are called 'peripheralist' theories, in opposition to 'centralist' ones. The former term is used here somewhat in the sense of Hull's term 'molar',[1] that is, it applies to a theory which attempts to correlate grossly observable elements of environment and behaviour, as opposed to a theory which tries to account for behaviour in terms of the underlying neurological laws. But this form of the distinction may mislead. For we are not talking about the type of distinction mentioned by Deutsch[2] between an explanation in terms of generalizations about behaviour and one in terms of the underlying mechanism. For virtually all 'peripheralist' accounts hazard some hypotheses about the form of the mechanism underlying behaviour, even if they are relatively vague about its physiological embodiment.[3]

A 'peripheralist' theory in the sense meant here is one which tries to account for behaviour as a function of the condition of the environment and, perhaps, of certain internal states of deficit or need, without using in any way concepts involving intentionality. A 'centralist' theory, on the other hand, would, at this level of explanation, make use of concepts analogous to those involving intentionality; that is, in accounting for the effect of environment on behaviour, it would invoke certain states of the system with properties analogous to those usually ascribed to organisms by means of psychological terms, states of desire, knowledge, intention; but, at the same time, it would attempt to account for the properties of these states in turn by more basic (neurophysiological) laws, the given states being shown to result from certain initial conditions according to these laws.

A 'centralist' account would thus not involve explanation by purpose or the use of genuinely psychological concepts, but it would resemble explanation by purpose in this, that its first level

---

[1] I.e., the term 'molar' as used by Hull—he didn't invent it.

[2] *The Structural Basis of Behaviour*, Chapter I.

[3] In this sense, Deutsch's theory is on a level with Hull's in spite of his attempt, op. cit., Chapter I, to distinguish them. The type of mechanism suggested by Deutsch is simply more sophisticated. But in either case the verification lies in the behaviour correlations derived and not in observations of the mechanism, since little or nothing is said about its embodiment; and in either case the behaviour correlations are derived from a specific type of mechanism. Hull, no more than Deutsch, tries simply to collect facts about the regularities of behaviour.

laws relating the condition of the environment to behaviour would invoke states of the organism analogously characterized. The properties of these states whereby they are analogous to 'intentional states' stem from the fact that they involve processing —that is, selecting and interpreting—information about the environment and the organism's own condition and behaviour by which behaviour is directed or guided.[1] The 'centralist' thesis is that this processing is a constant feature of the organism, such that, while it is affected by experience, the effect of experience itself depends on the way in which the events concerned are processed. And that is why, on this view, behaviour can never be made a function of the condition of the environment by laws which make no place for intentional states or their analogues.

Now, in discussing 'neo-behaviourist' theories we shall be concentrating on accounts of a 'peripheralist' kind. The ground for thus narrowing our scope is not only that to go beyond this would involve writing not one book but several. The fact is that 'centralist' theories are still too speculative and indefinite to allow a fruitful discussion. The question posed by this type of theory must, therefore, remain open.

But it may still be valuable to see if a 'peripheralist' science of behaviour which eschews explanation by purpose is possible, and it is this question that we hope to answer, or come some steps closer to answering, in examining these theories. If the answer is positive, then the claim we have been discussing in the last chapters will be shown to be unfounded; if the answer is in the negative, then we will have some, however incomplete and inconclusive, evidence for its validity. And even if the answer is inconclusive, we can hope to illustrate how it can be answered once more knowledge has been gathered.

---

[1] We can speak about 'information' here not only because the condition of the environment is selected and interpreted, but also because the processing results in variations in the way it affects behaviour.

PART TWO

THEORY AND FACT

VI

THE DETERMINANTS OF
LEARNING

I. S–R THEORY

THE neo-behaviourist or stimulus–response (S–R) theories, which we shall be dealing with in this part, are, in many ways, the descendants of classical empiricism. This is visible not only in the epistemological beliefs which we discussed in Chapter IV, which S–R theorists, virtually without exception, hold to, and which they put forward as a justification of their theory; we can also see it in the theory itself and its attempt to account for behaviour by 'associations' formed in learning. But the distinguishing feature of the modern theory is that the associations hold no longer between 'ideas' or 'impressions', but between what has replaced these, viz. 'stimuli', and responses. The attempt is thus to account for behaviour by correlating certain types of behaviour event and certain types of event in the organism and environment.

In choosing what kind of events should be so correlated, S–R theorists, like all others, start from the intuitively recognized fact that our behaviour is a function of what in ordinary language would be called our 'desires' and of the situation in which we are placed, or rather, of the situation as we know it. Behaviour is thus a function of two ranges of independent variables. So much is common to many theories. What marks S–R off is the terms in which they classify these events:

It is the primary task of a molar science of behaviour to isolate the basic laws or rules according to which various combinations of

III

stimulation, arising from the state of need on the one hand and the state of the environment on the other, bring about the kind of behaviour characteristic of different organisms.[1]

S–R theorists wish to do away with all notions involving intentionality. Indeed, under the influence of empiricist epistemology, they tend to believe that these notions are not genuine empirical concepts, and cannot be given a definite empirical sense unless operationally defined.[2] Otherwise, these concepts will be applied in an arbitrary and incommunicable way, on the basis of 'introspection', and their use would make an intersubjectively verifiable science of behaviour impossible.

Thus, for Hull, 'instead of furnishing a means for the solution of problems, consciousness appears itself to be a problem needing solution'.[3] The data language must contain only terms belonging to the physical thing language.

Thus, in characterizing the situation in which behaviour takes place, which is one of the factors behaviour is a function of, S–R theorists do not speak of the situation as it is known to the organism as we might spontaneously describe it in ordinary language, but rather of how it impinges on the organism via the organs of sense. They therefore speak of the 'stimulus', identified either as the object which gives rise to the stimulus, or as, say, the pattern on the retina in vision, or perhaps in terms of the current discharged up the 'afferent' channels. Similarly, they do not speak of the 'meaning' of the situation for the organism, i.e., what the situation would 'call for' granted the purposes of the organism. This kind of description is not only ruled out because it is 'intentional' but also because the situation characterized in this way is an antecedent condition of a teleological type. Thus Skinner:

> The independent variables must also be described in physical terms. An effort is often made to avoid the labour of analysing a physical situation by guessing what it 'means' to an organism or by distinguishing between the physical world and a psychological world of 'experience'. This practice also reflects a confusion between dependent and independent variables. The events affecting an organism must be capable of description in the language of physical science.[4]

[1] Hull, *Principles of Behaviour*, p. 19.   [2] Cf. Chapter IV.
[3] 'Mind, Mechanism and Adaptive Behaviour,' *Psychological Review*, 1937.
[4] *Science and Human Behaviour*, Chapter III, p. 36.

Here Skinner is not only objecting to the vagueness of the description and its 'subjectivity' but also to the fact that dependent and independent variables are 'confused', for as in all teleological laws, the independent variable (the situation) is characterized in terms of its relation to the dependent variable (the action) as one which 'calls for' this action (granted, of course, the purposes of the organism). And this, on empiricist assumptions, is inadmissible.[1]

Secondly, the internal conditions of behaviour cannot be characterized by terms which involve the notion of a disposition to behave in a certain way. This not only operates against ordinary language terms like desire. Spence, in his article 'The nature of theory construction in contemporary psychology',[2] makes a list of rejected terms in which scientific constructs like 'libido' are lumped together with such ordinary language terms as 'mind' and metaphysical terms like 'elan vital'. All of these, according to Spence, suffer from the same disability: they lack a definite empirical sense.

Thus the internal conditions of behaviour must be characterized in a way which does not involve the notion of a disposition to behave in a certain way, and hence for these the notion of 'need-' or 'drive-state' has been evolved, which either refers to some physiological condition which can be measured directly, or may be conceived as an intervening variable, as in Hull's system, linked to such antecedent conditions as hours of food deprivation and so on.

From what has been said above it is obvious that, once we turn to the response side of the correlations, the use of action concepts is also rejected by S–R theorists. They are, of course, aware that we usually classify behaviour by these concepts. They do not object to classifying sequences of behaviour by their results. But action concepts do not classify behaviour sequences by the results they end in only, but by the goals that are aimed at in them, and thus by the description they have for the agent. These concepts are therefore rejected as 'anthropomorphic' and 'introspective'.

Now for certain rough practical purposes the custom of naming action sequences by their goals is completely justified by its convenience. It may even be that for very gross molar behaviour it can usefully be employed in theory construction, provided the

[1] *Psychological Review*, 1944.　　　[2] Cf. Chapter I.

theorist is alert to the naturally attendant hazards. These appear the moment the theorist ventures to draw upon his intuition for statements concerning the behaviour (movements) executed by the organism between the onset of a need and its termination through organismic action.[1]

Thus our use of terms which classify behaviour by the end-results which 'terminate the need' must not lead us into explaining this behaviour as the result of desire or any disposition to try to bring about the result-event in question. On the contrary,

> An ideally adequate theory even of so-called purposive behaviour ought, therefore, to begin with colourless movement and mere receptor impulses as such, and from these build up step by step both adaptive and maladaptive behaviour.[2]

This is the basic goal of all S–R theorists. They do not want to deny that our ordinary action concepts have a utility in ordinary language. But they will not accept what is implicit in our ordinary notion of action, that it must be explained in terms of purpose and cannot be explained by connexions between 'receptor impulses' and 'movements'. On the contrary they want to account for the whole range of behaviour we usually describe in these terms by just such connexions.

> The present approach does not deny the molar reality of purposive acts (as opposed to movements), of intelligence, of insight, of goals, of intents, of strivings, or of value; on the contrary, we insist upon the genuineness of these forms of behaviour. We hope ultimately to show the logical right to the use of such concepts by deducing them as secondary principles from more elementary objective primary principles.[3]

Hull's insistence on the 'genuineness' of these forms of behaviour must not mislead us.[4] For he is categorically against the view that 'what is called goal or purposive behaviour . . . cannot be derived from any conceivable set of postulates involving mere stimuli and mere movement',[5] and yet this is what is essential to our ordinary notion of action.[6]

---

[1] Hull, *Principles of Behaviour*, p. 25.   [2] *Principles of Behaviour*, p. 25.
[3] *Principles of Behaviour*, pp. 25-6.   [4] Cf. supra, Chapter IV.
[5] Loc. cit.   [6] Cf. supra, Chapter III.

This insistence on the kind of connexion between 'receptor impulses' and 'colourless movement' is the essential principle of S–R theory and is what has earned it this name. The question, then, is whether laws linking events of this kind can be discovered which will account for behaviour. It is this question which we shall try to answer in this chapter and the succeeding ones.

2. LEARNING AS CONDITIONING

One of the cardinal features of the behaviour of animate organisms which has to be accounted for in any explanatory theory is learning, the capacity of the organism to adapt its behaviour to a new environment as a result of its experience of this environment. Since learning plays such an essential role in what we call adaptation, learning theory should be a good context in which to examine the question whether we can account for adaptive behaviour without the use of a teleological notion of adaptation or some analogue of it.

The notion of adaptation is of course implicit in the ordinary language teleological form of explanation where action is frequently explained in terms of its propitiousness for certain purposes i.e. by its 'adaptiveness' in respect of these ends. The aim of S–R theories on the other hand is to explain behaviour without using a notion of this kind. Thus for Hull it is one of the tasks of a molar science of behaviour to explain why behaviour is adaptive, why 'it is successful in the sense of reducing needs and facilitating survival',[1] a task separate from though closely related to that of explaining why the behaviour of different organisms is as it is. Adaptiveness is thus an explicandum for S–R theory. It is not a principle to be used in the explicans.

But learning theory is of especial importance for neo-behaviourism since, true to its empiricist heritage, it puts inordinate weight on learning in any explanation of behaviour. Just as the old empiricism held that the mind at birth was a *tabula rasa*, devoid of innate ideas, so S–R theorists pay little attention to 'instincts', or those behaviour sequences, often very complex ones, which are innate and emerge in the activity of the growing animal regardless of training. The attempt is rather to explain behaviour by

---

[1] *Principles of Behaviour*, p. 19.

connexions born of previous experience. Learning theory[1] is thus the best place to start if we are to test the adequacy of modern behaviourism.

The modern theory grew out of older empiricism as a radical solution to the dualism endemic in this latter, and to the problem that this posed, viz., that observable bodily events were always explained by unobservable mental ones. It was Thorndike who cut the Gordian knot by the introduction of his famous 'Law of Effect'. Thus the old view was that action was governed by pleasure and pain, that is, that human and other animate organisms sought the one and avoided the other. The survival value of this procedure lay in the fortunate congruence of pleasurable activity and activity needful to the organism on one hand and of painful experience and experience harmful to the organism on the other. This congruence was not, of course, complete, but it was wide enough to ensure survival. The explanation of this congruence varied. Locke, e.g., attributed it to the wisdom and bounty of the Diety. When the problem of adaptation really came to the fore with the discoveries of Darwin, the tendency was to account for the congruence by natural selection. No species was guaranteed that their pleasure would correspond to their need, but over time it would tend to be the case that all or most species would exhibit this congruence since those which did not would become extinct.

But explanations in terms of pleasure still had two disadvantages from an empiricist point of view. Since pleasure was an inner state only contingently linked with the activities which gave rise to it, animals and men could only discover by experience what produced pleasure and what pain. The experience of a constant conjunction between a certain action and pleasure would lead to the frequent occurrence of this action. But this raised two problems. First as an explanation of change of behaviour it involved the invoking of a totally unobservable condition in the organism in question, viz., the state of pleasure. Since pleasure

[1] We shall be dealing here with only one kind of learning, learning about the environment, and not, e.g., with the acquisition of motor skills or of new goals. This restriction is made necessary by the fact that, while the distinction between the different kinds is not accepted in S–R theory, this was really mainly devised to account for learning about the environment. In fact, it cannot deal with motor learning at all. Cf. below, Chapter IX.

was only contingently linked with the activities which gave rise to it and since, according to empiricist theory, any feeling was only contingently linked to the behaviour which we normally take as expressive of it, there was no way of establishing by the observation of behaviour from the outside whether the organism concerned was in a state of pleasure or pain. Thus to explain the increased frequency in the emission of a certain type of behaviour, say, by invoking a state of pleasure in the organism was to offer a purely verbal explanation, since our only evidence for the state of pleasure is that the behaviour with which it is putatively associated occurs more often.

The second problem is summed up in the question posed by Thorndike, how does one 'get to' the response? The first problem, that posed by the supposed unobservable nature of states of pleasure, could perhaps be solved by introducing a physiological theory and giving 'pleasure' a physiological definition. Spencer seemed to be proceeding along this path in adumbrating a physiological theory, although the conversion from classical empiricism was not complete and the notion of cognition was still given a role. But the second problem is more intractable. For the postulation of states of pleasure in order to explain adaptation is not enough, one has also to postulate the operation of an 'idea of pleasure' in order to account for certain cases. Thus Bain held that pleasure involved an increase in vital energy which induced the organism to continue doing whatever gave rise to it. But the problem remained of explaining why, on another occasion, this action would tend to be initiated. In this case one seems forced to say that the action is associated not only with pleasure but with the idea or memory of pleasure, which association will lead, on another occasion, to the action's being initiated. Thus we must posit a second unobservable state. But there is worse. We seem to be adopting a teleological type of explanation in saying that whatever leads to pleasure will tend to occur; that is, we are explaining behaviour by what it tends to bring about. Thus in trying to avoid a teleological form of explanation of adaptation in terms of the goal of survival we will simply have introduced another teleological explanation in terms of the goal of pleasure. In other words, once one has posited a connexion between a certain action and pleasure, the problem still remains of explaining how this association will affect behaviour. This is the problem of 'getting to' the response. And the only way to solve this seems to be to invoke a teleological principle.

It was considerations of this kind which led Thorndike to start afresh with a system of explanation freed of all cognitive elements. The response was held to be invoked directly by the situation and not to depend on any known link between this response and a resulting state of pleasure. 'Pleasure' entered the explanation in a different way. The thesis was that those responses which led to pleasurable states tended to become associated with the stimuli which were impinging on the organism at the time they were emitted, and on future occasions these stimuli would tend to evoke these responses. This is the substance of the 'Law of Effect' which has become a central principle in many S–R theories of learning. The notion is that a connexion between S and R is 'stamped in' by being 'reinforced', that is, followed by a 'satisfying' state of affairs, and is weakened if no such state of affairs ensues. Thus the Law of Effect can yield a way of explaining adaptation which does not involve the invocation of an unobservable cognitive state or a teleological principle of explanation.

The Law of Effect is, however, challenged by another group of S–R theorists who hold that it still suffers from the defects of the explanation it replaces. For while the second problem, that connected with the idea of pleasure, may have been removed, the first remains. How do we know, in fact, what is a reinforcing state of affairs, except by seeing which S–R connexions are in fact strengthened? Is not the definition of a re-inforcing state of affairs circular in that we define it as one which strengthens connexions between stimuli and responses, while at the same time we try to explain the strengthening of these connexions by their connexion with a re-inforcing state of affairs?[1] It has been held by proponents of the Law of Effect that the circle is not a vicious one since we could easily discover in the first instance what states of affairs were re-inforcing by seeing where connexions were strengthened and then go on to predict in future what connexions would be strengthened.[2] This procedure is perfectly legitimate

[1] Cf. Postman's 'The History and Present Status of the Law of Effect', *Psychological Bulletin*, 1947.

[2] Cf. P. E. Meehl: 'On the Circularity of the Law of Effect,' *Psychological Bulletin*, 1950.

provided we are specific and exact enough in our specification of the states of affairs in question. But it involves abandoning the specific content of terms like 'desire', 'satisfying', 'reward' and so on, for we are only saying that there is an empirical connexion between an S–R pair occurring together with a state of affairs of this kind and its occurring more frequently in the future. Or— and this has been the tendency of most re-inforcement theorists— we can posit mechanisms of a quasi-physiological kind which constitute 'satisfaction', e.g., 'reduction of the hunger drive' or 'need', and call these reinforcing states of affairs. It might be objected that the basis in physiological theory for these mechanisms is still fairly insecure, but S–R theorists usually get over this by planning experiments in which the 'reward' answers what everyone will recognize to be a need, such as hunger or thirst, avoidance of pain or harm, etc.

But this answer has failed to satisfy many S–R theorists, and they have evolved theories which were much closer to old-style associationism; except that what is associated is not ideas but stimuli and responses. Watson was one of the pioneers of this kind of theory, which also owes a great debt to the researches of Pavlov. Watson and those who follow him hold that stimuli are associated with responses, that is, acquire the tendency to evoke them, simply by virtue of occurring simultaneously with them. The strength of the association may depend on the frequency of association or the recency of the last occurrence or on the time interval between S and R, or the association may reach its full strength on one occurrence. S–R 'contiguity' theorists (as they are called to distinguish them from the re-inforcement theorists) differ in their views about the laws governing association, but they have in common a rejection of the Law of Effect and a theory of association by contiguity. The adaptive nature of learned behaviour is explained by Guthrie, one of the prominent members of the school, by the hypothesis that the achievement of a need-reducing goal so alters the stimulus situation, at least by removing the internal drive stimulus, as to mark a sharp break in the animal's environment. Thus, by the principle of recency, the last action committed before this change of situation will be conditioned to the stimuli obtaining before the reduction of drive and this will tend to recur when the situation recurs. Performance will become more 'adapted' in the sense of more successful in meeting needs.

But whether of the reinforcement or the contiguity type, the aim of S–R theory is to account for the adapted performance of men and animals arising from learning in terms of connexions between stimuli and responses formed in previous experience. The notion of what strengthens a connexion is in dispute, as is that of what constitutes a connexion. Most theorists seem to see this on the model of a reflex, but some, e.g. Skinner, make a distinction between reflex action which is 'elicited' and 'operant' behaviour which is 'emitted'. The pecularity of operant behaviour is that it doesn't need to be called forth by a stimulus, although it can be connected to a distinctive cue, and is subject to re-inforcement. But what all have in common is the desire to do away with the cognitive element in learning and to explain the improvement in performance in terms of the increased likelihood of certain movements occurring given certain stimuli or distinctive cues.

3. THE PROBLEM OF 'SET'

This account of learning is in sharp contrast with any account in terms of purpose. For an explanation of the latter kind attempts to account for behaviour as action, that is, as directed to a goal.[1] The fact that behaviour takes the form that it does is explained, therefore, in a teleological way, by what the environment makes propitious granted the goal. For instance, we might say: the animal ran down that path because it was the shortest way to get to the food. Now the type of learning we are dealing with here is learning about the environment, where behaviour in a given environment changes over time without any change in the environment or in the goals pursued by the animal. But, if both the old and the new behaviour are to be explained by what 'the environment' makes propitious granted the goal, there must be some sense of 'environment' in which we can say that it changes during learning. Thus any purposive explanation always posits a distinction between the environment *tout court* and the environment as it affects or is known by the animal.[2] It is this

[1] Cf. supra, Chapters I–III.

[2] As a matter of fact, all explanations of behaviour of a teleological or semi-teleological kind which are intended to account for learning must posit an analogous distinction, which we find, e.g., in Gestalt theory in the distinc-

latter, the 'intentional environment' as we may call it, which is correlated with behaviour. The change in performance in the same environment as a result of learning is then accounted for by changes in the 'intentional environment' and it is this change which constitutes learning. In ordinary language we often speak of learning as a change in our knowledge of the environment.

The issue is thus sharply drawn between S–R and purposive explanations in learning theory around this question of the use of cognitive terms. It should be possible, therefore, to establish the differences between the kinds of correlations which these two kinds of explanations would posit to account for the phenomena of learning. Let us take our examples from the field of discrimination learning, that is learning to respond differentially to discriminably different stimuli, such as takes place, e.g., when rats are trained to jump towards the white card of a pair, one black, one white, which is presented. Now S–R theory holds that it comes about this way:

> so long as the subject is receiving discriminably different stimulation from the positive and negative discriminanda during the pre-solution period, differential associative tendencies will be developed with respect to them. According to this theory, discrimination learning is conceived as a cumulative process of building up the excitatory strength (habit, associative strength) of the positive cue as compared with the competing excitatory strength of the negative cue.[1]

Thus each of the crucial stimuli becomes more or less associated with the response, that is, capable of evoking it, depending on the degree to which response to this stimulus is re-inforced or leads to some change in the animal's drive state. In the end the 'correct' stimulus, that is the one made correct by the experimenter, becomes much stronger than the other, so that the animal will respond to it virtually 100% of the time. The problem is then learned.

[1] Spence, 'Theoretical Interpretations of Learning', in S. S. Stevens, *Handbook of Experimental Psychology*, p. 719.

---

tion between the 'geographical' and the 'behavioural' environments; cf. Kurt Koffka, *Principles of Gestalt Psychology*. *A Fortiori*, a theory which uses the concept of action must make the distinction. Cf. Chapter III.

For a theory using the notion of cognition what occurs in the course of learning is that the animal discovers that jumping, say, towards the positive stimulus (towards the card of the type the experimenter has made positive) leads to reward. The process of learning is that of acquiring an intentional environment in which the action of jumping to a card with the right kind of markings is a way of getting food. What the rat learns is what Tolman calls the 'instructions', e.g. 'jump to the white card'; he acquires an 'expectancy' that jumping to the white card will bring a reward. On the cognitive view, then, the rat, once he has learnt the problem, is not simply responding to a certain stimulus but is acting on an expectation. Now in the presolution period, before the rat has 'caught on' to the right 'instructions' the cognitive view is that he is also acting on an expectancy, but not as yet the correct one. The process of learning is not the strengthening of certain associative connexions between stimuli and responses but the confirmation and disconfirmation of certain expectancies. Failures on this view do not 'stamp out' certain S–R connexions but show certain expectancies to be wrong and lead to their abandonment. For if we hold that the animal's behaviour is to be accounted for in terms of his intentional environment, then his 'maladaptive' behaviour must be accounted for by positing an incorrect intentional environment just as his adaptive behaviour is accounted for by a correct one.[1]

Now at the moment these two accounts represent simply two different ways of describing the behaviour of the animals concerned. It would seem to be difficult to find a way of deciding which is more helpful or informative. This issue is continuous with that which arises with animals at a higher phylogenetic level, concerning the use of the term 'insight' to describe the phenomena of learning, such as, e.g., when a monkey learns to use a stick to get some fruit which is otherwise out of reach.[2]

This issue is often misidentified as one concerning the continuity of behaviour through learning. S–R theorists are held to favour continuity since learning involves the slow building up of

[1] Of course the presolution period may be marked in some animals by a lesser degree of certainty about the intentional environment. The criteria for this are the behavioural marks of hesitation which some animals including the rat exhibit, and the greater lability of the intentional environment.

[2] Cf. Köhler, *The Mentality of Apes.*

S–R connexions over many trials, whereas cognitive theorists are held to found their case on the sharp discontinuities which occur at the moment of insight when animals suddenly begin to behave in a new way. Thus Spence (a continuity theorist) holds that the empirical ground on which theories of insight are built is the occurrence of a sharp drop in the number of errors or mal-adaptive actions, the readiness with which the correct response is repeated and the resistance the animal shows to forgetting it.[1] Now it is true that a cognitive theory would lead one to expect sudden changes in behaviour as the animal changed his expect-ancy, but, as has been pointed out many times, the 'continuity' theorists can also account for this and it is hardly crucial evidence. Thus Krechevsky[2] claimed to have found empirical evidence for the claim that rats in the presolution period of a discrimina-tion problem act on 'hypotheses'. Their behaviour, he claimed, is systematic. They make systematic runs to one dimension, e.g., a series of right-going responses or a series of responses to white, and then shift if this doesn't bear fruit to another, until they hit on the correct one. Now this is certainly what one should expect on the basis of a cognitive theory, but it can also be accounted for starting from the premises of S–R theory, as Spence[3] tried to show. One only needs to make certain quantitative assumptions about the strength added or subtracted from an association on each trial and one can predict that one particular one, say that which led to a right-going response, could suddenly become prepotent over the others and maintain this for some time, thus giving the appearance of systematic trial and error behaviour. Of course, it is another question whether these quantitative assumptions can be verified or not. At the moment S–R theory is, in spite of certain grandiose pretensions by some of its pro-tagonists, too vague and qualitative to permit the verification of hypotheses of this kind. But in any case we cannot hope to find crucial evidence here at this time.

Another misunderstanding which might arise from the terms 'continuity versus discontinuity' is the view that cognitive theorists claim a form of learning which constitutes a radical

[1] In S. S. Stevens, *Handbook of Experimental Psychology*.
[2] ' "Hypotheses" in Rats', *Psychological Review*, 1932.
[3] 'The Nature of Discrimination Learning in Animals,' *Psychological Review*, 1936.

break with past experience. But this is not what is at stake. It is easy to show that apes who have played with sticks and become accustomed to using them as functional extensions of their arms will solve the problem of getting at the fruit out of arm's reach much quicker than those who have no such experience.[1] But this evidence proves nothing one way or the other in this particular question. What is at stake is not the role of experience but whether that role can be accounted for in terms of the establishing of S–R connexions.

What, then, really divides the cognitive view from the S–R theories? We must look, as was said above in Chapter V, to the type of correlations which the latter seeks to establish. Now the idea of S–R theory is, as we have seen, that responses become conditioned to stimuli, either simply by occurring concurrently with the stimuli, or else by occurring concurrently with them in a context of reward. Thus, in either case, the type of correlation which we should look for holds between the responses made to a given set of stimuli in the training period and the responses made subsequently to this same set of stimuli, the latter being a function of the former.[2]

Now on the cognitive view learning is not a function simply of the responses occurring concurrently with the stimuli, or with the stimuli together with reward, but also of the way the stimulus situation is seen by the animal. Thus learning depends not just on the sequence of stimuli and responses but also on the 'hypotheses' or 'expectancies' that the animal is testing on these trials, in other words on his intentional environment at the time. But then it is possible, and in some situations likely, that the law-like relation posited by S–R theory between response history and current responses will not hold. Thus, to take an example from the range we shall be discussing, that of discrimination learning: The fact that a rat's jumping to what is in fact a white card is followed by reward may not serve to strengthen the tendency to

[1] Cf. Birch, 'The Relation of Previous Experience to Insightful Problem Solving', *J. comp. Psychol.*, 1945.

[2] The notion 'stimulus' here needs some examination, which we shall put off till the next chapter. For the moment, in the context of discrimination learning, 'stimulus' can be taken to mean 'a property of an object response to which can be linked with reward,' e.g., the colour of a card, where the animal must be trained to jump to a card of a certain colour. This is often spoken of as a 'cue' as well.

jump to the white card in future. For the rat may not have been 'paying attention' to the colour of the card but might have been 'testing the hypothesis' that jumping to the right-hand card brings reward. In other words, the 'intentional description'[1] under which the rat jumped to it was 'card on the right-hand side' and not 'white card'. But then if the 'solution' is jumping to the white card, i.e. if reward varies only randomly with position, but is constantly linked with colour, this trial will not have helped in any way to strengthen the correct response, even though the card jumped to was white and reward followed.

Hence on the cognitive view it matters what the rat is *doing*, that is, what action he is performing, and thus what intentional description the action has for him, whether 'jumping right' or 'jumping to white', whereas on the S–R view, the response is not an action, the intentional description is irrelevant, and it matters only what descriptions the card actually bears to which the rat jumped.

It should, then, be possible to see whether the correlations of the kind demanded by S–R actually hold or whether learning is also affected by the selective attention of the animal. Now the evidence for this latter alternative is not lacking. The term 'set' has been coined to cover these cases of selective attention.

The set in an animal can in fact usually be controlled by the pre-training which precedes the problem in which the set will be in operation and it is thus possible to test for the influence of sets on learning. Thus, for instance, Lashley[2] trained rats to jump towards a large circle where the alternative was a smaller circle. After a certain amount of training he substituted an equilateral triangle of about the same size for the large circle. The transfer was perfect and the rats continued to jump to the large triangle when this was presented along with the small circle. After a further training of 200 trials in which jumping to the triangle was rewarded, Lashley presented the rats with a choice between a triangle and a circle of intermediate size. The rats showed no preference for the triangle. They were then retrained on the choice

[1] This term is used throughout these chapters, of course, in its extended sense; cf. Chapter III. We mean here, e.g., 'the card as it is relevant to the animal's behaviour in jumping'. The term 'intentional description' will do duty for a more cumbrous locution of this kind.

[2] 'An Examination of the "Continuity Theory" as Applied to Discriminative Learning,' *J. gen. Psychol.*, 1942.

between the large triangle and the small circle and presented with a choice between a large circle and a small triangle. All chose the larger circle.

Now about this one is tempted to say that the preliminary training with circles of different size induced a set to size which led to the animals' ignoring the difference in shape although the positive and negative figures did differ in shape for a large part of their training. The 'hypothesis' that jumping to the larger figure brought reward was consistently confirmed so that no attention was paid to the difference in shape and therefore a differential tendency to jump to triangles against circles was not set up. And, indeed, an interpretation in terms of selective attention seems inescapable.

4. S–R AND SELECTION

Perhaps, however, S–R theory can account for this selection in a way which does not involve appeal to cognitive theories, to the use of such notions as 'hypothesis' or 'intentional environment'. It might, for instance, do so by invoking a mechanism which selects between the various stimulus elements in the field so that some are more prominent than others and so that some may even be 'dormant', their occurrence along with a response not leading to any association with that response. This involves a modification of the original S–R thesis to the effect that 'all the stimuli are associated' but this modification is clearly necessary.

There is one principle of selection, of course, which is clearly in accord with common-sense. It is obvious that not all the objects in the field affect the receptors, do not 'impinge on' the organism, or at least not to the same degree. An object, for instance, at the very edges of the perceptual field would not stimulate the receptors to the same degree as one closer to the centre. This principle of selection has been used to explain those cases where animals learnt a discrimination problem which involved a reversal of previous training, that is, where the previously positive cue was now negative and vice versa, as quickly as other animals who had no such contradictory pre-training. Thus Spence criticized[1] Krechevsky's results of this kind on the grounds

[1] 'An Experimental Test of the Continuity and Non-continuity Theories of Discrimination Learning,' *J. exp. Psychol.*, 1945.

that the relevant stimuli didn't really impinge on the rats' receptors. And similarly Ehrenfreund[1] showed that where the relevant
stimuli were on the upper portion of the cards which the animals
were to jump towards, and thus were not likely to be 'noticed',
the animals could reverse the response easily. But where the
stand was raised so that they could not avoid seeing the relevant
portions of the cards, they could not learn to reverse this discrimination as fast as other animals without this preliminary
training. Thus it would seem that, in this case, the effect of 'set',
of 'not noticing' certain stimuli, can be accounted for simply
in terms of their position *vis-à-vis* the sense organs. Objects
not directly in the line of vision will not tend to yield stimuli
which become associated with the responses which occur.
Thus we have no need to account for these phenomena by
some cognitive theory in terms of the 'hypotheses' the rats are
acting on.

But it is obvious that we cannot explain all the cases where
learning involves the operation of a set in terms of the relative
position of the stimulus objects *vis-à-vis* the receptors. This will
not do, for instance, in the case above where the animals were
'paying attention' to the size and not to the shape. Some other
mechanism of selection has to be evoked. Thus Lawrence put
forward a theory of the 'acquired distinctiveness' of cues or
stimulus elements. Having established that animals could learn
a discrimination problem more quickly on cues with which they
were familiar, that is, had been trained on in the past, even if this
involved learning a different response,[2] and also that associations
with these cues are stronger and show more retention,[3] and having
established that variations of a cue not relevant to solution could
take place without any loss to the associations set up to this cue,
as long as the animal was responding systematically to other
cues;[4] in other words, having shown the operation of set in

[1] 'An Experimental Test of the Continuity Theory of Discrimination
Learning with Pattern Vision,' *J. comp. physiol. Psychol.*, 1948.

[2] 'Acquired Distinctiveness of Cues; I, Transfer Between Discriminations
on the Basis of Familiarity with the Stimulus,' *J. exp. Psychol.*, 1949.

[3] 'Acquired Distinctiveness of Cues; II, Selective Association in a Constant
Stimulus Situation,' *J. exp. Psychol.*, 1950.

[4] 'Systematic Behaviour During Discrimination Reversal and Change of
Dimensions,' Lawrence and Mason, *J. comp. physiol. Psychol.*, 1955.

discrimination learning, Lawrence tries to put forward a theory to account for it:

> If the S [the subject of the experiment] is trained to respond to some aspect of the situation other than the initially dominant one, then this new aspect will tend to become more distinctive and the other aspects relatively less distinctive. Consequently, when this same cue appears in another discrimination problem, it will be more readily associated with the instrumental behaviour demanded by the new problem than it would be without the previous training. Thus the previous experience of the S with various cues, irrespective of the instrumental behaviour associated with them, becomes an important determinant of the rapidity of learning in a new situation involving the same cues.[1]

Thus Lawrence hopes to account for the phenomena described by the term 'set' by invoking the previous learning of the animal, itself accounted for in S–R terms. While accepting the fact of selective attention, he claims to avoid the usual conclusions drawn from this in cognitive theory to the effect that the rat tends to select certain hypotheses or have certain expectancies in the new situation. The effect of set on learning can be perfectly well accounted for, he claims, if we assume that certain stimulus elements become more distinctive, more easily and more strongly associated with whatever responses occur along with them in the reward situation, and others become less so. We do not need to assume that what is strengthened is an expectancy of a certain kind.

Thus there are two elements in learning: '(a) the learning involved in the acquisition of the correct instrumental responses in a discrimination situation and (b) the learning involved in modifying the initial order of distinctiveness among the cues.'[2]

Restle[3] puts forward a similar hypothesis to the effect that cues which are not correlated with success in the solution of the problem become 'adapted', that is, non-functional, and cease to be associated with any response. They will thus be relatively less prominent in a new situation. Similarly a relevant cue becomes 'conditioned' and is therefore more prominent in a new situation. Broadbent[4] puts forward a somewhat similar theory of selection,

---

[1] Loc. cit., *J. exp. Psychol.*, 1949; p. 770.　　　　[2] Op. cit.

[3] 'A Theory of Discrimination Learning,' *Psychological Review*, 1955.

[4] *Perception and Communication*, Chapter X.

a 'filter' theory, but he attempts to account for a much wider range of phenomena and elaborates a theory of greater generality. In his system, only a certain range of stimuli pass the 'filter', that is, are actually functional for behaviour. The determinants of what passes the filter include not only previous experience but also certain properties of the stimuli themselves, e.g., their 'intensity'.

A theory of selection might thus be able to account for the operation of sets in learning. This would still remain within the limits of S–R theory because learning would still be accounted for in terms of connexions established under specifiable conditions (contiguity or reward) between stimuli and responses, even though the stimuli concerned would be only a proportion of those impinging on the organism; and, secondly, the prominence of some stimuli over others could be explained by certain properties of these stimuli or by their past association with responses of the organism.

Now a theory of this kind could account for the phenomena observed by Lashley and Lawrence which were mentioned above. For in these cases it is simply a question of selecting among a number of cues present in the situation. But this is not the only way in which a set can operate. This we can see with the results of Harlow.[1] Harlow established what he called 'learning sets' in monkeys. The animals 'learned to learn', and transferred their know-how from one problem to the next. Harlow trained his monkeys on a set of discrimination problems; the monkeys were rewarded for picking one object out of two presented to them on a tray. In one range of experiments, the animals had to learn a number of object–quality discriminations, that is, the 'correct' object was correct in virtue of being an object of a certain type. In another range, the animals learned position discrimination, the 'correct' object was always in a certain position, right or left. In both cases, the animal's performance improved from problem to problem, even though different objects or different positions

---

[1] 'The Formation of Learning Sets,' *Psychological Review*, 1949. Similar experiments were reported, e.g., by Hayes, Thompson and Hayes, 'Discrimination Learning Sets in Chimpanzees', *J. comp. physiol. Psychol.*, 1953, by Riopelle; 'Transfer Suppression and Learning Sets', *J. comp. physiol. Psychol.*, 1953; and 'Learning Sets from Minimum Stimuli', *J. exp. Psychol.*, 1955.

were 'correct' from one problem to the next, to the point where they needed only one trial, an 'information' trial, to solve the problem; that is, if the object picked, or the position chosen, on the first trial was wrong (unrewarded), they immediately turned to the other, if not, they remained with their first choice. The animals were also trained on discrimination reversals, that is, after a certain number of trials, the object previously 'incorrect' became the 'correct' one. Here, again, the animals showed steady improvement, until they needed only one 'information' trial, and shifted their choice following only one trial in which the previously correct object was not rewarded. The animals could also learn more than one such set (Harlow taught them object–quality and position sets) and could alternate them, so that they tried one 'hypothesis', seeing if the answer depended on the type of object, and immediately shifted to position if this was unfruitful. As Harlow put it, the monkeys developed 'a generalized ability to learn *any* discrimination problem or *any* discrimination reversal problem with the greatest of ease'.[1]

Now this result cannot be accounted for by the acquired prominence of certain cues. For the cues which were relevant changed with each problem. Thus each problem presented a different pair of objects, and the cues differentiating the correct from the incorrect one therefore varied from problem to problem. But at the same time performance improved. We must say, with Harlow, that the animals 'learned to learn', that is, they learned what a given negative or positive trial *'proved'*. Thus, after a while, one negative result would lead the animal immediately to choose the other object; this negative result showed that the other object was the rewarded one. But the animal could only see more quickly what a given trial 'proved' because he was more aware of the type of problem he was dealing with, he had 'got the point', e.g., of the object–quality discrimination. And this means that his attention was focused not on certain *cues*, for these varied from problem to problem, but on certain *cue-dimensions*, that is, the animals learned to focus on quality of object, and not colour, size, position, smell, or whatever, as the relevant dimension. But *this* cannot be accounted for by a 'filter' hypothesis, whereby certain stimuli are 'let in' and others are filtered out; for what the animal learns is not to concentrate on certain particular

[1] Op. cit., p. 59.

features of the objects, such as 'red' or 'white', or 'left position' or 'right position', but, for any situation, to concentrate on that feature of the objects, whatever it be, which falls in a particular category. This result is in no way altered if we try to account for the improvement, as Harlow does, on the hypothesis that 'disturbing factors' are eliminated. For whatever these factors are, what remains is the concentration on features of a certain category.

But if we have to allow for selective attention to different cue-dimensions in this case, why not in the cases cited by Lashley and Lawrence? That is, why shouldn't we say simply that the animals respond to the problem as one of a certain type, as one where, say, size, and not shape or colour, is the relevant cue-dimension?

Now it is clear that the prominence of a cue-dimension, unlike the prominence of a cue, cannot be accounted for in S–R terms. There thus seems little way to avoid using concepts involving intentionality for learning of this kind, that is, we seem forced to say that the animal's improvement is due to the fact that the problem comes to have a certain 'description' for him, as one where correlations of a certain kind hold. In order to account for this learning in S–R terms we would have to invoke a set of 'determinable' or 'categorial' cues, that is, 'being determinable in respect of its type' would have to be a 'cue-property' of an object, as 'being an inkwell' could be. For this is what the animals learned to concentrate on from problem to problem; and this, as a cue, would of course not be enough, for being determinable in this way would be a property which both positive and negative objects shared. But apart from this, the suggestion is, of course, absurd that 'being determinable in respect of X' should be considered a *stimulus*-property of an object, if we mean by this a property which makes a certain kind of effect on the receptors, as 'white' or 'square' can be assumed to do.

But a suggestion of this kind is what is implicit in Restle's theory, which thus adequately illustrates the limits of S–R theory. Restle[1] struggles with the data of Harlow in an attempt to account for them within the confines of S–R theory and his own selective theory of learning, mentioned above. He admits that it seems impossible to reduce the data about learning sets to 'simple processes characteristic of naïve rats', 'but an attempt to formulate

[1] 'Towards a Quantitative Description of Learning Set Data,' *Psychological Review*, 1958.

the intuitively sensible hypothesis that monkeys gain an abstract understanding of the situation puts a great strain on current theoretical resources'.[1] Restle is, of course, referring to the theoretical resources of the S–R theory. But his theory puts no less of a strain on this doctrine:

> Monkeys, with extended experience, can transcend the concrete stimulus characteristics which ordinarily form the basis of discrimination responses, and respond to conditional cues such as 'the object which was correct on the previous trial', etc. These contingent cues are analogous to the cues, whatever they may be, in conditional discriminations.[2]

The problem which is to be solved by the invoking of 'conditional' cues is this. In the course of a single discrimination problem the animal learns to respond to an object of a certain type. But over the course of many problems he acquires a learning set which cannot be accounted for in terms of a tendency to respond to a specific type of object, because the type varies from problem to problem. We might put it by saying that the animal, instead of learning to respond to a specific type of object as in the single problem, learns to respond to any type of object provided it is being currently rewarded. Thus we might say that the animal learns to respond not to any specific properties but to the fact of being rewarded on the last trial.

Now Restle's hypothesis, taking off from this point, introduces a 'conditional cue' 'rewarded on the last trial', a stimulus property which attaches to whatever object was in fact so rewarded. His explanation is that, as the animal runs through a number of problems, responses to particular properties of the objects are inconsistently rewarded, because a given property, say red, which might hold of the positive object in one problem might belong to the negative object in the next. These properties are thus 'adapted' or made non-functional, they become less prominent. But the one property response to which is always rewarded is 'having been re-inforced on the last trial'. This therefore becomes more prominent and as the animal comes to respond to this one alone his performance improves in the way observed by Harlow and other experimenters in this field. The monkey 'is responding to the property of having been re-inforced, as distinguished from

[1] Op. cit., p. 77.   [2] Op. cit., p. 89.

other properties such as size, colour, spatial shape, arrangement of parts, etc.'[1]

But although the property of having been re-inforced is certainly a property of the object itself separate from the other properties of size, shape, etc., it cannot as a *stimulus* property be so separated. For in order for it to hold as a stimulus property the animal has to recognize the object as that object which was in fact re-inforced on the last trial. And in order to recognize something as the object which was re-inforced, one has to know some other description true of it besides simply that of 'having been re-inforced'. Thus the conditional cue cannot just be 'object which has been re-inforced', but 'object identified in such and such a way which has been re-inforced'. As Restle himself says, such cues are 'compound', 'one part . . . being the characteristics of the object, the other part being previous re-inforcements given and perceived by the animal'.[2]

But then, out of one given re-inforced trial, several different conditional cues might arise on the next trial depending on the way the animal identified this object as the same one. It is clear that the acquisition of a learning set would involve selecting the right one. For instance in acquiring the learning set for positional as against object–quality discrimination problems the animals would have to learn to respond to the object which resembled that which was correct on the previous trial in position, and not in type. Thus in learning the object–quality discrimination game, the animals have to learn to respond to a conditional cue of a certain type out of those present. But which type? Any particular cue, e.g., 'object of type X which was re-inforced', 'object of type Y which was re-inforced', etc., would itself not be re-inforced consistently throughout the whole range of problems beyond the one in which X or Y was the positive object. It is quite possible that they might be, over the whole range, less re-inforced than that of the position last rewarded provided position alternation didn't occur on every trial. Why does the re-inforcement of the cue 'object identified as A which was re-inforced on the last trial' in problem a and that of 'object identified as B which was re-inforced on the last trial' in problem b, and so on, increase the likelihood that the animal will respond to 'object identified as N which was re-inforced on the last trial' when it comes to problem n?

[1] Op. cit., p. 79.   [2] Op. cit., p. 89.

The answer is, of course, clear, that all these cues have in common that they distinguish the object from its rival by the type to which it belongs and not by, say, position, order, the reactions of the experimenter, degree of attractiveness, and so on. These properties fall in a certain *category*, and it is, of course, by tumbling to this that the monkeys come to solve the problems with increasing speed. Thus having learned to focus on type on a number of occasions they begin to look for differences of type. When they are rewarded, they therefore know to pick the right object as the one which resembles the rewarded one in type and not in position, etc. Restle covertly assumes this categorial selection when he speaks of the 'object last rewarded' as a cue. This is not one 'cue' (if this term can be used at all), as we have seen, but several. There is no reason why responses conditioned to one such cue should also be conditioned to others, unless we accept the principle that responses to shape properties also 'generalize' to colour properties and so on, which is absurd. Nor can we say that these cues resemble each other in being conditional cues relating to re-inforcement on the previous trial, for the cue 'object having the same position as that rewarded last' is also in this class. The only recourse of S–R theory would be to introduce a categorial 'stimulus' such that all objects had the property of being objects characterizable by type as well as being objects of this or that type. But here we have left the realm of neo-behaviourism.

It would thus appear that some phenomena of 'set', or selective attention to aspects of the situation cannot be accounted for in S–R terms as the acquired distinctiveness or greater prominence of certain cues. Experience may not only bring certain cues to the fore but may bring to the fore what we would normally call a certain way of looking at the situation. It may show a problem to be of a certain type, or narrow the range of 'hypotheses' to be tried. In the above case it shows the animals that the problem is a discrimination problem which hangs on properties of a certain category. It is because of this that cognitive theorists have tended to talk of 'insight'; not because learning shows discontinuous jumps in the number of errors—though it sometimes does—but because the effect of experience, even the slow effect of a 'gradual learning history' can often be most aptly understood as a growth in insight.[1] In this way the solving of discrimination problems connects with the other problem-solving behaviour of apes of the kind mentioned above. What induces us to speak of 'insight' when the ape picks up the stick to reach the fruit is not the abruptness of the change in behaviour, but the nature of the solution. Spence[2] tries to explain this solution in terms of the particular 'receptor-exposure adjustments' that the animal learns to make.

> That is, once this particular orientation of the sense-organs (particularly eyes) occurs, the subject will, because of past learning, make the appropriate perceptual response that leads directly to the correct overt act.[3]

But this is no explanation of insightful solution. The importance of past learning is not in question. But the 'appropriate perceptual response' is here none other than seeing the solution to the problem, seeing that the stick can be used to get the fruit. It is this which 'leads directly to the overt act'. This explanation turns out to be a redescription. It is difficult to see how this change between seeing and not seeing the solution could be accounted for in terms of differential stimulus elements.

[1] Harlow misidentifies the significance of his own results for this issue. He says,

> The field theorists, unlike the neo-behaviourists, have stressed insight and hypothesis in their description of learning. The impression these theorists give us is that these phenomena are properties of the innate organization of the individual. If such phenomena appear independently of a gradual learning history, we have not yet found them in the primate order. (Op. cit., p. 65.)

But the issue is not whether this behaviour is 'innate' or 'learned'. Indeed, if behaviour occurred independently of learning history, we could hardly speak of it as learned behaviour. No one disputes that the improved performance is the result of experience; what is in question is not the importance of experience but its role.

[2] In S. S. Stevens' *Handbook of Experimental Psychology*.

[3] Op. cit., p. 718.

VII

WHAT IS LEARNED?

THE attempt to introduce 'categorial' cues shows the confusion which surrounds the notion of 'stimulus'. In fact S–R theorists are generally imprecise in their use of this notion. 'Stimulus' can generally mean any one of four different types of element. Sometimes it is used for the various objects in the field and their cue-properties, e.g., the white card, or the markings on the card. This is sometimes referred to as the 'distant stimulus'. Or 'stimulus' can be used for, say, the light-waves emitted from the distant stimulus which impinge on the retina. Thirdly, it sometimes means the 'proximal' stimulus, the pattern of excitation on the receptors, e.g., the pattern of the retina. And fourthly it can also be used to refer to the (postulated) afferent impulse sent by the receptors to the brain.

This uncertainty is not necessarily a disadvantage at an early stage in any science. It may not yet be clear for which type of stimulus element the regularities hold. But what is essential is that it be clear, for any type of stimulus, what will count as a stimulus element. For, if the responses emitted in a situation are a function of the response history in this situation or in other similar ones, then it is essential if we are to be able to predict behaviour, that we be able to identify a situation as similar or as of the same type as another in which certain responses were emitted, or emitted in the context of reward, and to which type, therefore, these responses have been conditioned. But to say 'same type' is to say 'similar in stimulus elements' or 'producing similar stimuli'.

136

Thus, if we are to predict, we must be able to give a definite sense to 'the stimuli which the situation contains or produces'.

But to achieve this kind of definiteness it is not enough just to single out a certain kind of stimulus, say the 'distant' stimulus, or stimulus object, and to characterize a situation as consisting of such and such stimulus objects, say, white and black cards, or three alleyways painted different colours, and so on. The question can still arise, what are the stimulus elements in this situation? For any object or set of objects can bear an indefinite number of descriptions. In order to specify what the stimuli are we have not only to name the objects in the situation, but also the descriptions under which they operate as stimuli. Thus any set of objects can be classified in an indefinite number of ways, by their shape or size, by their relative position, their configurational properties, their physiognomic properties ('very like a whale'), they can be picked out singly for description, or in groups of various sizes and compositions, and so on.

Now, if any one or group of these objects under any of these descriptions can count as 'the stimuli produced by the situation', then this expression has no definite sense, that is, there is no finitely enumerable class of things which falls under it in any situation. And if this is so then an S–R theory will be totally empty. For if 'the stimuli produced by this situation' is indefinite, then so is 'the same (type of) situation' (i.e., situation similar in stimulus elements). If we allow the objects under *any* classification to count, then *any* other situation can be said to resemble this one in *something*, if it be only the number of objects involved, and therefore to be, in some sense, the 'same situation', and similarly any situation can be said to differ from this one in something, and so to be a 'different situation'. But then it will be impossible to tell of any previous situation whether it is relevant to present behaviour. It will be impossible, in other words, to tell which part of the animal's behaviour history will determine his present behaviour in a given contemporary situation. Similarly, we shall never be able to predict, from an animal's behaviour history in one situation, what he will do in future, for the response 'learned' here might just as well generalize to *all* other situations as to none.[1]

[1] Of course, we might still be able to identify the 'same situation' in the sense of 'numerically same situation', if the criteria of this were simply

In effect, to allow the notion 'stimulus' to range this widely would be to abandon the S–R theory of learning. For in order for learning to take place there would have to be some selection of the 'stimuli' to be 'associated', that is, some selection would have to occur from among the many descriptions that the objects could bear, of those which were relevant, which defined the situation as a situation of a certain type, that type for which this behaviour had been discovered to be appropriate. For the phenomenon we are trying to explain involves the acquisition of a response specific to this environment, either because it is seen as appropriate, or, following the S–R theory, because the connexion between it and the situation is 'stamped in'. But, if this is to be the case, then the environment must be marked off in some way from others in which this response is not called for, and for this some specific description of it must be singled out, by which it is recognized as this (or this type of) environment, or under which the response is conditioned to it. For otherwise any response rewarded, or otherwise 'stamped in', in this situation would tend to generalize to all other situations, and the responses acquired in all other situations would tend to generalize to this, and no selection among responses would take place at all, i.e., no specific response would be acquired. Or else, if *all* the (indefinite number of) descriptions were relevant, then the most trivial change would cancel all previous learning, and there could be no response at all to a novel situation, not even one of exploration.

This can readily be seen in the case we are discussing, that of discrimination learning. For this involves the selection of one path or card, or box or whatever among two or several alternatives. But if the response conditioned to the 'correct' object is conditioned to it under *any* true description, then since there will always be some respect in which the current object resembles the incorrect ones, the response will generalize to these latter, and no learning will take place; in other words the response cannot be conditioned to *this object* unless it is conditioned to it under a

---

geographical location in a wider environment. But this is rarely the feature of the situation to which learned behaviour is tied. Learned behaviour is usually behaviour adapted to the nature of an environment, and would not survive if this nature were totally changed even if we could still speak of it as the 'same spot'.

description which marks it off from the others, *qua* type of object which the others do not exemplify. And if the response is conditioned to it under *all* true descriptions, then the most trivial change will totally disorient behaviour.

Thus the problem of accounting for learning includes that of accounting, in some way, for selection. But selection of this kind is something that S–R theory cannot account for. For the response is held to be conditioned to all the stimuli impinging at the time, and therefore cannot select between them, even when they are indefinite in number. Nor could it account for the selection by some special hypothesis, such as the 'filter' hypotheses which we discussed in the last chapter. For if these hypotheses are to remain within the bounds of S–R theory, they will have to account for the selection in terms of the properties of the stimuli themselves, that is, selection itself would be a type of 'response' made to certain stimuli and not to others. But, if we allow no limit to the ways in which we can classify the stimulus objects, then the number of types or classifications of stimulus objects will be indefinite. But then for each type or classification we would have to pick some property or set of properties which determined which objects of this type were selected. Thus colours might be selected on the basis of the intensity of the light waves emitted, shapes on the basis of regularity of form, and so on. But neither of these would do to select between objects of different sizes, or between objects classified by relative position, or physiognomic properties, and so on and so on. But since the number of types is indefinite, the number of criterial properties would be indefinite too. And this means that we should never be able to determine finally what properties are selected in any given situation.[1]

Thus an S–R theory must put some restriction on the notion

---

[1] There is, of course, a property which would apply to 'stimuli' of all categories, that of being associated with a response in (some) previous learning. But this criterion could never be sufficient for selection, because, unless there was some prior selection, we would never be able to say what previous learning situations were relevant, and even if we could, the stimuli associated with the response in those situations would still be indefinite in number. If the notion 'the stimuli in this situation' designates an indefinite number of things, then so does the notion 'the respects in which this situation resembles past ones'. To invoke past experience just puts off the problem of selection, it does not solve it.

'stimulus'. And the restriction must be such that the expression 'the stimuli produced by this situation' will always designate a finitely enumerable set of elements. For otherwise we could make no definite predictions from an animal's behaviour history in one situation how he will behave in others.

This requirement is little discussed among S–R theorists because it is generally assumed that it is enough to say that only expressions belonging to the 'physical thing language' will be used. But the sense of this expression is by no means clear in this context. It rules out, of course, the use of psychological concepts, but no one would be tempted to use these to characterize an environment consisting wholly of inanimate things, such as the average test apparatus used in learning experiments. To say that we should describe the contents of such an environment, e.g., jumping stand, cards, etc., as physical things seems redundant. And it is also not definite enough. Because resembling something else in colour, or having been painted by Jones, is just as much the property of a physical thing as being red, and being the third square thing from the left is just as much a property of a physical thing as being square. The types of classification which can be said to belong to the physical thing language are indefinite in number.

But, of course, the understanding here is that we are talking not just about the physical properties of things in general, but about their stimulus properties; and for this we could add an additional requirement: Something is a stimulus property if it can be supposed to bring about a specific type of effect on the receptors. Some additional requirement of this kind seems to be assumed by S–R theorists, and it would rule out such properties as that of having been painted red by so-and-so, which could not be discriminated from that of simply being red on this criterion. But this would still not be enough to give a definite sense to the expression 'the stimuli in the situation'. For the number of elements in the stimulus situation would still be indefinite. In order to have an enumerable list of elements we must introduce a third requirement, that there be a principle of counting the parts of the stimulus field, objects or part objects, such that in any situation there are a definite number of such parts. In other words, there must be some restriction on the way the parts of the stimulus field can be singled out for description, such that only properties of these parts can be called stimulus properties, or 'cues'; for, if the number of parts is indefinite, then the number of cues will be as well.

This rules out such properties as, e.g., the configurations of the whole field or sub-sections of it. For if the only cues are the properties of the field parts, then the configurational property of the whole would not be a cue, but only the properties of all the parts which made up this whole. And, although the whole would only have this configuration because the parts had the properties that they did, to say that they had these properties would not be the same as saying that the whole had this configuration, that is, the two would not be equivalent descriptions. The configurational property, then, would not be a stimulus property. And it is clear, as we said above, that it must be ruled out, if we are to have an S-R theory. For the configurational property can only be singled out as against the properties of the parts if we allow as cues properties of the whole or of other sub-sections of the whole as well. But if we do this, then there is no limit to the number of possible sub-sections that could be singled out, depending on the way we decided to divide up the situation. But each of these subsections would have its own configuration, or arrangements of parts, or, in some cases, shape. The number of such configuration or shape properties would thus be indefinite, and there would be some respect in which the situation bore a resemblance to almost any other situation. For learning to occur, one way of dividing it up, one way of individuating parts would have to be singled out. But this selection could never be accounted for by S-R theory. For, as stimuli, the configurational property of the whole would be indistinguishable from the properties of the parts in virtue of which it had this configuration. For the two could not be assumed to bring about a distinguishable type of effect on the receptors, as e.g., the colour and the shape of a thing could be. A 'filter' theory would thus be of no use here.[1]

[1] This problem is the same as that raised by Gestalt theory by the question 'why do things look as they do?'. Once we admit, as Gestalt theory claims, that the same stimulus elements can result in different structures being seen, then we cannot account for the structure simply in terms of the properties of the elements. Some other factor has to be introduced to account for the variations. And it goes without saying that the operation of *this* factor cannot be accounted for in terms of the properties of the elements either, i.e., in S-R terms. Cf. Koffka, *Principles of Gestalt Psychology*.

Similarly, 'relative' or 'extrinsic' properties are ruled out. A relative property is a property such as 'bigger than Y' or 'resembling X in shape', whose holding of an object, O depends in part on the properties which hold of another object, N. Now O's being, say, of a lighter shade of grey than N would not be a cue property of the field distinguishable from O's being, say, of an intensity a, while N was of an intensity b, which is darker; that is, it would have no effect on the receptors distinguishable from Oa and Nb. Thus there is no way of accounting for the selection between relative and 'absolute' or 'intrinsic' properties by an S–R 'filter' hypothesis. But learning plainly requires a selection between the two, if both are possible stimulus elements. For, if we allow relative properties, then each part of the stimulus field will be the locus of a vast number of cues. For each stimulus object will not only have a colour, but also n other properties, viz., the properties of resembling or differing from each of the n other objects in the environment in respect of colour, and also another n set of properties, that of being brighter or darker in colour than each of the n other objects, and each stimulus object has not only a shape, but n other relative shape properties, and so on. In some of these properties, e.g., differing from X in shape, it will resemble a vast number of other objects, in fact most others, and therefore any response conditioned to this object will generalize to these, in fact all objects except those of shape X. But since it will also differ in shape from Y which in turn differs from X, the response will also tend to generalize to X-shaped things. If any learning is to take place at all, i.e., if there is to be any selective response, there must be some selection of certain properties as relevant. But a selection between absolute and relative properties is the type of selection which S–R theory cannot account for.

Thus the requirement that stimulus properties be of the kind which can be said to 'impinge on the receptors' is not sufficient to restrict the meaning of 'stimulus' in the way that is required by S–R theory. For the 'effect on the receptors' can itself be classified in different ways, different units can be picked out, comparisons can be made, and so on. In order to give a definite enough sense to 'the stimuli in the situation', we have to posit a unit of stimulation, and call 'cues' only the intrinsic properties of such units.

This third requirement seems to be tacitly demanded by S-R theorists. The reason why it is so little discussed can perhaps be found in the empiricist assumptions which many of them seem to share and which were discussed in Chapter IV. For it was often assumed by those thinkers who adopted this epistemology that there was such a thing as a sense-datum unit, a spatio-temporal unit of impression. This is another point, therefore, where psychological and epistemological doctrines influence each other. It would not be unilluminating to think of the S-R theory as a mechanistic transposition of the traditional empiricist views on epistemology. In both cases, there is a restricted 'data language', which is in one case the language describing immediate experience, and in the other the properties of a situation which can be called its cue-properties.

And in both cases this approach conflicts with a view which gives a place to the notion of intentionality. In one case the 'thesis of intentionality' is invoked to reject the notion of a single data language: Seeing is always seeing under a certain description, with some 'interpretation', and nothing is therefore 'immediately seen' in the empiricist sense, that is, no level of description is more basic than all the others, the foundation, as it were, of all the others. In the case we are discussing here, the notion of intentionality can be invoked to reject the narrow definition of a cue-property. For if a given set of objects may bear a number of different descriptions, there is no reason in principle why they should not have a number of 'intentional descriptions' for an animal. And, if some selection must take place between these for learning to occur, this does not have to be accounted for by a 'filter' hypothesis, in terms of the cue-properties of the objects themselves, which requirement, as we have seen, imposes a narrowing of the definition of 'cue-property'. For the shift from one type of description to another could take place simply because no solution to the problem can be found in the first type. That is, the fact that reward varies randomly with position will be enough to induce the animal to abandon the 'set' to position and adopt one, say, to size.

There is thus another way in which the correlations sought by S-R theory differ in nature from what one would expect on any view which accepted the notion of intentionality. For if cue-properties are confined to the intrinsic properties of the parts of the stimulus field, then all learning must be the conditioning of responses to such properties. But then the 'correlations' learned by the animal, so to speak, those on which he acts, must be restricted to those which link responses to such properties with reward. That is, the relevant properties for any discrimination problem, say, must be the intrinsic properties of stimulus parts if the animal is to solve the problem. For the result of learning can only be that some such property comes regularly to evoke a response. Should reward, then, be linked to some other property, the configuration of the whole, say, or some relative property, no regular link could be established between the relevant property and a response, and the discrimination could never be mastered (unless, of course, there is some other intrinsic property also linked with reward). For a cognitive view, on the other hand, no such limit can be established *a priori* to the types of correlation an animal can act on, and therefore to the type of problem he can solve. If there are limits to the intentional descriptions under which objects can fall they are limits set by the intelligence of a given animal or a given species. But these limits must be discovered empirically in each case. We cannot say *a priori* that learning *must* be acquiring a response to an object of a certain restricted type.

Thus we have in a different form the same question as we discussed in the last chapter, whether learning must be considered as related in some way to the intentional description under which the situation is subsumed by the agent. There we raised the question whether what is learned in any trial depends on the way the situation is seen. Here the question is whether the limits of what can be learned are set by the type of stimulus element in the situation, or whether they can be wider and depend rather on the limits of intelligence, the limits to the ways the animal can see the situation.

2. EMPTINESS OF THE 'STIMULUS'

Now it should be possible to determine which of these views is correct by examining what animals actually manage to learn, and in order to do this we will turn once again to cases of discrimination learning. Of course, in any experimental situation, there may be a large number of cues on which the response *might* be conditional. How can one test what is actually learned? A way in which it can be done is, after a given learning series, to test the responses of the animal in other situations which differ from the training ones in certain respects. If the training is 'transferred' to the new situation, then this is evidence that the respects in which the situation has been altered are not the crucial respects, that is, the respects in which the situation or stimulus object has become connected to the response through training. Or to put it in another way, if the test situation differs from the training situation in that the description 'P' no longer holds of it, and if the training is transferred, then the response cannot be said to be conditioned to P; the connexion learned is not that between responding to P and reward. The description which holds of all the test situations to which transfer takes place and the training situation is the invariant, and we have some evidence for saying that the connexion was set up between the situation under this description and the response.

Now for S–R theory the invariant is the situation, or the crucial stimulus, characterized as a set of stimulus elements, that is, as the intrinsic properties of certain spatio-temporal units of stimulation. Variations in any other respects should have no effect on training, that is, transfer should take place. But variations in this respect should hinder transfer.

Of course, with a small variation, transfer should still take place, although the response might not be as strong. Thus it is generally agreed that 'a response conditioned to one stimulus (or set of stimuli) will be elicited by or will occur in the presence of another stimulus (or set of stimuli) which is similar to the conditioned stimulus or discriminative stimulus although there has been no specific training to it'.[1] By 'similar' of course, is meant 'similar as a stimulus element'. But, aside from such small changes which permit transfer, it should not take place if the stimulus properties, or the ones which have become conditioned are changed, although any other change should not hinder it.

Unfortunately, the vagueness which surrounds the above principle of 'primary stimulus generalization' makes this claim difficult to test. For it is not clear how big a small change can be, nor is it exactly clear what are the continua along which it is to be measured. Hull[2] distinguishes between a 'stimulus

---

[1] Verplanck's 'Glossary', *Psychological Review*, 1957. p. 35
[2] *Principles of Behaviour*, Chapter XII, p. 188.

dimension', that is, a dimension along which stimuli can vary, such as the rate or intensity of auditory vibration, and an 'afferent generalization continuum', that is a dimension along which the degree of change can be measured for the purposes of establishing the scope of stimulus generalization; In other words, a 'small difference' to the animal may not be the same as a small difference along a stimulus dimension. This doesn't make nonsense of the notion of stimulus generalization as Lashley and Wade seem to think,[1] for tests could presumably be devised which could show how these afferent continua were related to stimulus dimensions; but until the nature of these continua is actually established it will be difficult to tell in some cases whether a given case of transfer can be accounted for by stimulus generalization or not.

Thus an animal trained to respond to a circle when presented with a circle and a triangle may transfer this training to a new choice between another figure with round contours and one with jagged edges, and respond to the former. Now we would ordinarily say that the animal had learnt to respond to the circle under the description 'round-contoured figure'. But this would be to use the cognitive principle that what is learnt is not determined by the stimulus elements but depends also on how they are seen. For we couldn't say that the circle had two stimulus properties, that of being a circle and that of being rounded in contour. Of course the description under which it fell for the animal would depend on the context of choice. If we trained an animal to distinguish between a circle and an ellipse, then he would not transfer this to all round-contoured figures in other situations.

This fact, of course, is the starting point of the S–R explanation in terms of stimulus generalization. The explanation is that the width of generalization, that is the distance away along the afferent continuum from the original conditioned stimulus at which a stimulus will evoke the response conditioned, can be narrowed if one simultaneously 'stamps out' response to a stimulus within the original range. For we will then have two generalization gradients, one centring around S_1 to which a response has been conditioned, and the other around S_2 to which non-response has been conditioned. Then, even if S_2 is within the usual range of generalization from S_1, that is, even if a response conditioned to S_1 would usually be evoked by S_2, this will be counter-acted

[1] 'The Pavlovian Theory of Generalization,' *Psychological Review*, 1946.

in this case by the negative conditioning undergone with S_2. Thus, in the above case, although all rounded figures might be within the usual range of generalization from the circle, this is counter-acted in the second case where response to the ellipse is 'stamped out'.

But this explanation is uncheckable until we have established what is the 'afferent continuum' on which a circle-shape is placed, and what the 'slope' of the gradient of generalization is, that is how strongly a response conditioned to a certain strength to S_1 would tend to be evoked by S_2. And we still seem a long way from obtaining such exact quantitative data, if, indeed, we ever will.

A second element of indeterminancy enters with the notion of 'secondary stimulus generalization'. Hull's[1] account of this is in terms of 'receptor–effector convergence'. Several different stimuli might separately acquire the power to evoke a response. In this case it sometimes happens that when a new response is conditioned to one of these stimuli, the others also tend to evoke it. The response is 'generalized' to other stimuli not on the same afferent continuum. Hull points to conditioned response experiments in which this has been demonstrated. This mechanism could presumably be evoked to account for those cases where a response was learned to an object under a description which was not connected with the stimulus properties of the object. Thus a child might be taught to fear animals from one unfortunate experience with a dog. But it is difficult to find common stimulus elements' such that the stimuli produced by all animals could be put on an afferent continuum. We might assume, then, that the various different species of animal stimuli had all been conditioned on separate occasions to some common response. Thus, in this case, the newly learned fear-response would generalize to them all. Just as in the case of primary generalization above, this highly unlikely explanation could not be really tested until the conditions of secondary generalization have been more closely stated.

But although these generalization hypotheses do introduce fairly large elements of indeterminacy into S–R theory, they do not make it impossible or unfruitful to try to answer the question, viz., is there a limit to the connexions which can be acquired

---

[1] *Principles of Behaviour*, Chapter XII.

such that the response must be conditioned to stimuli of a certain range of descriptions?

In a well-known experiment, Köhler[1] trained chickens to respond to one of two grey objects, the positive one being the lighter. When the animals were presented with a new choice between the previously positive shade and one even lighter, they chose the lighter shade. This was taken as evidence that the animals hadn't learnt to respond to the originally positive object under the description 'grey of such and such a shade', but under that of 'lighter of two greys'. In other words, the crucial properties of the stimuli here were not the absolute, intrinsic properties, but the relative ones.

Spence[2] tried to account for this result by invoking the principle of primary stimulus generalization. The conditioning of the response to the lighter shade (G_2) in the original training would naturally induce a tendency to respond to other shades of grey, although the tendency would naturally not be as strong. Similarly, the non-reinforcement of response to the darker shade (G_1) would tend to condition non-response (inhibit response) not only to G_1 but to a less degree to other points on the afferent continuum. The result might easily be, if we make certain quantitative assumptions, that the tendency to respond to the new shade (G_3) might be not only stronger than the inhibition, but G_3 might even have a net 'excitatory' power greater than G_2. For inhibition would have been generalized from G_1 to G_2 as well as to G_3, and the excitatory power of each will therefore depend not just on the strength of the tendency to respond, but on the *difference* between this and the strength of the inhibition. If the gradients have the right slope, then, G_3 will be prepotent over G_2. Thus by making suitable assumptions Spence believed he could account for the case of relative transposition, and not only that, but also give an account of those cases where transfer breaks down, as it often does for absolute values of the stimuli which are far removed from the original ones. Of course, there is no way of testing this hypothesis until the conditions are made clear for both the height and the slope of the gradients as they

---

[1] 'Simple Structural Functions in the Chimpanzee and in the Chicken,' in W. D. Ellis: *A Source Book of Gestalt Psychology*.

[2] 'The Differential Response in Animals to Stimuli Varying Within a Single Dimension,' *Psychological Review*, 1937.

arise in learning, but in any case this offered a way of accounting for the facts of transposition without invoking relative properties.

But it is difficult to see how this hypothesis can account for the result of Lawrence and de Rivera.[1] These authors trained rats to jump to the right when, on the two cards which faced them, the top half was lighter than the bottom, and to the left when the top half was darker. During the training period, the bottom half of the cards was always the same intermediate shade, so that conceivably the animals could have ignored it and conditioned their differential response to the top half which differed absolutely in the two cases. Then, in the test trial, a great variety of different shades were used, such that, had the animals been trained to respond to the particular shades previously associated with jumping right and jumping left, either no transfer or negative transfer would have taken place. But the animals showed a very high degree of transfer in these cases. There is little doubt, then, that relations between stimuli play an important part in learning.

But animals cannot only learn to respond to an object which has more or less of a certain property than another object. They can also be trained to pick an object which resembles a standard in a certain respect. Thus Nissen[2] reports a matching experiment where monkeys had to pick from two objects lying on each side of a third, the one which had the same colour as this middle one. Nissen tries to account for this by supposing a 'perception of identity and difference'.

The sense organs of all organisms are being exposed constantly to identities and differences of environmental energies. The very essence of a 'stimulus' lies in spatial heterogeneity or temporal change in those energies. It would be most surprising, therefore, if organisms were not provided, innately or through very early experience, with a mechanism for perceiving and responding to this most elementary and ubiquitous feature of their sensory world.[3]

[1] 'Evidence for Relational Discrimination,' *J. comp. physiol. Psychol.*, 1954.
[2] 'Sensory Patterning versus Central Organization,' *J. Psychol.*, 1953.
[3] Op. cit., p. 281.

Similarly,

> A central mechanism for the perception of 'more' and 'less',
> similar to that for identity and difference, would provide an
> explanation for the vast array of relational (transpositional)
> behaviour displayed in all sense modalities by minds from amoeba
> to men.[1]

But this addition virtually amounts to an abandonment of
stimulus–response molar theory. Of course, there may be such
a 'mechanism', although whether we can explain the perception
of identity and gradients of more or less in terms of a mechanism
is a question which 'molecular', physiological theory has yet to
solve. But, whether or not there is such a mechanism, to invoke
it at this stage is to abandon hope of establishing an S–R molar
theory. For it means that we introduce, besides 'absolute'
properties, a whole range of relative properties as cues. But
then, as we have seen, it is difficult to understand how any learning can take place. For if we condition a given response to a red
object, which also has the property of being different in colour
from the experimenter's tie (which is green), then why will the
response not be conditioned to the 'stimulus property' 'differing
from the experimenter's tie colour' and thus be generalized to a
yellow object which shares this property? It is clear that if we
are going to call both absolute and relative properties equally
'stimuli' or 'perceived properties', then we have to account for
the fact that learning involves not only the conditioning of a
response to a stimulus or perceived property, but the selection of
the perceived property which is to be conditioned; for a response
conditioned to the absolute and all the relative properties of a
given object would be 'generalized' to virtually every other
situation; there must be some selection if learning is to take
place. But this is a type of selection which cannot be accounted
for by S–R theory.

Nissen's perception of 'likeness' and 'difference', and 'more'
and 'less' is a paradigm of the special hypothesis introduced to
save a theory which solves none of the problems it was meant to
answer;[2] rather it serves to reveal more clearly where the theory is
inadequate. Nissen, in effect, is abandoning the view that the
effects of the stimulus objects on the receptors must be classified

[1] Op. cit., p. 285.   [2] Cf. supra, Chapter V.

in a certain restricted range of ways. And, of course, there is no reason to believe that the effects of 'stimulation' on the cortex, or on behaviour, can be understood if we classify it in this restricted way—'cognitive' theory has always claimed the contrary —but once we abandon this then the notion 'the stimuli in this situation' has no definite sense, and prediction by S–R laws, therefore, becomes impossible; or else, based on the same sort of hunch that all non-theorists use.

But it is difficult to see how the restriction can be maintained. There are other relative properties besides likeness and difference, more or less, which can be seen to play a role in learning. For instance, Hamilton[1] placed some monkeys in a box with four exits. On each trial one door was open, but always a different door than the one which was open on the last trial. The monkeys learned to neglect this door and try the other three. As a discrimination problem, this involves training the animals to approach only doors with the description 'other than the door opened on the last trial'. Yerkes and Coburn[2] in an experiment with pigs placed the animals before nine compartments. On each trial three were open, but the three varied on each trial. The animals learned to get food in the compartment first from the left of whatever combination of compartments were open. They also learned to take food from the compartment first from the right, and then to alternate.

But it is not only relative properties which we must admit. There is also lots of evidence that configurational properties can be crucial. Thus Teas and Bitterman[3] established that rats can be trained to go right when the stimuli in the field are of one kind and left when they are of another. The animals in each case were faced with a set of two cards with different markings. But they jumped left or right whenever the appropriate pair was presented regardless of the order of the cards. The response was therefore not conditioned to one of the cards in each case, but to the global effect of both. Thus in this case the animals were trained to respond to the global properties of the whole and not to punctual properties of the parts.

[1] Reported in Maier and Schneirla, *Principles of Animal Psychology*, pp. 458–9.

[2] Reported in Maier and Schneirla, op cit., pp. 459–60.

[3] 'Perceptual Organization in the Rat,' *Psychological Review*, 1952.

Again, O. Koehler[1] trained birds to respond to the number of stimulus elements as against their size, shape, colour, etc. A raven and a grey parrot were trained to open a box with the same number of spots on the lid as a 'key' card lying on the ground in front of the boxes.

It is clear, from this and other evidence, that we cannot place an *a priori* limit on the type of property which can be crucial in learning, and therefore on the type of correlation which an animal can learn. But, if this is so, then the attempt to establish an S–R molar theory is bound to fail. We will have to admit, on the contrary, that a given situation can bear many descriptions for the animal, and that, on a 'molar' level, something like the notion of intentionality must be given a place. It is possible, of course, that we may one day be able to account for mental activity in terms of some non-teleological neurological theory. This day is still a long way off, and for this reason, among others, this possibility is outside the scope of this book. But, whatever the outcome of this question, an attempt to account for learning by the conditioning of responses to stimuli seems to be misguided, for the crucial fact which needs to be accounted for is the selection essential to learning, and this an S–R theory cannot do.

3. RESPONSE OR ACTION?

Thus the restriction on the notion 'stimulus' or 'cue' required by S–R theory is found to be inadequate to the facts. But the same is true of the S–R theory of a 'response'. For a response is meant to be understood as a movement, whereas once we admit that learning depends on how the animal sees the situation, then we are classing it as *action*, for the nature of the response then also depends on the description it has for the animal, whether he is 'picking the white card' or 'picking the card on the left'. For the S–R theory on the other hand, the nature of the response must depend purely on the description which holds of it as a movement.

For the S–R theory, then, the difference in this case between picking the white card and picking the one on the left lies simply in the stimuli which elicit what is an identical movement in either case. Once we have abandoned the notion of stimulus, this

[1] Reported in Thorpe, *Learning and Instinct in Animals*.

account has no more point. But, even leaving this aside, it would still be clear that we cannot account for responses in this way.

For the relation between cue and movement is more complicated than this. For instance, it may be that a cue is linked with a movement of approach to that cue, or that the movement it elicits is one of approach to another cue, or even a movement of some other type. In other words, the question whether a given identical movement is one of two responses may not hinge simply on the cues which elicit it; for even when we know the cue, the question may still arise what type of response it is, e.g., is it a response of approach to the cue, or is it simply the movement of certain muscles which in this case happens to bring the animal nearer the cue? Once we have observed movement and cue, their relation to each other may still be in question.

The description that a movement may have *qua* response may thus vary more widely than the S–R theory can allow. For if there is more than one way in which a cue may be relevant to the response in learning, then learning must require some selection; something must determine whether the animal is learning to emit the movement now being rewarded as an approach to this cue, or as some other type of movement to be made if this cue appears, and which in present circumstances happens to bring him closer to the cue; for instance, something must determine whether a rat is learning to approach card X, or simply to go right whenever card X is presented (it happening to be the case that card X is always presented on the right side). But this selection cannot be accounted for in S–R terms, for in either case in the training situation cue and movement are identical; if two different responses can nevertheless be learned, it can only be because the cue-response relation is *seen* in a different way by the animal. In other words, the difference between the approach-description and the other description will not lie either in the nature of the movement the animal is now executing—*ex hypothesi* —or in the nature of the cue, which is the same in either case; it must lie, then, in the description which, in some sense, the response has for the animal.

If this variation is permitted, then, we will not be able to determine the nature of the response simply by observing the movement emitted, or even by singling out the cue which elicits it as well, for the question can still arise under what description this movement is a response of the organism. And, if this is so, we will not be able to account for learning in S–R terms, that is, as the conditioning of movements to cues; for any theory of learning will also have to account for the selection of the description under which this movement is 'conditioned' to the cue. Thus it is essential to S–R theory that there be no such variation, that is, that the responses conditioned to the stimuli be all of the same type of description, such that there be no doubt, once one has observed the movement, what the response is. Thus, in connexion with the response, too, the S–R theory requires that there be a limit on what can be learned, on the correlations by which we can account for behaviour which is adapted to the environment through learning.

These limits on the response type seem to be generally assumed among S–R theorists, and in the debates on the subject, they tend to refer without question to *the* nature of the response. But the question arises whether the facts of learning can justify this limitation. And this can be decided by the empirical evidence. The question concerns what is learned, in the sense of, which of the many descriptions which a movement emitted in a given situation can bear does it bear as a response? And, as with questions about the nature of the stimulus, we can discover this by seeing in what ways training is transferred to a new situation, whether and in what ways the response will alter, and therefore what are the invariants, the description under which the response is the same as the one learned in the original training. For this will define the learned response, that is, the way the animal's behaviour has been altered by learning.[1]

Now if the response is unitary in type, what is this type? It seems clear that the original Hullian notion of 'colourless movement', that is, movement identified by the effectors used, cannot apply to all learning situations. This arises clearly out of an experiment of Nissen.[2] Nissen trained chimpanzees with a box with two panels which could be pushed in to allow access to the

---

[1] This method is applied by Campbell, 'Operational Delineation of "What is Learned" via the Transposition Experiment', *Psychological Review*, 1954, but Campbell is still interested in discovering what the nature of the response is in general, whereas the question we want to pose is whether there is such a unitary nature.

[2] 'Description of the Learned Response in Discrimination Behaviour,' *Psychological Review*, 1950.

food chambers inside. One of the panels was white and the other black. The animals were trained to push in the white panel when the box was arranged so that the panels were alongside each other, whether the white one was on the right or the left. It would seem natural to say that the response which the animal had learnt was 'reach for the white panel'. But it could still perhaps be maintained that it had learned to reach right (i.e., make certain muscular movements) when the positive panel was on the right, and reach left when it was on the left. This interpretation is ruled out, however, by the next stage of the experiment. Nissen put the box on its side so that white was above or below black, and the animals transferred their training almost perfectly. There seems little doubt that the animals had learnt to reach for the white panel.

This, and many other features of discrimination learning, has led a number of S–R theorists, e.g., Nissen himself, and Spence,[1] to abandon the Hullian notion of 'colourless' movement (one which Hull himself doesn't seem to have stuck very faithfully to) in favour of a classification of movement in terms of 'approach' and 'avoidance' (Nissen) or 'non-approach' (Spence).

It is not entirely clear what is meant to fall under this classification. Nissen[2] accepts

> the logical necessity, in some instances, of describing the discriminative response as an act, that is, in terms of its consequence or effect (usually with reference to a goal or an altered organism–environment relationship.)

Now this goes far beyond what we would usually class under 'approach' or 'avoidance' behaviour. It would also apply to such things as 'pushing the lever down' as well as to 'going towards the red square'. If we gave this a wide interpretation, then we should fall into exactly the same problems as were mentioned above in the case of 'response'. For 'alteration in the organism–environment relationship' is as unclear and multivalent as 'response'. For any such alteration can be classified in a great number of ways. The only type of response-classification which would be ruled out by this is one which would specify responses purely

---

[1] 'The Nature of Discrimination Learning in Animals,' *Psychological Review*, 1936.

[2] Op. cit., p. 130.

by the changes in the organism itself (movement of muscles, etc.) which we sometimes use in talking about reflex responses.

Moreover, if we adopt a classification of response by the result achieved, then an important concession is being made which undermines the whole basis of S–R theory. For, unless we can account for the occurrence of such responses in terms of others not defined by their results, we shall be left with S–R correlations of a teleological form (e.g., 'on the occurrence of S, the animal will emit that behaviour which in the situation will achieve G, the goal by which R is defined'). It is, of course confidently—and wrongly—believed by S–R theorists that an account of this kind can be given.

But, if we leave this difficulty aside for the moment (in order to return to it in Chapter IX) and concentrate on cases of discrimination learning, the thesis of Spence and Nissen is simply that the response type is invariably one of approach or avoidance (or 'non-approach'), i.e., that the movement elicited must always be classified as approaching or going away from a cue-object. The introduction of 'avoidance' and 'non-approach' raises further ambiguities which we shall take up in a minute, but for the moment we can interpret Spence and Nissen as saying that, in cases of discrimination learning involving reward and not punishment, the response can invariably be classified as an approach to something, and the response type is therefore constant.

But this claim cannot be upheld.

Already Nissen's 'approach' interpretation is strained by the results of Weise and Bitterman[1] where rats were trained not only to go into a lighted alleyway and avoid a dark one, but also to go right when both alleys were lighted and left when both were dark. Now, if the first result squares with the 'approach' interpretation, the second doesn't seem to. For when the animal goes right when both alleys are lighted, he cannot be said to be 'approaching the lighted alley'. Nissen tried to account for this by invoking 'kinaesthetic stimuli' connected with turning right which together with the lighted alleyway were associated with approach. The animal thus learned to 'approach' his own kinaesthetic stimuli! But even if a clear sense could be given

[1] 'Response-selection in Discriminative Learning,' *Psychological Review*, 1951.

to this latter hypothesis, it is ruled out by another experiment by Teas and Bitterman.[1] These authors showed how rats could respond by jumping one way to one pair of discrimination cards, and another way to another pair, even if they were reversed. Thus we must admit that some spatial movements cannot be described in terms of 'approach'.

Then, of course, Spence's and Nissen's classification in terms of 'approach' and 'avoidance' or 'non-approach' is itself ambiguous. For what movements are 'approaches' to something and what 'avoidances'? Generally we know quite well because of our 'anthropomorphic' specification of the experimental situation with such refined methods of torture as electric grids. We are then quite safely certain that the rat is 'fleeing' the shock. Or by placing sunflower seed in the goal-box, we know that the rat is 'going to' it. But then it is difficult to see wherein lies the greater exactness in the language over that used in everyday contexts or by cognitive theorists. Moreover, there are, of course, a whole range of actions which cannot be characterized in terms of spatial change of position *vis-à-vis* some landmark, such as 'grabbing', 'biting', 'putting on', and so on. Here, of course, the context usually tells us quite unambiguously what 'the animal is doing', that is, in what way to characterize this 'alteration in the organism–environment relationship'. When the ape goes to get a box from the next room and stands it upright and climbs on it and gets the fruit, we know that the point of carrying the box is not that it should no longer be in the next room, but that it should be used as a 'stool'. The ape is 'bringing the box here', not 'taking it away from there', or just 'carrying it about for a while'. We are simply adopting the ordinary language notion of action. But in doing this we are not only introducing a teleological element, but we are abandoning the claim to explain learning in terms of the conditioning of movements to stimuli, since, on any set of criteria for a movement, we will also have to explain the selection of the description under which the response is being conditioned. For, for any movement, or change in the environment, there may be a number of actions, and the question of what the animal is doing in the training situation is not settled by reporting his movements.

In connexion with the discrimination learning examples above,

[1] Op. cit.

157

we might also put it in this way: The relation of stimulus to response may vary. That is, the relevance of a stimulus for a response which the animal learns to emit in its presence will not always be the same. This variation is often covered over by the formula 'the response is conditioned to the stimulus'. The relation may be that the animal learns to approach or bite or pick up a given kind of object, or it may be of the 'if-then' type, the animal learns to do X when Y. Thus the animal must not only learn which are the relevant cues, he must also learn what their relevance is for behaviour.

Hull tries to account for this conditional relation by one of his more implausible mechanisms, that of 'afferent neural interaction'.[1] This is the thesis to the effect that each distant stimulus alters the effect of each other distant stimulus on the organism itself, so that the afferent impulses arising from distant stimulus S will be altered, by the presence of Sx, to $\acute{s}$. Now $\acute{s}$ is considered to be some distance from s along a generalization continuum, so that, granted certain quantitative assumptions, the response conditioned to $\acute{s}$ may not occur if Sx is absent, and therefore S results in s. The response R to S can therefore be conditional on the presence of Sx. The thesis is, of course, wholly unverifiable. Hull[2] tries to answer the criticisms that his thesis is too vague by citing the example of conditioned reflex experiments. He quotes Pavlov's experiments which show that, once a response has been conditioned to a stimulus, it may easily not be evoked if some new stimulus is introduced along with the CS. Pavlov called this 'external inhibition'. We can thus measure the degree of interaction by the loss in readiness of the response when the new extraneous stimulus is introduced. But, if we turn to Hull's discussion in his *Principles of Behaviour*, we find that this is not the whole story. For sometimes the introduction of an extraneous stimulus, as Pavlov found, can serve to revive a conditioned reflex which has been partially extinguished. The effect of 'afferent neural interaction' can thus be both to increase and to decrease

---

[1] Cf. Hull, *Principles of Behaviour*, pp. 287–9, and 'The Discrimination of Stimulus Configurations and the Hypothesis of Afferent Neural Interaction', *Psychological Review*, 1945. Cf. also Spence's 'Sensory patterning' in 'The Nature of the Response in Discrimination Learning', *Psychological Review*, 1952.

[2] *Psychological Review*, 1945.

'reaction potential'. Hull's explanation of this, following Pavlov, is that the response builds up a certain conditioned inhibition, and this is also weakened by the change in the stimulus produced by interaction. Thus both the tendency to emit and the tendency not to emit the response are weakened. This is of course compatible with virtually any result whatever. Hull's only comment is that a 'mild' extra stimulus will tend to disinhibit more than weaken the response, whereas a harsher one will not.

But, of course, this hypothesis cannot help us to re-interpret the behaviour observed by Teas and Bitterman[1] as 'approach-behaviour'. Nor can it account for such learning as can be seen in conditional matching. Nissen[2] reports an experiment where monkeys were trained in matching, that is, picking an object which resembles a standard object, and trained to pick the object resembling the standard in colour when the background was of one kind, and to pick the one resembling it in shape when the background was of another kind. Here the differential condition governed attention to a certain stimulus dimension, and not a reaction to a given stimulus. And this can hardly be accounted for by afferent neural interaction.

The response learned, then, is not invariant in type. And, just as was shown in the discussion of 'stimulus', the correlations between environment and behaviour by which we account for learning can be shown to vary beyond the limits demanded by an S–R theory of learning. That is, the type of correlation which S–R theory seeks to establish does not hold. The mere fact of the contiguity of stimulus and response, or their contiguity in a context of reward, doesn't determine what is learned. For, beyond the question of what movements are being emitted, we also have to know what the animal is *doing* in the training situation. For on this depends whether he learns to 'do X when Y' or 'get Y'. Any S–R theory therefore has a problem of explaining the selection of a particular description under which the response is to be conditioned. And it is difficult to see how this could be accounted for in S–R terms, since the difference concerns not a selection between stimuli or cues, nor, *ex hypothesi*, a difference of movement, but rather a determining of the relevance of the cues to action. That one thing is learned, then, and not another

[1] Op. cit.
[2] 'Sensory Patterning versus Central Organization,' *J. Psychol.*, 1953.

depends not only on the movements emitted or reward received, but also on the structure which the situation has for the animal. The attempt of S–R, therefore, to do away with the notion of intentionality fails on the level of a molar science of behaviour.

The results of the discussion in this chapter, then, confirm those of the last. For the selection between different intentional descriptions of the situation which, we saw, had to be supposed in order to account for the direction and speed of learning has been found here to be necessary to account for the variety in what can be learned. And this, although it conflicts with the principles of neo-behaviourism, is what one would expect on the assumption that explanation by purpose is valid.

VIII

SPATIAL ORIENTATION

---

1. IMPROVISATION AND LATENT LEARNING

1. IMPROVISATION AND LATENT LEARNING

THE problem that was raised in the last chapter was that of discovering what the animal has learned to do. This question cannot be answered simply by discovering what movements it is making. We very often have to test in varied situations in order to discover what the animal was 'trying out' in the training situation, and therefore what he has learned to do.

Up to now we have been mainly discussing cases of discrimination learning, where the animal is trained to respond in a certain way to an object of a certain kind, e.g., to jump at the red card, or pick up the square object, etc. But the problem of what the animal has learned to do arises with maze learning as well, where the animal is trained to go down certain paths and find his way to reward, say in a food box. Now the standard S–R theory is that what is learnt here is a series of responses to stimuli. Each 'choice point' in the maze, where the animal has to choose, in other words, whether to go into a blind, say, or to take the 'true' path, becomes conditioned to the correct response, e.g., 'going right', as a result of the reward which follows this correct choice. The reward is either held to 'stamp in' the correct response, or to change the stimulus situation so that the last response made to this situation, which is the one which leads to reward, tends to be repeated. Of course, certain problems arise concerning the time-factor, since correct responses at the beginning of the maze are not rewarded for quite some time after they are made, until, in fact, the animal has run the rest of the maze. Special hypotheses are adduced to account for this, notably that of 'secondary re-inforcement': The sight of a choice point higher up on the 'true' path which the animal comes to as a result of making a correct choice farther back itself is held to acquire some reward value, thus stamping in that previous correct response. There are grave difficulties connected with this notion of secondary re-inforce-ment, but we shall not discuss them here, for they are not central to the issue of spatial orientation.

Now the thesis that maze-learning can be accounted for by the acquisition of a series of S–R connexions is called into question by the evidence of improvisation. For instance, Tolman, Ritchie and Kalish[1] tested rats in an apparatus where they were trained, after running along a path to a table, to go left, right and right again, ending up at a point at an angle of some 45° from the starting point on the table. A light was placed at this point. On the test trial, the original paths were taken away and a set of eighteen paths leading from the table in different directions were substituted. Nineteen of the fifty-six rats took the path which pointed most directly towards the goal-box.

Now this result would seem to suggest that the rats had learnt not only a series of correct responses to the original apparatus, but that they had also learnt where the goal-box was (that is, where food was usually given) *vis-à-vis* their original starting point; in other words, that the goal-box was part of their inten-tional environment which had been extended by the training beyond the limits of what could 'impinge on the receptors', to what McDougall calls 'remote' objects.[2] When we ask ourselves what the animal has learnt to do in this case, it seems plausible to say that he has learnt to approach the goal-box, just as we might say in a discrimination learning experiment that he has learnt to approach the white card. For in both cases the behaviour seems, in varied circumstances and by varied means, to be directed to-wards these objects. The difference is that in one case the approach response is 'conditioned' to a present stimulus, in the other to a 'remote' one. And the notion of responding to an object which is not present is, of course, one that can have no place in S–R

[1] 'Studies in Spatial Learning: I, Orientation and the Short-cut,' *J. exp. Psychol.*, 1946.
[2] *Outline of Psychology*, 13th ed., p. 207.

theory. Some other explanation must therefore be found for the facts of improvisation.[1]

But the facts of improvisation also raise a deeper issue between S–R theory and the ordinary teleological view which was not touched on in the previous section. We asked above what the animal had 'learned to do', as though the results of training on the animal's behaviour could best be described in terms of the acquisition of a tendency to emit a certain response or responses in the situation. But it is a question whether this is always the case.

Now it is the claim of S–R theory that this is the case. For behaviour is to be accounted for by certain laws linking environmental stimuli and responses.[2] These connexions may be innate. But when we come to learning, that is, the case where behaviour in a given environment changes over time as a result of experience, the change is, of course, accounted for by postulating acquired connexions.[3] Thus, insofar as any given course of training results in a change in behaviour, the change can be described as the acquisition of a tendency to emit a certain response or set of responses in certain conditions.

According to the ordinary type of explanation, on the other hand, behaviour is explained by the total situation[4] according to

[1] A number of other experiments by Tolman's associates were also concerned with discovering evidence for learning to go to a place, as against learning to make certain responses at certain points, the so-called 'studies in spatial learning', e.g., 'II, Place Learning versus Response Learning', *J. exp. Psychol.*, 1946; 'IV, The Transfer of Place Learning to other Starting Paths' and 'V, Response Learning versus Place Learning by the Non-correction Method', *J. exp. Psychol.*, 1947.

[2] Some of these laws are conditional for their operation upon certain states internal to the organism, as we shall see below, the so-called 'drive' states, but this does not alter the basic form of the theory.

[3] Learning must be distinguished from maturation. For instance, the behaviour of the individual in early ontogeny changes as certain motor skills develop. But this change may not be attributable to learning in the sense that it may be independent of the experience or practice of the animal prior to its development. Certain experiments with birds seem to indicate, for instance, that this is true of 'learning' to fly.

[4] I say 'total situation', and not simply 'environment', because in some cases certain conditions internal to the organism, e.g. hunger or thirst, are also relevant to behaviour. This is also recognized by S–R theory which introduces the notion of 'drive' to account for it. The essential difference is that, on the ordinary view, hunger and thirst condition behaviour as elements

teleological laws, by what the situation calls for or makes propitious, granted the goals of the organism. In some cases we might speak of learning as the acquisition of new goals, for instance, when an animal by experiment learns that a new substance is edible, and therefore acquires a new goal object. But in other cases—and this includes that of maze learning—we cannot account for it in this way, or at most only in part. In these cases the role of learning is to effect a change in the intentional environment, usually to bring it more in line with the geographical environment, and thus to bring about adaptation by 'orienting' the animal. Thus the effect of learning on behaviour is accounted for on the teleological view not by the conditioning of certain responses to certain stimuli but by certain features of the environment becoming known to the animal and therefore relevant for behaviour.

In a sense it might be said of the S–R theory as well that it accounted for learning in terms of certain features of the environment becoming relevant to behaviour. But by this would be meant simply that certain responses are conditioned to these features. Their relevance to behaviour can therefore only be univocal, that is, they can only serve to evoke a certain response or set of responses according to S–R laws. But on the view that the animal's behaviour is determined by what the total situation makes propitious granted the goals of the organism, the relevance of a feature may not be univocal. On the contrary it may play a part in many total situations, and therefore may be relevant to behaviour in many ways, depending on the other features of the situation. Thus, a given path which we know leads to a certain spot may serve as an escape route if there is danger, as a route to food if food is there, and so on. Or a hammer may be used to drive in a nail, or as a weapon, or as a paperweight, etc. In each case its presence in the field, its being an element in the total situation, is relevant to behaviour; it 'directs' it, in the sense that the hammer is chosen as an instrument. But that it is relevant

---

in a total situation, and thus contribute, like the other elements, to the 'direction' of behaviour, whereas for S–R theory, the role of drive is that of 'sensitising' the S–R connexions which alone direct behaviour. Cf. discussion below, Chapter X. There is a broad sense of 'environment' in which it includes the 'internal' environment, but it will be clearer to use the restricted meaning.

and what its relevance is—that is, what role it plays in the situation—depends on the other elements in the situation.

But, if the relevance of a feature of the environment to behaviour may not be univocal, then to say that a given course of training has had the result that certain features of the environment are known, i.e., relevant to behaviour, may not be to say that it has had the result of increasing the tendency to emit a certain number of responses in defined conditions. It may be to say much more than this. For a given feature may be relevant in an undelimitable number of ways. If I know my own neighbourhood, the particular shape of the environment will play a part in 'determining my response', i.e., setting the particular route I take, when I go to the barber; it will play a different part when I am going to a restaurant, another again when I go to the shop for cigarettes, and so on *ad infinitum*. Thus we cannot trace the result of the original 'training' period when I learnt this environment on my behaviour by enumerating a number of actions I should take (directions I should walk in) at certain points and given certain goals. For, however long, the list is bound to be incomplete. At any point in the neighbourhood, and given the goal of reaching any other point, my behaviour will differ from that of the stranger who hesitates, tries the wrong route, or waits for someone to ask.

This knowledge is what we normally call 'orientation'. It is not a form of 'knowing that', but a kind of 'know-how'; that is, its content cannot be expressed in a list of facts known about the environment, but it is a more general capacity to get around, to go from any point to any point in the environment. The question is: Can this kind of knowledge be the result of learning? S–R theory is bound to answer in the negative because this would mean that the effect of learning on behaviour could not be accounted for in terms of a list (however long) of acquired S–R connexions, and this would call into question the whole enterprise of a science of behaviour consisting of laws linking stimuli and responses. The ordinary view of learning, on the other hand, answers in the affirmative.

An issue is therefore posed by spatial orientation learning which did not arise in connexion with discrimination learning, but which is nevertheless of fundamental importance. It concerns ultimately, as we shall see below, the question of the direction of behaviour, whether we can account for the new behaviour arising from learning purely in terms of the history of the training period, that is, in terms of the responses conditioned then, or whether the role of training is to make possible certain adaptive responses, whose occurrence has to be accounted for on other grounds. The S–R theory tries to account for oriented behaviour in terms of a number of stimulus–response connexions set up in training; the behaviour is explained by the fact that these laws now hold. For the ordinary view, the training serves to familiarize the animal with the maze environment, to make therefore the adaptive 'oriented' behaviour possible. This, when it occurs, is explained by the goal towards which it is directed. To put it in anthropomorphic terms, the S–R account of orientation learning is rather analogous to saying that the animal learns a number of 'directions'; as though the animal had learnt that at choice point A he had to 'go right', at choice point B 'go left', and so on. To be oriented on the other hand is to be able to dispense with directions, or rather, to know more than can be set down in any list of directions.

Now in discrimination learning, or even in the ordinary case of maze learning, where the animal on the test trial runs the same path as on the learning trials, there is nothing to choose between the two accounts. We can say either that the animal chooses the 'true' path on the teleological ground that, because of learning, he knows it leads to food, or on the non-teleological ground that certain responses are conditioned to certain stimuli. There is no way of deciding between the two explanations. But in the improvisation case, we seem to have a phenomenon which is comprehensible on the first account but not on the second. For if we allow that the animal can learn the whereabouts of the goal-box, or its general direction from the starting point, that is, if this feature of the environment can become relevant to behaviour, then it may continue to be relevant in the new situation created by a rearrangement of the paths, and the new adaptive response may occur as a result. But if the learning consisted of the conditioning of the correct path responses to the stimuli at the choice points in the old 'true' path, then it is entirely irrelevant to the new situation in which the old paths cease to exist, and there should be no 'transfer of training' whatever.

It would seem therefore that the animal can become 'oriented' in training, so that in a changed situation it can improvise a 'correct' response, that is, one which gets to the goal without using the 'directions' or stimulus response 'habits' (*sHr*'s) connected with the original true path. Similarly, an animal can improvise a correct response which involves changing the order of importance of the original habits. A number of experiments have been made which bear on this. For instance, Tolman and Honzik[1] tested rats in an elevated maze with three possible paths to the goal. The paths were of different lengths, and the animals acquired a preference for the paths in inverse proportion to their length. That is, when path 1 (the shortest) was blocked near the beginning, they took path 2; when this was blocked, path 3. But paths 1 and 2 had a final common segment as they entered the goal area. A block was placed in this segment. The question was: Would the animals when they found path 1 blocked try path 2 as they had done before when path 1 was blocked near the beginning, or would they realize that path 2 was also blocked, and straight away turn to path 3? Tolman and Honzik's results were positive, as were those of Caldwell and Jones[2] with a similar maze.

In these cases of improvisation, the goal, and therefore the general direction of the correct path, was already established in the learning trials since these were run to reward. But the best known experiments which bear on the question of spatial orientation are those designed to test for 'latent learning' or the ability to learn by random exploration in a maze without reward. For in these experiments the animals familiarized themselves with an environment before this environment was given a specific relevance by the introduction of a goal-object at a specific point in it. One of the first of these experiments was that by Blodgett[3] in which hungry animals ran a maze without reward, and showed little improvement in consequence. As soon as reward was introduced, however, their performance markedly improved, up to the level of the control animals which were trained from the beginning with reward. It seemed therefore that exploration

---

[1] ' "Insight" in rats,' *Univ. Calif. Publ. Psychol.*, 1930.
[2] 'Some Positive Results on a Modified Tolman and Honzik insight Maze,' *J. comp. physiol. Psychol.*, 1954.
[3] 'The Effect of the Introduction of Reward upon the Maze Performance of Rats,' *Univ. Calif. Publ. Psychol.*, 1929.

without reward also produced learning. A spate of experiments followed this, some of the original 'Blodgett' type, others with different variations. In some cases the animals were allowed free exploration, and then were put directly into the goal-box and fed; their performance in the maze was then tested. In others, two distinctive goal-boxes were used in the training non-reward period. The animals were then put directly into one of them and fed, and their subsequent performance in the maze was tested. In another type of experiment, animals were run in a T- or Y-maze when satiated which had food in one arm and water in the other. They were then made either hungry or thirsty to see if they could find their way to the appropriate arm. The greater part of these tests were positive.[1]

Now these results are difficult to accommodate within the framework of an S–R theory. The point of these experiments is that the environment in the training trials has not got the specific relevance it will have on the test trials, and therefore it is hard to see how we can account for the improved performance after learning by the acquisition of just those habits needed to run what will eventually be revealed as the correct path. This is not always understood. Some theorists seem to think that latent learning is mainly a problem for reinforcement theory, and that it can be answered by postulating new types of 'rewards' in the training period. Thus MacCorquodale and Meehl[2] discuss the possibility of accounting for Blodgett's results by assuming that the animals were building up a tendency to take the 'true' path throughout the exploration period (rewarded probably by getting out of the maze), but that the full effect of learning on performance only showed when they had an adequate incentive.[3] And in this case, of course, the learning would consist simply in learning to make the right responses to the appropriate choice point stimuli which together constitute the taking of the correct path. But while this might be assumed in the case of Blodgett's experiment where the rats on the unrewarded trials ran always from the starting point to the end, we cannot assume this is the case of an experiment

[1] For a summary and discussion of many latent learning experiments, see Thistlethwaite, 'A Critical Review of Latent Learning and Related Experiments,' *Psychol. Bull.*, 1951.

[2] In Estes, et al., *Modern Learning Theory*.

[3] Op. cit., pp. 199–206.

like Buxton's[1] where the rats on the different exploration trials were always put into and taken out of the maze at different points. Yet here there was evidence of latent learning. Nor can the thesis that exploration results in an increased tendency to take the correct path account for the results of Herb[2] where, after exploration, the animals discovered food in one of the blinds, after which their tendency to enter blinds sharply increased. Nor can it account for cases where an experiment is conducted with two goal-boxes, and after exploration the animal is fed in one; or where, after being fed in two boxes, the animals are shocked in one,[3] which results in their taking, or in the latter case avoiding, the path to this box. The question is not therefore whether an animal can learn the true path without reward; the point is that in the exploratory period, there is no 'true' path. The true path only emerges with the reward or punishment given later. Thus we cannot account for latent learning in terms of a tendency to take one path rather than another, or in terms of a set of stimulus–response habits. It would appear more accurate to say that exploratory learning results in an increased capacity to get to any point which is later made a goal, by being shown to contain reward, that is, that it results in 'orientation'.

2. THE APPEAL TO 'STIMULUS ACTS'

Now it would seem fairly clear that S–R theory cannot account for the evidence of improvisation and latent learning without the addition of special mechanisms and hypotheses. And, after an initial period when they tried to reject the evidence, a great many S–R theorists have tried to develop special *ad hoc* explanations. The question is whether they are really adequate to the evidence. Some of them clearly are not. Thus an attempt by Birch and Bitterman[4] to use the notion of 'sensory integration' to account

---

[1] 'Latent Learning and the Goal Gradient Hypothesis,' *Contr. psychol. Theor.*, 1940; also reported in Thistlethwaite, op. cit.

[2] 'Latent Learning—Non-reward Followed by Food in Blinds,' *J. comp. Psychol.*, 1940; also reported in Thistlethwaite, op. cit.

[3] Tolman & Gleitman, 'Studies in Learning and Motivation, I,' *J. exp. Psychol.*, 1949.

[4] 'Sensory Integration and Cognitive Theory,' *Psychological Review*, 1951; also, 'Reinforcement and Learning,' *Psychological Review*, 1949.

for these data can hardly be sustained. The rule they invoke is that:

> When two afferent centres are contiguously activated, a functional relation is established between them such that the subsequent innervation of one will arouse the other.[1]

They apply this to the case of cul-avoidance, the tendency of the animal to avoid blinds once he has learned his way around the maze. Thus:

> When motivational conditions are such that avoidance behaviour would be evoked by the cul-end, this behaviour will now be evoked by the cul-entrance.[2]

But, of course, that mechanism could not explain improvisation. Nor can it explain why one path is chosen rather than another when there are two goal-boxes of which one has been shown to be positive. Nor can we see why, on this hypothesis, the animal does not start eating the maze at some early choice point, since the cues at this point will have been 'activated contiguously' with the food stimuli to which this is the appropriate response.

But this brings us to one of the most important mechanisms adduced by S–R theorists to account for the data of improvisation and latent learning, viz., the 'fractional anticipatory responses' (r_g's). It was Hull's claim[3] that precisely such an anticipation of the goal-response tends to occur. That is, that the response which is conditioned to food at the end of the maze tends to become conditioned to the stimuli which occur at earlier points in the maze. If this response occurred in full, of course, if the animal started to chew up the maze, it would totally disrupt behaviour. Fortunately, however, the conditioning of other incompatible, 'adapted' responses, like running down the path, to these earlier stimuli is too strong, so that the animal tends to inhibit this action. Some part of it, however, that part which is compatible with the adapted response, will occur and this is the 'fractional

[1] 'Sensory Integration and Cognitive Theory,' *Psychological Review*, 1951, p. 358.

[2] Ibid., p. 359.

[3] Cf. 'Goal Attraction and Directing Ideas Conceived as Habit Phenomena', *Psychological Review*, 1931. 'The Concept of the Habit Family Hierarchy and Maze Learning'. *Psychological Review* 1934; and 'The Mechanism of the Assembly of Behaviour Segments in Novel Combinations Suitable for Problem Solution', *Psychological Review*, 1935.

anticipatory goal-response' (rg). As examples, Hull cites[1] salivating and licking the chops. Now the rg is a 'pure stimulus act'; its role is to produce proprioceptive stimuli (sg). And these, according to Hull and many other S–R theorists, play a crucial role in directing behaviour. They are cast for the role that in ordinary 'anthropomorphic' speech we would attribute to ideas. And in fact, 'Pure stimulus acts are the physical substance of ideas'.[2]

Now how can this help us to account for such data as those, for example, of improvisation? For this Hull invokes a new mechanism, the 'habit family hierarchy'. The hypothesis is that an animal will many times in its experience have been in a position where it could, starting from one point, take several paths and reach the goal. This would particularly be the case for 'locomotion in free space'—e.g., in an open field where several routes were possible. In such a situation, all the different responses which were each the first in a chain of responses which terminated in the goal, i.e., the responses which consisted of 'starting on' the different paths, would be conditioned to the stimuli at this starting point. This set of paths following which is conditioned to the same starting point and which ends in the same goal is called a 'habit family'.

> A family of habits may be defined in general as a group of two or more habit sequences, all of which may be initiated by a particular stimulus and terminated by a particular reaction.[3]

Hull does not wish to confine this term to the 'field of spatial orientation'. 'It is operative in all situations wherever there is more than one distinct action sequence which will lead to the attainment of a particular goal or sub-goal.'[4] His main examples, however, are taken from the field of locomotion in space.

But some habit sequences in any given family will reach the goal quicker than others. The responses initiating these, by the 'goal gradient hypothesis', will be more strongly conditioned to the stimuli of the starting point than the others. Thus we can speak of a 'hierarchy' in the habit family. The favoured member will naturally be evoked on any occasion. But should this for

[1] Cf. 'Goal Attraction and Directing Ideas Conceived as Habit Phenomena', *Psychological Review*, 1931.

[2] Ibid., 1931, p. 505.   [3] Ibid., 1934, p. 39.   [4] Op. cit., p. 40.

some reason be impossible (e.g., the path be blocked), the next strongest member will tend to occur. Thus Hull hopes to explain detour behaviour.

But how does this apply to improvisation behaviour? Here Hull makes use of the notion of transfer. In various situations in the past the responses initiating various sequences in a habit family will have occurred along with a fractional goal-response (rg) for the goal which terminated those sequences. Thus the corresponding sg will have had all these initiating responses conditioned to it as well as the stimuli of the starting point. And the responses higher in the hierarchy would have been conditioned more strongly to sg. Now supposing, in some new situation, the animal learns to respond to some new stimulus with a response initiating a sequence very similar to one of the less-favoured sequences in such a habit family. The animal will continue to emit this response and run through the sequence, receiving reward each time. But gradually over several trials the goal-response will become conditioned to the stimuli which occur earlier in the series, and since the full response is impossible, a fractional component of it will occur (rg). This will in turn set up a proprioceptive stimulus (sg). Finally, the rg will be conditioned to the stimuli of the starting point, and therefore will occur at the beginning. Now this sg has conditioned to it not only the response initiating the habit sequence which has already been emitted up to now, but also the initiating responses of the whole family. It has also more strongly conditioned to it the favoured member of this family. Therefore this response will tend to take the place of the response occurring up to now, and the animal will 'improvise' by taking a short cut. In other words, improvisation occurs because

> when one member of a habit family hierarchy has attained a goal in an objectively novel situation, the learning thus acquired is transferred without specific practice to the remaining members of the hierarchy.[1]

Now this is the classic example of an account which simply poses again the question it was meant to solve. For the question is how the animal knows that, when it follows a path forward and then right for food, say, the most direct path lies at 45° right

[1] Op. cit., p. 41.

from the starting point. This is very schematically the problem set, for instance, by the experiment of Tolman, Ritchie and Kalish. Hull's answer is that the original roundabout response belongs to a habit family of which the most favoured member is the response along the short-cut. Thus once the less-favoured response is conditioned, the more favoured one becomes conditioned too, and the animal takes the short-cut. But the problem is precisely to explain why just *this* habit family comes into play here. The animal will doubtless have been in positions in the past where the response of running straight ahead was the most favoured of a given family, or where this response was one of the less favoured ones, but where the response of going 45° left was the most efficient. Why are these families of responses which are also in the animal's repertoire not also conditioned? Why does the animal pick, out of all possible families, just that one which will lead to the adaptive response? It must be that he recognizes the response of going straight ahead and then right as 'belonging' to that habit family of which the most favoured member is going 45° to the right. But then the intervention of the habit family cannot account for the fact that a given response is favoured; on the contrary, we have to account for the intervention of the habit family from the fact that a given response is favoured. So we might as well drop the habit family altogether, and say simply that the animal knows from the kind of roundabout route he is taking what the more direct route is. And this cannot be explained in S–R terms.

Hull's notion of *sg* and the explanations derived therefrom are attended with an additional question-begging ambiguity which has been pointed out by Deutsch.[1] We can see this if we take the example of Hull's projected explanation of phenomena such as that cited by Tolman and Honzik[2] where animals learn a three-path maze so that when the common part of paths 1 and 2 is blocked they take path 3. Hull[3] widens his notion of fractional goal-response to include responses to sub-goals, like 'entering the final pathway'. Thus the stimuli at the entrance of both paths 1 and 2 tend to have the fractional 'response' conditioned

---

[1] 'The Inadequacy of the Hullian Derivations of Reasoning and Latent Learning,' *Psychological Review*, 1956, reprinted in Deutsch, *The Structural Basis of Behaviour*, 1960.
[2] Op. cit. Cf. supra, p. 167.   [3] Loc. cit., *Psychological Review*, 1934.

to them whose integral version is conditioned to the final common pathway (perhaps a special preparatory licking of the chops before entering the goal-region). When this response is inhibited by the blocking of the pathway, the conditioning of the response to the earlier stimuli is weakened as well, and hence rg occurs less strongly, and so hence does sg. Thus the tendency to take either of these paths is weakened in favour of the third path.

Now this last step is illegitimate on Hull's premises. For sg is a stimulus like any other which tends to have conditioned to it the responses which occur along with it in a context of reward. Thus if the sg 'representing' the final common pathway of 1 and 2 occurs at the entrance to the maze, it will have conditioned to it *all* the responses which occur there which are followed by reward. But this means it will be conditioned to going down all three paths, just like the maze-entrance stimuli, but more strongly conditioned to 1 than 2 and to 2 than 3. Thus the weakening of sg will simply weaken all the responses proportionately, and will have no tendency to weaken 1 and 2 in relation to 3.

As Deutsch points out, Hull's derivation would work if he assumed that the sg was not just like any other stimulus, responses being conditioned to it simply when their conjunction was followed by reward, but if he assumed that an R would only be conditioned to sg when it was followed by the particular goal-response which sg 'represented'. In this case, the sg of the final common path to 1 and 2 would only be conditioned to the response of running down one and two, and its weakening would weaken these responses in relation to three. But this, of course, would be to make the notion 'sg' like the notion 'expectation'. Its connexion with a response would not so much be 'reinforced' as 'confirmed'. And this would be very far from Hull's intentions. It is clear, however, that his notion of sg as it stands cannot account for the data of Tolman and Honzik, or for a whole range of latent learning experiments which involve different paths to different rewards, and so on.[1] For—and this is the upshot of

[1] Cf. the discussion in Deutsch, loc. cit., *Psychological Review* 1956, and *The Structural Basis of Behaviour*, Chapter VII. In the above discussion we have seen that the 'habit' of sg-R must function like an 'expectation' of what will follow R. But the fractional response rg can function like an expectation too, that is, if rg is only conditioned to S when it is followed by the goal-response of which it is a fractional component, and not simply when it is followed by any reward whatever. This is the type of expectation which Deutsch mainly

Deutsch's criticism—it is clear that the 'stimulus act' hypothesis cannot solve what one might call the 'true path' problem, the problem of explaining the high level of the animal's performance on the path which is made 'correct' on the test trials, although neither this nor perhaps any other path was the 'correct' one during training; or—to put the point in another way—it cannot show how a change at one point (say the introduction of reward at the end of a path) can influence behaviour at another (say the choosing of the right path at the beginning). For although—via the notions of 'fractional anticipatory response' and the accompanying 'sg'—some 'stimuli' connected with the end point are present at the beginning, they can have no selective influence on behaviour, since both 'correct' and 'incorrect' responses will be conditioned to them.

3. S–R 'EXPECTANCY' THEORY

It is difficult to see how explanation by 'pure stimulus acts' could account for the phenomena in question, unless these were made much more like the 'ideas' of which they are held to be the 'physical substance', unless, that is, the theory moves in the direction of expectancy theory. There certainly has been a trend in this direction among S–R psychologists in recent years.[1] An attempt to evolve a more successful account of latent learning in

---

[1] Cf. Ritchie, loc. cit.; Seward, in *Essays Presented to R. S. Woodworth*; Hull's later theory also reduced the importance of reinforcement for learning, and the effect of the goal object was mainly to operate as an incentive. This change was probably not made in order to account for the latent learning phenomena, but it could be used for this—although it obviously came no closer to answering the 'true path' problem.

---

discusses, for in the cases he deals with, the Hullian derivation will only work if this change is made. For otherwise an rg, originally conditioned by being rewarded by its 'own' goal response, can be stamped in to other stimuli by some totally irrelevant reward, thus failing to discriminate between them as it must if the adapted behaviour is to be explained. This is the case, for instance, where we have two paths to two different rewards. Cf. Kendler's experiment, 'The Influence of Simultaneous Hunger and Thirst Drives upon the Learning of Two Opposed Spatial Responses of the White Rat', *J. exp. Psychol.*, 1946, and the discussion of it in Ritchie, 'Explanatory Process of the Fractional Antedating Response Mechanism', *British Journal of Psychology*, 1959.

terms of 'stimulus acts' by Seward[1] illustrates this point. The trend is also visible in the attempted 'formalization' of expectancy theory undertaken by MacCorquodale and Meehl in their commentary on Tolman.[2]

Of the two the latter is probably more worthy of study. In fact on the level of molar correlations the two theories are very similar. The difference mainly lies in that Seward's attempt still involves the invocation of the implausible inner machinery of 'stimulus acts'. But, apart from the intrinsic improbability of the terms used having any empirical foundation (different surrogate 'responses' representing all the different sections of the maze— we might just as well speak of 'ideas' except that this word is banned from behaviourese), they are used simply as intervening variables; that is, propositions containing them are not independently verifiable; the validity of the laws mentioning them stands or falls entirely with that of the molar correlations, between observable stimulus and response elements, which are derived from them. There are thus no *empirical* differences between the theories on this score. And insofar as there are differences in the molar correlations, the advantage lies clearly with the formulations of MacCorquodale and Meehl. Their theory seems therefore superior to Seward's in the line of S–R approaches to expectancy theory, and it is to an examination of this that we now turn in order to assess how adequately this type of hypothesis can account for the data of latent learning and improvisation.

From the fact that this is an 'expectancy' theory, we must not conclude that it is a step in the direction of cognitive theory. It remains very much an S–R theory, since the attempt is to account for the results of learning in terms of the conditioning of responses to stimuli. It only introduces a more complex relationship between stimulus and response elements. The principal hypothesis is to the effect that the occurrence of R_1 to S_1 when this is followed by S_2 leads to an 'expectation' S_1–R_1–S_2. This is used to predict that, should S_2 become a goal, or connected with a goal, R_1 will tend to be emitted to S_1. Thus instead of

---

[1] 'A Theoretical Derivation of Latent Learning,' *Psychological Review*, 1947; 'Secondary Reinforcement as Tertiary Motivation: a Revision of Hull's Revision', *Psychological Review*, 1950; and 'Introduction to a Theory of Motivation', *Psychological Review*, 1952. Mowrer, 'Two-Factor Learning Theory Reconsidered', *Psychological Review*, 1956, expounds a similar theory.

[2] Cf. the chapter on Tolman in Estes, et al. *Modern Learning Theory*.

saying that an R becomes conditioned to an S when it occurs along with it and is followed by reward, it also allows for the case where an R is conditioned to an S because its occurrence along with it was followed by another S which is later connected with reward. This is simply a special extension to take account of some of the phenomena[1] which seemed to call for an account in cognitive terms. This is the closest it comes to cognitive theory. The aim is still to predict the behaviour which results from learning on the basis of connexions between stimuli and responses or stimulus response habits. Only the conditions in which stimuli can evoke responses are made more complex.

The difference between MacCorquodale and Meehl's 'expectancy' theory and a teleological one can be seen in the fact that their 'learning about the environment' plays an univocal role in evoking behaviour. For, if learning is the acquisition of a set of 'expectancies' of the kind S_1–R_1–S_2, then we can account for it in terms of a set of tendencies to emit a number of responses, R_1, and so on, although the conditions in which these tendencies will be 'active' are more complex than the drive-conditions usually cited in S–R theory. For MacCorquodale and Meehl, then, the role of the environment in behaviour is univocal: It can be understood as the evoking or as the tendency to evoke a certain finite list of responses. And therefore learning about the environment is acquiring a number of such tendencies although many may be 'latent'. In anthropomorphic terms, orientation learning is reduced to a series of 'directions' (if you are at S_1 and want S_2, then do R_1), and is not conceived as a general capacity to find one's way around. And, of course, the cognitive element even in the notion of 'directions' is removed by the fact that the conditions for 'wanting S_2' are very strictly laid down in drive and stimulus terms.

MacCorquodale and Meehl's theory thus seems to be the solution which S–R theorists have been looking for, a way of accounting for the phenomena of latent learning which remains within the framework of S–R theory. For they seem to have solved the problem of the 'true' path. The solution consists in assuming that the animal builds up in training a latent tendency to take each of the possible paths, one of these being activated only when

[1] Notably those of latent learning experiments where the animal is fed separately in the goal-box before being put back in the maze.

the stimuli at its end point are paired with reward. In this way, they can explain how the introduction of reward at a given point leads to the animal's selecting a path and to his showing proficiency in running it (avoiding errors, blinds, etc.). They have thus found a hypothesis which will do the job that the Hullian 'fractional anticipatory goal response' was meant to do but couldn't, show how changes introduced at the end of a path (say, the introduction of reward) can influence behaviour at the beginning (say, choosing the right path). For the stimuli associated with the end point are connected not with all the responses emitted at the beginning point which were followed by reward, as was the case with the 'sg', but only with those which led to this end point. And this is the force of the term 'expectancy'.

But what the solution of MacCorquodale and Meehl gains in comprehensiveness, it loses in definiteness. For the solution consists in liberalizing the conditions under which a stimulus–response habit may be acquired, while adding to those which may have to obtain for it to be activated. The usual conditions for the acquisition of an sHr are that the stimulus and response occur concurrently in a context of reward; but here the simple running through a sequence S_1–R_1–S_2 may lead to S_1 evoking R_1 on a future occasion. Correspondingly, the conditions of activation are more stringent: The usual theory is that it only requires that the animal be in a drive state for the habit to be activated; here it must also be that the second stimulus (S_2) has been paired with reward. But this liberalization of the conditions of acquisition of sHr's makes the theory—at least in its present form—that much more difficult to verify. In the case, say, of Hull's theory, one can, by observing the behaviour of an animal in a maze, say with some degree of precision what habits it is supposed to have acquired; with MacCorquodale and Meehl's theory this is much more difficult. How many times must an animal run through a given section of the maze for him to build up an 'expectancy'? In the case where an animal explores a maze at random, entering and leaving it at different points, under what conditions does he form a 'chain' of expectancies? That is, when does he 'recognize' points approached on different occasions from different directions as the same? There are many questions of this kind which remain unanswered and this uncertainty makes the theory very difficult to verify. To the extent that this is the case, of course, it fails of its object. For we cannot tell whether we can account for orientation learning by the acquisition of a finite set of 'habits' unless we have some way of determining in each case exactly what habits are acquired. It is always possible that by making the conditions of habit-acquisition indefinite enough S–R theorists could 'account' *ex post* for any oriented behaviour whatever, but this would be of little use.

But although it is less definite than orthodox S–R theory, MacCorquodale and Meehl's 'formalized' expectancy theory is definite enough to show that it cannot account for oriented behaviour. Thus the condition for the acquisition of an expectancy $S_1-R_1-S_2$ is that the animal move from S_1 to S_2 'via' R_1. This sequence in the training period therefore could not account for an expectancy of the reverse order, $S_2-R(-_1)-S_1$. Therefore MacCorquodale and Meehl's theory could be shown to be inadequate if, say, animals trained to go through a maze in one direction could run it with fewer than chance errors in the other (say, if they were fed at the starting point and then introduced at the end). It is possible, of course, that an experiment of this kind would be negative because retracing one's steps is often difficult if one has been confined to a closed pathway (as for instance in an Underground station). But there is the result obtained by Köhler, where rats trained in a maze could master another maze which was a mirror image of the first more quickly than animals with no such training. Since this would mean that all the expectancies built up in previous learning would be inapplicable, it should retard learning according to the hypothesis.

The last example, showing as it does 'transfer' of training, brings us to improvisation. And it is here that MacCorquodale and Meehl's theory is most clearly inadequate. For the crux of the theory is that it liberalizes the conditions of habit-acquisition. Thus it might serve to account for those cases where the animal, during free exploration, runs through the path which is later to become the true path, even though no reward is given. But in cases such as those studied in Tolman, Ritchie and Kalish's short-cut experiment, the 'true' path on the test trial does not exist at all during the training period, and therefore the adapted response is entirely new. The theory therefore cannot account for an important feature of oriented behaviour—viz., what is called in ordinary speech 'a sense of direction',—which may be relatively independent of particular known paths.

MacCorquodale and Meehl attempt to fill this gap by means of another special hypothesis. The mechanism is somewhat reminiscent of Hull's habit family, but escapes some of its difficulties. The account starts from the notion of a chain of expectancies, where $S1-R1-S2$ is linked to another expectancy $S2-R2-S3$, and so on. Then from this is introduced the notion of a 'circular set'. This is a chain of expectancies in which $k-1$ form a chain and the kth has as its elicitor ($S1$) the elicitor of the first expectancy of the chain, and as its expectandum ($S2$) the expectandum of the last expectancy in the chain. An example of such a set would be the case of simple relations in space. Thus the chain $S1-Rx-S2$, $S2-Ry-S3$, where Rx is 'go ahead' and Ry is 'go right' might form a set with, as kth member, $S1-Rz-S3$, where Rz is 'go right 45°'. Now when both the chain and the kth member of a set are confirmed, we have a 'confirmed circular set'. Now circular sets can be 'isomorphic' when (a) the number of expectancies is the same, and (b) 'the response terms in corresponding positions in the two sets are so similar in topography that near-perfect primary induction would occur between them'. A number of isomorphic circular sets is called a 'family' of sets.

Now the mechanism operates simply in this way. If a number of sets in a given family are confirmed, and the chain of $k-1$ expectancies of a new family of that set is confirmed, this will tend to make the animal acquire the kth expectancy, and thus act on it.[1] Thus, since the animal has found many times that going forward and going right leads him to the same place as going 45° right, he will tend, in each new case in which he gets somewhere by going forward and going right, to head for the short-cut and go 45° right.

Now this gets around the Hullian problem of explaining why the adaptive response arises. Here the response of going right 45° is picked by the nature of the chain of responses. But the 'explanation' is either almost entirely verbal or false. It is false if we take seriously the notion that only responses 'close in topography' to the original confirmed set, i.e., resembling it in terms of limbs or movements, will mediate transfer to a new situation. For this would mean that the basic rules about spatial orientation which we learn, say, on land, would totally desert us when we came to swim, or that we would have no notion about what was a short-cut when we learned how to drive, until we had laboriously acquired the experience. It is verbal if we allow that there is 'induction' between all the different ways of locomotion.[1] For then we are saying that the animal learns a great number of rules of the form 'going forward and going right get one to the same place as going a little to the right'. In other words, the animal learns in general how to take short-cuts and orient himself in space.

Of course, this might still be considered as an S–R 'explanation' of orientation in that we would account for this ability in terms of the acquisition in experience of a finite number of such 'maxims' or behavioural rules, each independent of the others. As it stands, of course, it is virtually impossible to confirm it. We have no way of predicting which circular sets will be operative in an animal's behaviour (i.e., have been confirmed) and which will not. Indeed, we have no principle of counting for types of 'families' of circular sets. When an animal goes forward and then two yards to the right, is there a different set operating from the case where he goes five yards to the right? And if so, where is the boundary between these two?

But once we have posed this question, even the indefiniteness of the circular sets thesis cannot hide its inadequacy. For first we are asked to believe, for instance, that there is no connexion between an animal's knowing how to take the diagonal as a short-cut to a point two sides around a square and, say, his knowing how to go right as a short-cut to the point which is three times around a square. Or the animal might know both of these, and yet be at a loss when he had run two and a half sides. Now, of course, this *might* happen in an unfamiliar environment. And this brings us to the second point. According to the thesis, having a sense of the direction from A to B depends on the confirmed circular sets, that is, the general 'maxims', in the animal's experience. But then it is impossible to see why the animal's familiarity with—that is, 'orientation' in—a particular environment should make any difference. Thus it should be the case

---

[1] Which there most certainly is: Rats trained to run a maze can swim it, and rats trained by being pulled through on a basket can run it. Cf. McNamara, H. J., Long, J. B. and Wike, F. L., 'Learning Without Response under Two Conditions of External Cues', *J. comp. physiol. Psychol.*, 1956.

either that the animal be able to take a short-cut in any environment of a given shape where he had developed an expectancy chain, so that he could run an indirect path to reward, or that he should be able to do so in none of this shape. His ability should depend purely on the spatial structure of the path and short-cut. For instance, there should be no difference between the animal's improvisation performance in a closed maze and in an open one respectively of the same shape. And this is not borne out by the evidence.[1] Thirdly, on this hypothesis, the sense of direction should be either quite accurate or totally absent, depending on whether the chain of expectancies belongs to a family with many confirmed members or not. But, of course, this is not the case. Sometimes we know only the 'general direction', that is, that the true direction may lie within a certain range. Thus the animals in Ritchie's spatial orientation experiment,[2] when the apparatus had been reversed, tended to go towards the wall where they had been fed rather than taking the direct path to the exact point on the wall.

It is thus difficult to see how MacCorquodale and Meehl can account for improvisation, or the taking of short-cuts, except by invoking a sense of direction in the animal. But then their hypothesis would cease to be an S–R one. For this would be to say that the animal can sometimes learn not just a set of 'directions', but also the general direction of points from each other, i.e., the relation to each other in space of various points. And this knowledge, as we have seen, cannot be accounted for in terms of a set of stimulus response connexions, but only in terms of a general ability to 'get around' from one point to another in a given environment.

4. THE MACHINE WITH 'INSIGHT'

So far, improvisation has been the most difficult feature of behaviour for S–R theories to account for. But there is a new and imaginative hypothesis by Deutsch, one of whose principal claims is that it can account for these data. The major new feature of Deutsch's theory[3] is that the stimulus is not held to evoke

---

[1] Cf. Restle, 'Discrimination of Cues in Mazes', *Psychological Review*, 1957.

[2] 'Studies in Spatial Learning: VI,' *J. exp. Psychol.*, 1948.

[3] Cf. *The Structural Basis of Behaviour*, and 'A New Type of Behaviour Theory', *Brit. J. Psychol.*, 1953; and 'A Theory of Insight, Reasoning and Latent Learning', *Brit. J. Psychol.*, 1956.

behaviour but to terminate it, or perhaps one could say more accurately, to steer it.[1] The theory has been applied mostly to problems of spatial orientation and maze learning, and a machine has been constructed with some of the features,[2] which is said to exhibit 'insightful behaviour'. This was done 'to show that this theory was really the description of a mechanism in general terms and not a redescription of the behaviour of an animal in high-falutin' language'.[3] But of course this does nothing to show that the theory *is* an account of the animal's behaviour.

Deutsch accounts for the effects of learning on behaviour in terms of a hierarchy of cues which the animal picks up on the learning trials. As the animal runs through the maze in the ordinary type of experiment, he picks up a number of cues which are then arranged in the order in which he comes across them. When the animal comes across some cue already known, such as the reinforcement at the end of the maze, then the cues become fixed in this order. On future occasions when the animal is hungry, say, the cues connected in a chain with past cases of reinforcement will become active, that is, they tend to draw the animal to them. But their arrangement in a hierarchical order means that those cues higher up will draw the animal more strongly than those lower down.[4] This hierarchical order will account for the by-passing of blinds on subsequent trials which were entered on the earlier trials. For the cues of the pathway beyond the blind will have been encountered after the cues of the blind, and being nearer to the goal will be higher in the hierarchy. The animal will therefore be drawn more strongly along the true path. Similarly, the hierarchy can be used to account for improvisation. For if a short-cut is opened in the maze, then a cue much higher up in the hierarchy will enter the animal's field at an early stage (the cue, say, for the final passage-way which is now visible near the beginning of the maze), and

---

[1] In fact the whole behaviour sequence is terminated not by the making up of a need-deficit, but by certain key stimuli; but the role of environmental cues is to direct behaviour. Cf. *The Structural Basis of Behaviour*, Chapters III and IV.

[2] 'A Machine with Insight,' *Quart. J. exp. Psychol.*, 1954, reprinted in *The Structural Basis of Behaviour*.

[3] Deutsch, *Brit. J. Psychol.*, 1955, p. 30.

[4] In Deutsch's theory, the presence of a cue higher up in the hierarchy in the stimulus field will 'switch off' the cues lower down.

this will take precedence over all the cues lower down, and draw the animal directly to it. With the aid of an additional hypothesis[1] Deutsch also claims to account for the results of the Tolman and Honzik type experiment, where the animals 'inferred' from the closing of path 1 that path 2, with the same final segment, was also closed.

It is clear that the ability of Deutsch's theory to surmount, or appear to surmount, the obstacles on which other S–R theories have foundered arises not only from the idea of a hierarchical order of cues, but also from the hypothesis that the cues serve to steer rather than to evoke behaviour. For in the case of improvisation it would make no difference that a cue higher in the hierarchy appeared, if it served to evoke the same response on each occasion. For the cue in its new position relative to the animal requires a different response. This classification of the basic response as an 'approach to' a given stimulus constitutes the important break which Deutsch has made with most previous S–R theories of maze learning. For in these the thesis usually is that the stimuli at the choice point evoke the response previously stamped in. But on this type of theory improvisation cannot be accounted for, for this requires a new response which has not been conditioned to any stimuli in past training. Thus neither Hull's theory, nor the various 'expectancy' theories could account for these phenomena, since they were all based on a notion of stimulus–response connexion of this type. Deutsch's theory, on the other hand, promises to surmount this difficulty. And yet it remains recognizably an S–R theory, in that learning is accounted for by a series of S–R connexions and is therefore univocally related to behaviour. Orientation learning is not the acquiring of a general capacity to get from place to place, but the acquisition of a set of tendencies to approach a certain number of cues in hierarchical order.

In this way, Deutsch's theory approaches S–R theories of discrimination learning in which the basic connexion is held to be of this type, i.e., a connexion between a stimulus and approach behaviour. But in this it runs into the difficulty that we analysed in the previous section, viz., that it involves a teleological element in the explanation of behaviour. For behaviour characterized as 'approach' to a certain object can vary very widely in its

[1] Loc. cit., *Brit. J. Psychol.*, 1956.

topography. McNamara, Long and Wike[1] have shown that an animal can even learn a T-maze if it is drawn through it in a basket. Thus, to say that an animal learns approach behaviour is to say that it learns to do whatever will bring it near that object, which is to say that we are explaining the responses emitted by their results.[2] Secondly, Deutsch's theory would not hold for that kind of discrimination learning which does not involve learning to approach an object of a certain kind, but where the connexion is of the 'if . . . then' type, such as, e.g., the conditional matching experiments discussed in the last chapter.[3] Deutsch is aware of this fact:

> It is doubtful, however, whether this explanation could cover all forms of conditional learning. Neither will it account for many other phenomena customarily included under the heading of higher mental processes such as delayed reaction, double alternation, abstraction and the perception of relations.[4]

But since the theory is mainly meant to account for orientation learning, it would be best to leave these difficulties on one side and see how well it can deal with the phenomena in this field.

Now Deutsch's theory, like that of MacCorquodale and Meehl, is hard to assess because of its indefiniteness. We have no way of telling *a priori* what the cues are which are picked up by the animal in learning. We cannot even conclude from the fact that an object is prominent that it becomes one of the cues conditioning approach. Thus Blodgett and MacCutchan trained rats in a T-maze with a lighted disc at one end. The animals were trained to go to the arm containing the disc. If the end at which the disc was placed varied during learning, the animals could be trained to approach the disc, but if it remained at one end, then a shift of the disc after a certain amount of training did not induce the

[1] 'Learning Without Response Under Two Conditions of External Cues,' *J. comp. physiol. Psychol.*, 1956.
[2] This point will be discussed at greater length in the next chapter. Deutsch, *The Structural Basis of Behaviour*, p. 35, speaks of a behaviour sequence as 'a set of tropisms', but we cannot assume that he believes the mechanism involved to be the simple one described by Loeb.
[3] Cf. supra, p. 159.
[4] Loc. cit., *Brit. J. Psychol.*, 1956, p. 124.

animals to go to the other end. Their behaviour could not thus be described as 'approaching the disc'.[1]

But the theory in its present form can nevertheless be seen to be inadequate. The principal difference from an ordinary teleological cognitive view of learning is, as we said, that it accounts for learning in terms of the acquisition of approach–responses to a series of cues. This means that Deutsch's remains an S–R theory in the sense that the environment learned is related univocally to behaviour, whereas for cognitive theory learning the environment is giving the animal the capacity to do a great many different things. Like the other S–R theories, then, Deutsch's runs into trouble in accounting for the learning gained by free exploration, i.e., he encounters the 'true path problem'. When the animals run the maze in the same direction each time, then the order in which they pick up the cues is more or less set; but in the case of an experiment like Buxton's where the animals are put in and taken out of the maze at different points, what is to guarantee that the cues are acquired in the order needed to exhibit the test behaviour? The notion of a hierarchy of cues is fairly plausible in the ordinary case of learning, for the particular features of the maze environment lend themselves to being seen as a set of 'objectives' to be reached one after the other, just as they do to being seen as a set of 'directions'. But not all environments to be learned are like mazes, and not all of them are learned in the same order as they will have to be run in future.

Now Deutsch[2] tries to account for this by the hypothesis that rows of cues can be attached to other rows when a series is run through and terminates in a cue which is already attached to a row. Thus, in a maze with many arms which meet at some midpoint, the animals will set up several rows of cues which will be connected at this particular point. Thus, in a complex maze, we will have not only a main hierarchy of cues which the animal will run to, but also a set of 'branch lines' extending into other parts of the maze. Thus, if the animal is placed in any part of the maze,

[1] 'Place versus Response Learning in the Simple T-maze', *J. exp. Psychol.*, 1947. Blodgett and MacCutchan seem to claim that this shows prevalence of 'response learning' over 'place learning', contrary to the hypothesis of Ritchie; but of course the rats went always to the same place; we might just as easily interpret this as showing the predominance of 'place learning' over 'approach learning'.

[2] Loc. cit., *Brit. J. Psychol.*, 1956.

once he has learned it, even in a corner off the main path, he can find his way to the goal by following the 'branch line' to where it joins the main hierarchy, and then up to the goal.

Now the only problem with this is that it cuts across Deutsch's hypothesis of the hierarchy. For there is nothing to guarantee that, say, the cues in the branch line are acquired in the order in which they will have to be used in the future. An animal might easily explore a side path by running up it and back again. Now if the order of cues in the system is as first acquired, then they will be in the wrong order to mediate a successful solution if the animal is placed at the end of this side path in future. For the cues farther down toward the main path will be 'switched off' by the cue at the end. Or again, if an animal explored a maze by being placed halfway along the true path, and going forward to the goal and backward to the start, he would be unable to run the maze in future. An extreme case of this would be that in which the animal learned the maze in reverse order to that in which he had to run it on the test trials. This is the counter-example which was also suggested for the theory of MacCorquodale and Meehl. If evidence of this sort could be found, it would weigh against Deutsch's theory as well in its present form.[1]

The theory might be amended, however, by dropping the hypothesis that the hierarchy depends on the order in which stimuli are first encountered. We might assume that the order of stimuli in relation to each other is recorded in the system, but that this does not mean that the order of prominence is thereby set. We could say that the order of prominence could run in either direction, depending on circumstances. But then what would determine which cue was more prominent than which other? To answer this we might use one of Deutsch's hypotheses to the effect that when a row of cues ends in reinforcement, then on future occasions when the animal is in a drive state this row and those connected with it—its 'branch lines'—are activated. Now since the excitation of the row is held to flow from a certain goal-cue representing reinforcement, might we not assume that the excitation diminishes as it flows through the row, so that cues

[1] Deutsch, *The Structural Basis of Behaviour*, pp. 114–15, claims, of course, that his theory could account for the animal's finding his way in either direction. But this is nowhere reconciled with the hypothesis that the cues are arranged in hierarchy by the order in which they are experienced.

farther away from the goal are less potent than those nearer it? This would account for the hierarchical effect which mediates the avoidance of blinds and short-cut behaviour, without the inconveniences of a fixed hierarchical order.

Now the amended theory (which I have no evidence that Deutsch would accept) might seem to account for the greater part of the phenomena of latent learning and improvisation. And yet it would be an S–R theory, in that learning would be accounted for by assuming what might be called a certain number of 'objectives' which the animal is induced to reach, the order of the objectives depending on the final objective in each case. But there would be a finitely enumerable number of 'objectives' and of hierarchies of objectives, so that there would be no need to account for learning in terms of the acquisition of a general capacity to go anywhere from anywhere. The environment would therefore still be univocally related to behaviour in that it would serve to call forth, in appropriate conditions of drive, a certain number of approach responses.

But the problem is that Deutsch's theory, so amended, suffers from the same disability as that of MacCorquodale and Meehl, only to a greater degree—namely, that the conditions for habit-acquisition or, in this case, the picking up of 'landmark' cues are so indefinite that it seems almost totally unamenable to verification. And in fact a clear experimental test for the theory in its present form is very difficult to find, although perhaps not impossible.[1] But, even in the absence of an experimental test, we can go some way towards assessing the theory. The principal advantage in Deutsch's theory is, as we mentioned above, his notion of the role of cues in orientation learning. The function of these 'landmarks' is to induce approach behaviour on the part of the animal. Now a certain amount is known about the nature and role of cues in orientation learning and it should be possible to see whether this squares with an account of orientation in terms of the conditioning of approach responses to a series of cues.

Now *a priori* it might seem likely that it would square fairly well. The plausibility of Deutsch's theory rests largely on the way we usually think of the maze as a series of stages to be run, which we can express to ourselves as a series of objectives to be

[1] Cf. below, p. 193.

reached. But the problem arises of how these objectives are recognized as such. How does the animal manage to organize his environment into the right sort of 'map' in which the cues are arranged in the right lines and 'branch lines'? If we think of a maze with detour paths from the main one, which touch the main path at more than one point, we have to assume that the animal 'recognizes' a point on the main path as 'the same' whether he approaches it from the detour or from the main path.[1] Otherwise his avoiding the detour in future will depend on the order in which he first runs the maze.[2] Similarly in complex short-cut experiments like that of Shepard,[3] where, after learning a maze with many blinds, the animal discovers that the wall between one of the blinds and the path has been removed, thus opening a shorter path, the animal discovers this after he has passed the blind, for he cannot see that the short-cut is opened from the entrance to the blind. Shepard found that on the next trail animals tended to take the new path. But this depended on their recognizing the opening as coming at the end of what had previously been the blind in question. Now the question is, how does the animal recognize this?

We might assume that each portion of the maze has certain characteristic stimuli attached to it, a certain look or smell or feel, by which the animal recognizes it. The cues which are arranged in rows, then, are intramaze cues of this kind. But in actual fact mazes are often such that the variety of such intra-maze cues is very small, and they can be deliberately minimized. As a matter

[1] Deutsch, as a matter of fact, tries to have it both ways. He usually assumes that the same spot is recognized as the same, but in his discussion of the Hull–Leeper experiments, *The Structural Basis of Behaviour*, pp. 118–23, he has to posit a difference in the cues picked up in the same goal-box when approached from different angles in order to derive the result observed. If this degree of freedom is allowed, then virtually any result will 'confirm' the theory.

[2] If the starting point is A, the entrance to the detour B, and the exit D, the detour stimuli being C, then the animal may run $ABDBCD$, then on up to the higher points, E, F, etc. But unless D on the second occasion is recognized as the D of the first occasion, then the animal will take the detour; for if D the second time is seen as different, viz. D', then the order of cues will be $ABD(B'?)CD'$. C will thus be more potent than D and the animal will take the detour.

[3] Reported in Maier and Schneirla, *Principles of Animal Psychology*, pp. 468–9.

of fact, tests have shown that the cues which an animal uses in learning a maze are extremely varied and the animal can lean on some if others are not available[1] or even shift the weight if some cues, hitherto important, are 'scrambled' after learning—usually, however, after an initial period of disorientation.[2] Rats seem to rely heavily on visual cues if these are available, and a great deal on extra-maze visual cues.[3] At the limit a rat seems to be able to rely on no cues whatever if it is a question of learning a maze with some regular alternation of response (e.g., go right, go left).[4] Visual extra-maze cues are particularly important for cases of improvisation, or short-cut behaviour, that is, they are particularly important in those cases where the animal has to 'recognize' a new element, like a new path, as belonging to the complex in a certain way, as being in fact a short cut or the end passage of blind X.[5]

Now, if we consider the importance of the extra-maze cues, that is, the degree of disruption caused by their removal or 'scrambling', particularly in cases where the animal shows the capacity to improvise, then the simple structure presented by Deutsch's theory seems to be in need of amendment. For this means that a short-cut is often recognized as such, or the path at the end of the detour is recognized as the main path, largely by the cues from the environment outside the maze, and not simply by some special property of this path. The animal when the situation permits 'orients' by these cues. But then it is doubtful if we can still speak of 'approach behaviour' in the same sense, for the animal has not learned simply to go along the path with such

[1] Patrick and Anderson, 'The Effect of Incidental Stimuli on Maze Learning with the White Rat', *J. comp. Psychol.*, 1930.

[2] Tryon, 'Studies in Individual Differences in Maze Ability, VI', *J. comp. Psychol.*, 1939.

[3] Tsang, 1934, 1935, reported in Munn, *Handbook of Psychological Research on the Rat*.

[4] This is sometimes spoken of as reliance on 'kinaesthetic' cues, but this simply means that the rat knows that he has gone right and now must go left. It is difficult to see what is added by calling this a 'cue'.

[5] Restle, loc. cit., *Psychological Review*, 1957, points to this importance of extra-maze cues, as though it solved the problem which place learning and short-cut behaviour pose for S–R theory; but of course it does nothing of the kind, for the problem remains that the animal exhibits a new response, not previously conditioned to these cues. The problem concerns not the importance of extra-maze cues, but the role of these and other cues in orientation.

and such a look or feel, but to go along this path, if such and such a constellation of cues are present in the environment. Or, if we still wish to speak of approach behaviour, the description of the path to be approached is now a very complex one, including mention of its relation to extra-maze environmental cues. The animal in a relatively open maze sets up not so much an order of cues as an order of distributions of the same important environmental cues.

But if the extra-maze cues are important, then cues characteristic of the main path approached from the detour will certainly be very different from those characteristic of this portion of the path approached from the main path. And the constellation of stimuli which are opened by the short-cut where the animal can see a later part of the maze hitherto invisible from this point will certainly be very different from the cues previously associated with this part when it was seen from the immediately preceding section. How does the animal know that this set of cues is one to be 'approached'? Thus in the case of Tolman, Ritchie and Kalish[1] the rats who headed towards the goal point which had previously been in front of the light took a path which led somewhat to the left of it, although this path did not have the light shining directly down it as had the original goal path. Similarly, in Ritchie's[2] experiment where, after turning the maze around, the rats tended to head towards the wall where they had been fed before. They still knew the general direction of the goal. Can one say that they had learnt to 'approach' the wall? Then the question arises, which wall? Since one of the paths towards a wall resembled the original goal paths in having a light at the end, one would expect all the animals to take this path, but instead the animals who had been fed on the other wall took the path to it in spite of the differences. It is these cases where orientation is unsure, where only the 'general direction' is known, in which the account of improvisation in terms of approach to a certain cue is most clearly inadequate. But the difficulty clearly arises as well in those cases where improvisation is perfect and where the reliance is heavy on extra-maze cues. If one can give Deutsch's theory a specific meaning, it would seem to imply that short-cut behaviour would be more difficult if extra-maze cues are important, whereas it has generally been found to be less so.

[1] Op. cit.   [2] Restle, loc. cit., *Psychological Review*, 1948.

In view of this it seems unlikely that we can account for orientation behaviour in terms of the conditioning of approach responses to a series of cues. What, then, is the role of cues in orientation? The thesis that the various distributions of cues available at each point are unrelated one to another, and each have conditioned to them some response is improbable and does not seem to account for the facts. It is very much more likely that these various distributions of extra-maze cues in the partly closed situation of the maze are connected the way that they are in the open situation in that the distributions are expected to vary in an orderly way with the locomotion of the organism or changes in the dispositions of its sense-organs. It is in all likelihood in virtue of an expectation of co-variation of this kind that subjects with certain eye-muscles paralysed tend to 'see' the objects in the visual field shift in a direction opposite to that in which they have tried to move their eyes. Orientation in space is thus a matter of an expected co-variation between the locomotion of the animal and changes in the distribution of certain landmarks. If this is the case for open mazes, then there is no reason to believe that the case is any different for closed mazes where the 'landmarks' appear one after another. We should not assume that here the order in which the landmarks appear is unconnected with the movements which the animal has executed in helping to orient him. And this, of course, is what is assumed by Deutsch not only in the closed situation but in the open one as well. But it is much more likely that the animal's recognition of a certain pathway, his knowing 'where he is' in the maze, depends also on how he has just moved or been moved from a previous point. It seems fairly certain[1] that animals can learn to run a maze virtually without landmarks at all, simply by learning to take turns in a certain order. It seems unlikely that this knowledge of what turn has been taken plays no role at all in most orientation learning.[2,3]

[1] Cf., e.g., Hunter and Hall, 'Double Alternation Behaviour of the White Rat in a Spatial Maze', *J. comp. Psychol.*, 1941. Some landmarks seem necessary, however, in the training period.

[2] The evidence that animals can do without 'kinaesthetic stimuli' is irrelevant here unless one can show that knowing what one is doing depends on certain 'kinaesthetic stimuli', and this seems very unlikely. A very drunk man can be ignorant of where he has been wandering, as can one absorbed in thought, but they do not lack any 'kinaesthetic stimuli'.

[3] The notion of 'getting oriented' in a once familiar environment points

If this view is right, then improvisation occurs not because certain cues previously experienced are present, but because a distribution of cues related in a certain way to the previously experienced ones is experienced from a position in the maze which shows that a short cut has been opened to the goal. And the mere presence of cues similar to those experienced nearer the goal will not do if the position at which they are experienced is one which is far from the goal. And the type of cues which will count as representing a new shorter path to the goal will vary with the position at which they appear. Thus we can never account for orientation in terms of the conditioning of an approach response to a certain number of cues.

The issue between this view and the revised theory of Deutsch could perhaps be decided in part by an experiment of the following kind: In a maze with a distinctive covered goal-box, the animals are trained to run to reward. Then, once learning has reached a certain standard, the goal-box is placed, empty, beside the path in an early part of the maze. According to Deutsch's view, this should be similar in principle to opening a short cut. The animal should enter the box, and these stimuli should 'switch off' all the cues higher up on the path, so that, when the animal emerges, he will not tend to run farther up the maze. Moreover, according to a special hypothesis of Deutsch's, introduced to account for the Tolman and Honzik multiple path experiment, these stimuli should not be reactivated for some time. In this way we might have some evidence whether or not an animal can discriminate position in a spatial environment independently of the nature of the objects at that position, whether he can discriminate the change in order of stimuli represented by a real short-cut from that represented by the introduction of some new element. If he can do so it will be because known position in the environment is not entirely a function of the order of stimuli, and therefore, oriented behaviour is not 'a set of tropisms'. *A priori* the chances are that the animals will see that this is not a short-cut, and will thus not abandon hope, but will go on to see if a full goal-box is not in the original place.

---

to this fact of co-variation. One tries to find a point where one can enter the system of expected co-variation, as it were. One needs simply to get started, to discover where one is, and then one can find one's way about freely. In re-orientation, finding the initial position is everything.

There is as yet (to the writer's knowledge) no experimental evidence of this kind. But there is another somewhat similar class of results where we have evidence which seems to tell decisively against Deutsch's view, viz., cases of detour behaviour. Deutsch himself says that, where the animal can see the goal or a point near the goal, but cannot reach it by the most direct route because of some obstacle, he will fail to take an indirect route.[1] This seems an inevitable consequence, since taking the detour would involve steering towards landmark cues lower down in the hierarchy than the one seen, which are now, therefore, 'switched off'. But detour behaviour does occur in apes and dogs, and perhaps even, in some cases, in rats. And, where this is the case, position in the environment cannot be entirely a function of the order of cues, for the animal can 'steer' towards less favoured cues, even when the more favoured ones are present.[2]

It would seem from the above discussion that the chances are slim of accounting for the changes in behaviour as a result of maze learning in particular or any exploration of a spatial environment in general in terms of a series of acquired 'tropisms' or other tendencies to emit certain responses in certain conditions. At least, none of the theories put forward up to the present time seem to be adequate. For the evidence shows that animals and men can profit from exploration by improved performance on a great number of different paths—perhaps an indefinite number. S–R theories have not as yet adequately accounted for this fact and, to the extent that they have tried, it is by modifying their hypotheses in the direction of vacuity. And then animals and human beings can 'improvise'—e.g., by taking a new path, hitherto untravelled, to the goal. This phenomenon is the stumbling block of all theories with the apparent exception of the 'landmark' theory of Deutsch. But when we examine the evidence about the nature and role of landmark cues, this theory appears, to say the least, implausible.

---

[1] *The Structural Basis of Behaviour*, p. 38.

[2] Some evidence of the influence of cues in orientation might be gained by the following: in a T-maze with a covering over the choice point of the T, run the animals without previous training, and rotate the extra-maze cues 90° while the animal is making the turn, such that he emerges from the covered part facing in the same direction *vis-à-vis* the rotated environment, and see if this produces disruption of behaviour.

It would appear therefore that 'orientation' learning, the learning arising from spatial exploration, results in a general capacity to 'get about', to find one's way from any place to any other. The notion of position or place seems fundamental here. Knowing how to get from A to B for the properly oriented animal is more than knowing a path; it is having a sense of the general direction of B; that is, B in some sense has a position or place relative to the animal and to other positions. Our examination of the role of 'landmark' cues in orientation seemed to yield a similar result. For oriented behaviour does not seem to depend on the order of the stimuli alone, but on their order in relation to the locomotion, i.e., changes in the position of the animal. But then, too, it would seem that the notion of position, of knowing 'where one is' relative to other parts of the environment is fundamental to orientation. If this is so, then it will be clear why we cannot account for oriented behaviour in terms of S–R laws, i.e., the constant effect of certain stimuli on behaviour. For their effect will vary with position, that is, with the animal's knowledge of its position and thus, far from accounting for orientation by the constant effect of the stimuli, we have to account for the varied effect of the stimuli by the fact of orientation.

It seems likely then that orientation learning involves the acquisition of an intentional environment in which 'remote' objects—that is, those which cannot impinge on the receptors—have a place, just as 'present' ones do; that it involves, in other words, extending the area of the intentional environment. And this means that, in orientation, the effect of the remote environment on behaviour comes to resemble that of the present one, i.e., we can speak of 'approaching' a remote object as we do of a present one. In short, it would mean that the barrier between the 'open' situation—that 'in which the consequences of the alternative acts could be anticipated without actual carrying out of the act'[1]—and the closed one—which is so important to S–R theorists—would be shown to be an artificial one so far as the laws linking environment and behaviour are concerned. And in this case the much neglected question of the laws regulating behaviour in the 'open' situation would acquire a new and important relevance to the issue with which we are concerned.

[1] Spence, in S. S. Stevens, *Handbook of Experimental Psychology*, p. 718.

IX

THE DIRECTION OF BEHAVIOUR

I. THE OPEN ENVIRONMENT

UNDERLYING all the discussion on learning in the last chapters has been the issue about the nature of behaviour, whether it should be characterized as action or not. As we have seen, to characterize behaviour as action is to characterize it as directed towards some goal. Now this means that the particular form which it takes in any situation can be accounted for in part in a teleological way by what the situation requires given the goal in question. The issue about the nature of behaviour is, therefore, in part an issue about what could be called the direction of behaviour in a given environment: In what way does behaviour depend on or vary with the environment in which it is carried out? This question concerns what one might call the first-level correlations which hold between environment and behaviour, that is, the manner in which they are in fact found to vary together, however the holding of just these correlations is to be explained.

The alternative, then, is this: Must we account for the particular features of a response in a teleological way in terms of the goals pursued by the animal, or must we account for them on the hypothesis that a response with these features is linked in a law-like way with the stimuli obtaining at the time, and is constantly elicited by them? This is one of the crucial questions at stake between S–R theory and explanation by purpose. It is because the S–R theorists adopt the latter alternative on this basic question, as we have seen, that they must account for the changes in behaviour as a result of learning in terms of responses 'conditioned'; they must make learned behaviour, that is, a function of behaviour history, of the responses emitted in this or similar situations in the past (and, in the case of reinforcement theory, of the 'rewards' obtained as well), which confers on the situation the power to elicit some of these responses in the future.

On the other hand, if we adopt the other alternative, that behaviour is a function of what the situation calls for granted the goals of the animal, then the role of training will be different: It will be to change the operative or relevant features of the situation of which behaviour is a function, in short, to change the intentional environment. In this sense, of course, learning is held to change behaviour. But—and this is the crucial point—the change in the intentional environment will not be held to be a function of the learning history. On the contrary, a great many different learning histories can bring about the same change, and conversely, as we have seen above, the same history may bring about different changes in different animals. Learning, on this view, is thus simply a necessary condition for certain adaptive responses to be made, but not an antecedent condition which will vary with behaviour in a law-like way, i.e., not the independent variable in a functional law.

Thus, what is perhaps the most fundamental disagreement between the two views about learning comes to this: that for our ordinary view learning simply 'facilitates' certain responses, that is, it makes a range of responses possible, while for S–R theory it determines which responses will be emitted.[1] And this is closely connected with—indeed, is almost another way of stating—the issue about the direction of behaviour.

Now the evidence discussed in the last chapter seems to weigh against the S–R theory. For improvisation behaviour, or that which results from latent learning, does not seem to be a function of the animal's past behaviour in this or similar situations whereas

---

[1] By contrast, as we shall see in the next chapter, the positions on motivation are reversed. For S–R theory the role of 'drive' is simply to 'facilitate' responses without selecting them, while the ordinary view, as is implicit in the notion 'desire', is that the response is selected by the goal to which we are 'moved' or 'driven'.

these phenomena can be accounted for teleologically on certain assumptions about the animal's goals. These are cases in which 'adaptive' responses occur where the S–R theory would predict mal-adaptive ones. But there are also cases of the opposite which weigh against the S–R theory, where the response is mal-adaptive in a way it would not predict. Thus Tolman[1] reports an experiment where rats in a certain part of a maze suffered shock from an apparatus which was withdrawn from sight immediately afterwards. The rat, therefore, could not identify 'what hit him', and in these conditions the animals sometimes failed to take the 'adaptive' course of avoiding the danger spot, as S–R theory would predict they should do. Another example is an experiment by the McDougall's, where a rat had to undo a latch by undoing first another latch. Here, in spite of the fact that it sometimes hit on the right response by accident, it did not improve and could not master the problem. The emitting of the right response, that followed by reward, in other words, didn't seem to strengthen the tendency to emit it subsequently. We are tempted to say simply that the problem was too complex for the rat and that no amount of fortuitous success could induce learning.

The evidence within the field of orientation learning itself, therefore, seems to point to the ordinary teleological view. But there is no reason why we should restrict our attention to this type of case. A reproach which has justly been made against theorists of the S–R school is that they try to build a theory on too narrow a range of experiments. This approach, in fact, involves a double risk of distortion. In the first place the experiments are not placed in the context of a body of evidence gleaned from the observation of the behaviour of animals in their normal habitat, such as ethologists have obtained, and thus are liable to misinterpretation. In the second case, the range of experiments itself is extremely restrictive in the type of situation chosen—the maze- and discrimination-learning experiments make up a great part of S–R theorists' work—and are tailor-made to suit the theory. The latter is often given a spurious air of validity which disappears, or at least tends to tarnish, as soon as one looks beyond the narrow context chosen. Thus Pavlov's work on the salivation of dogs was well suited to a theory of conditioned reflexes, but when one turns to ordinary goal-directed behaviour,

[1] 'Cognitive Maps in Rats and Men,' *Psychological Review*, 1948.

one can see just how little basis there is for positing a mechanism of this kind as underlying the whole range of learned behaviour. Similarly, the ordinary type of maze experiment, where the animals run the same path on the training and test trials, was ideally suited to the S–R theory. For it introduced a certain rigidity into behaviour not found in the normal habitat. The animal was compelled, by the shape of the maze, to take only a limited number of fixed paths. What Tolman has called 'multiple-trackedness', the ability to take different paths to the same goal, was therefore reduced to a minimum. It remained largely to opponents of S–R theories to devise experiments, such as those on improvisation and latent learning, which called in question the orthodox view. For the ordinary type of experiment design had the effect of preventing these questions being raised.

But just as the ordinary type of maze-experiment—with training and test on the same path—was only one among many possible such experiments, so the maze environment is only one among many possible environments, and in many crucial respects not the most common. For alongside the 'closed' environment of the maze is the 'open' environment where the animal's choice is not narrowed to locomotion along a number of fixed paths, and where many more features of the surroundings are visible at one time. If our aim is to elaborate a theory of behaviour we should look here as well, and see what laws apply in this kind of situation.

And, if we are to make any progress on the question at hand, we have to look to the open situation. For the question concerns the role of goals and goal-objects in the direction of behaviour. Thus the assumption behind the ordinary explanation of 'short-cut' behaviour is that the improvised adaptive response does not need to be explained as one conditioned to a set of stimuli, but simply as one which has as its result this goal, the training having provided the necessary conditions in the animal's intentional environment. The assumption is therefore that food, say, functions as a goal-object in the animal's intentional environment; that its presence in the environment is not to be linked with a set of responses which have been conditioned to the stimuli accompanying it, or which—in the case of innate behaviour—attach to them innately, but with approach behaviour in general, that is, with responses which have the result of 'getting' this goal object. The role of training, then, is to make the goal object intentionally 'present' in the environment, and not to alter the animal's repository of 'habits'.

But this question of the role of goals and goal objects in behaviour is a general one which must be answered not only in the context of orientation learning. We have to discover, for instance, whether in general certain objects, say certain kinds of food, or a certain set of learned sub-goals, operate as goal objects in this sense, that is, whether they do not elicit more than only those responses conditioned to them or innately connected with them, whether their role is to elicit that behaviour which will end in a 'consummatory act'. And this question can hardly be answered by examining only the special case of orientation learning—a case which is 'special' in virtue of the complicating factor that the goal is not present to the animal's senses at the moment of choice—but must be tested in the general case, uncomplicated by such considerations, which is behaviour in the open situation where the terminating point of the animal's action, or the object affected by it, is visible to him.

The significance of the open environment for our discussion is, in fact, twofold. It is not only that the temptation is removed to see the choice before the animal as limited to a definite number of clearly demarcated behaviour possibilities; we are also shifting our attention from what are called 'behaviour sequences' to what is, in effect, the basic unit in the S–R account of behaviour, a response to a feature of the environment which is present, in the sense of 'impinging on the receptors'. Thus we shall no longer be discussing simply whether complex behaviour sequences can be seen as constructed out of such units—and the evidence of improvisation and latent learning seems to show that they cannot be—but the more radical question whether a unit of this kind exists at all, whether there is anything answering to the classical description of a stimulus–response connexion. That is, we shall be asking the question whether the simpler, shorter responses, which we might single out as units in a response sequence, can be understood as movements elicited by stimuli, or whether they must be accounted for in terms of the goals for the sake of which they occur. In effect, therefore, the question about the laws which hold in the open situation brings us back in some way to the question discussed at the end of Chapter VII, that concerning the nature of the response. The conclusion there was that there was no type of description (e.g., 'approach to X') which applied to all movements as responses. Here the question is the more general one, whether responses, i.e., the movements emitted in so far as they can be linked in a law-like way with the environment, are to be classified by their goals or what they achieve, or whether they should be classified in some other way, e.g., topographically, by the limbs or 'effectors' used and the processes they undergo.

2. THE RESPONSE AS ACHIEVEMENT

We turn, then, to examine cases of learned or innate behaviour in the open situation. Let us, for example, look at cases of the kind studied by Köhler[1] where chimpanzees learned to use sticks and boxes as instruments in getting to food which was otherwise out of reach. Now the evidence seems to show[2] that training is relevant here; that animals who have had an opportunity to play with sticks are more likely to use them than those who have not. But it is difficult to see how the occurrence of adaptive responses of this kind can be considered a function of the animal's past behaviour in this situation. This is not only because the response can sometimes occur without previous experience with sticks or boxes, but also because the past training which is relevant, where it is relevant, is not necessarily training in this or a similar situation, if 'similar' is taken to mean 'similar in stimulus content'. To put the point in another way, the resemblance between training and test situations lies simply in the fact that there is a role for a stick to play, something which could be done by a stick in each of them. Thus, if we can speak of the animal's acquiring a 'habit', it is that of using the stick where it is required. There is, of course, an ordinary language sense of 'habit', where it would be quite correct to say that the animal 'got the habit' of using the stick, but this is quite different from the sense the term has in S–R theory. It is not meant to explain his behaviour; we are just re-stating the fact that the animal is more likely after training in a situation requiring the use of a stick to use one. But we cannot say that the response is conditioned to a situation of the kind 'requiring the use of a stick for some goal'. For, if the animal can recognize a situation as of this kind, then he doesn't need to

[1] *The Mentality of Apes.*
[2] Birch, 'The Relation of Previous Experience to Insightful Problem-solving', *J. comp. Psychol.*, 1945.

learn to use a stick in it. The role of training must be to make him more likely to recognize situations as of this kind, to train him to see the situation in a certain way.

The nature of the animal's improvement in the 'Umweg' problems which require the use of some indirect means or path, also points to the view that the effect of training and practice is to allow him more readily to 'see' the solution. At first the solution comes with great difficulty. Conditions have to be very favourable. Sometimes the animals didn't 'get the idea' until fortuitously at one moment the stick was pointing in the right direction. Other animals didn't see that a box could provide the solution as long as another animal was sitting on it, fixing its behavioural relevance, as it were, as that of a 'seat'. But after some practice, animals can go and fetch boxes from another room if the situation requires it, or, when sticks are not available, some can break the branch off a tree as a substitute. The nature of this 'improvisation' behaviour shows that the situation was clearly recognized as one requiring this solution, even in the absence of 'props', like the stick pointing in the right direction. The role of training therefore is to 'facilitate' the response.

But whatever the accuracy of this hypothesis, it is virtually impossible to see how this type of improvisation behaviour can be accounted for in terms of conditioning—even more difficult than in the case of short-cut behaviour in the maze. For the absence of stick or box should mean absence of some of the original eliciting stimuli, which should weaken the response, rather than evoking the adaptive improvisation which alone can make it occur. On the other hand, both this and the original instrumental behaviour are perfectly comprehensible on the assumption that getting food is a goal for the animal.

But we do not need to look at the higher achievements of chimpanzees. This example only illustrates on a more striking—because more intelligent—level a feature which is present in all behaviour. It is the declared aim of most theorists of the S–R school to devise behaviour laws which will make mention only—to use Hull's terms—of 'colourless movements'. But in spite of this, they almost all use ordinary action terms in the correlations which they claim to have established. This is true of Hull himself, as Peters has pointed out.[1] For instance Hull describes the

[1] *The Concept of Motivation*, p. 114.

rat's behaviour with such terms as 'biting the floor boards' or 'leaping the barrier'. Thus the animal's behaviour is classified not in terms of the limbs and muscles, etc., used, and their movements and contractions, it is not what is called 'effector-defined', but in terms of the ends achieved, i.e., it is 'achievement-defined'. Similarly Nissen and Spence agree that the animal's behaviour in discrimination learning cannot be classed in terms of movements but must be spoken of 'as an act, that is, in terms of its consequence or effect (usually with reference to a goal or an altered organism-environment relationship)'[1] Even Guthrie, who is most consistent in eschewing achievement-defined terms, has only succeeded in adumbrating a correlation using movement terms in one highly artificial situation, and the validity of even this is doubtful.

Now it may be thought that this is not too much of a setback for S–R theory, and that laws using achievement terms are simply first approximations to be replaced later on by more exact laws using a classification of behaviour as effector-defined. But there is no reason to expect this whatever. Thus MacCorquodale and Meehl[2] base their optimism on the belief that 'any R-class (class of responses) specified by achievement is a truth-function of a finite set of R-classes specified by non-achievement flux-descriptions'.[3] Their grounds for this belief is that 'there is more than one way to get a lever down, but there is not an infinite number of ways'.[4] In other words, the statement that the rat got the lever down would be a truth function of the disjunction, 'the rat did so-and-so with his paws, or the rat did so-and-so with his teeth', and so on.

Now, of course, strictly speaking we cannot speak of a truth-functional relation here. It is not part of what is meant by the disjunction above that the rat got the lever down in the process. But this might be thought to be a mere quibble, if we could establish empirical laws to the effect that whenever an event of an achievement class occurred an event of a certain list of effector classes occurred, and that the same held the other way around.

---

[1] Nissen, 'Description of the Learned Response in Discrimination Behaviour', *Psychological Review*, 1950, p. 130

[2] In Estes, et al., *Modern Learning Theory*, pp. 219–231.

[3] Op. cit., p. 223.

[4] Loc. cit.

It is this claim that MacCorquodale and Meehl want to make when they say that there is not 'an infinite number of ways' to get a lever down. Now in a certain sense this is true, but it is not really helpful to MacCorquodale and Meehl. This is clear when we examine what is meant by a 'way' in the sense we should have to give it to make this statement true. MacCorquodale and Meehl define it as a 'sub-class defined by fairly restricted effector topography, but necessarily allowing for certain quantitative variations over its own instances'. Thus an animal like a rat, for instance, will only have a certain number of motor response-patterns in his repertoire, and to say that he got the lever down will inevitably amount to saying either that he got it down with his teeth, or that he got it down with his jaw, or his paws, etc. This much is certainly true, and if this is what is meant by a 'way', the statement stands. But, of course, we have not yet reached a set of effector-defined classes. The statement 'the rat pushed the lever down with his (right) paw' does not classify the action in effector only, but also in achievement terms. The question is therefore whether we can find an effector-defined movement such that it occurs whenever this statement is true. But, of course, when we examine the situation more closely we find that there are many paw movements which the animal can make which will count as 'pushing the lever down'; it all depends on the size and position of the lever, the position and stance of the animal immediately before, and so on. Perhaps, then, we need to break the action down even more finely, and make 'he pushed the lever down' 'truth-functional' of a more minutely described set of sub-classes. But here the concept of a 'way' begins to become more indefinite. For it is clear that with a motor pattern of this kind, we have to do not with a set of movements clearly differentiated, but with a pattern of responses which can vary finely and continuously in various ways and can be adjusted to the action in train. To say that there are a certain number of 'ways' of pushing down a lever is as arbitrary as saying that there are a certain number of points in a line. But the problem is more fundamental than this. For the various movements which the animal can make in pushing down the lever are each appropriate, that is, will each actually constitute pushing down the lever, only in certain circumstances. The movement which would get the lever down at this height and granted this initial stance, say, will utterly fail to do so granted another set of initial conditions. Thus even if it were the case that there were a definitely enumerable set of paw-movements which the animal emitted when it pushed down the lever, so that from the statement 'he pushed the lever down' one could infer that he must have done either X or Y or Z, etc., we still could not infer from the fact that he had done either X or Y or Z, etc., that he had pushed the lever down. For in certain circumstances, he might have emitted any one of these movements without doing so. Indeed, one of these movements might easily be emitted in the course of some quite different action, such as standing up against the wall to get something from a certain height, and so on.

Thus the truth-functional relationship is totally inappropriate to action terms and movement terms. We can indeed infer from 'the rat got the lever down' that he either got it down with his teeth, or his paws, etc., and we can certainly infer (in a stronger sense) from the fact that he got it down with his teeth or his paws, etc., that he got it down; but we cannot infer from the fact that he made any movement with his teeth, or paws, or chin, or rump, or whatever, that he got the lever down. For this depends on whether this movement was appropriate.

It thus follows that when S–R theorists establish 'stimulus-response' correlations using action and not movement terms, that they are not giving rough sketches of laws using only terms for 'colourless movement'. On the contrary, when they say that response R is conditioned to S, they are saying that, on the occurrence of S, the animal will do whatever is necessary within certain bounds[1] to achieve G, where G is the goal in terms of which action R is defined. And this, of course, is a correlation of a teleological form, where the action is explained in part at least in terms of the goal it is aimed at.

The fact that S–R theorists have been forced to give some place to a teleological type of explanation is significant, even if they seem largely unaware of its significance. It may appear that they use action terms only for the convenience that attaches to employing terms in common use, but the statement of Nissen and Spence on the evidence of discrimination learning shows that

---

[1] The bounds being set by the limits of achievement of a given motor habit, or—as we shall see later on—set of motor habits; obviously there will be some cases in which the goal will be beyond the animal's reach.

this is not the case. It is not just for convenience' sake but because the molar behavioural correlations which can be abstracted are on the level of actions and not on that of the various component movements, of which there is no definite number, which can each, in certain circumstances, constitute an action. Thus, as Nissen shows,[1] it is the action of reaching for the white door, and not certain muscular movements, which is 'conditioned' in the discrimination experiment. The problem is that what is almost invariably conditioned—except in certain extreme artificial situations, or those of conditioned reflex experiments which have very little to do with operant behaviour—is an action, that is, the effecting of a certain result. One cannot predict therefore from the *movements* emitted in the training period what the animal will do in future test situations, but only from what *action* he is learning to perform.[2]

S–R theorists sometimes talk as though this goal-constancy of action could be explained by some principle of 'induction'[3] to the effect that certain effector-defined responses are connected in such a way, that the strengthening of one to a certain stimulus will automatically strengthen the others. But this, of course, cannot serve as an explanation. For the class of responses which are strengthened along with the response, say, of pressing the lever are precisely those which will have the result of depressing the lever. We cannot find a characterization in movement terms for a set of actions which are strengthened along with a given action, and between which a relation of induction holds. It is possible, as we have seen, to 'induce' a quite different set of movements by 'strengthening' (rewarding) a given movement, if the action being accomplished by it is different, e.g., when the action is 'approaching the grey card' and not 'going right', or 'approach-the square card'.

3. RELEASERS AND DIRECTORS

The language of 'stimulus–response' is therefore quite misleading when one considers the correlations that psychologists actually work with. A much more adequate conceptual scheme for a non-teleological theory of behaviour is developed by Tinbergen

[1] Op. cit.   [2] Cf. above, Chapter VII.
[3] Cf. MacCorquodale and Meehl, op. cit.

in his study of innate behaviour.[1] Tinbergen distinguishes between the 'releasing' and the 'directing' functions of stimuli. The former simply set the motor activity going, or release the pent-up energy through the motor pattern; the latter 'direct an activity in relation to the spatial arrangements in the surroundings'.[2] Thus the problem of the variation of a response and its dependence on the situation is clearly recognized. But this, of course, provides no solution. The direction of the activity by a goal will not be explained by introducing the notion of 'directing stimulus'. As it is Tinbergen restricts the function of these stimuli to that of fixing the direction of movement or the orientation of the body. And here the notion of a directing stimulus makes sense, as a landmark or point to be steered towards. But, of course, the problem of goal-direction is much wider than this. All the motor patterns, grasping, climbing, walking, running, reaching for, pushing down with paw, etc., etc., are directed by the environment, that is, are adjusted in each case to a particular feature or features of what is being grasped, climbed, run over, etc. And here the notion of a 'directing stimulus', even of a 'configurational' sort, doesn't have the same clear application. Certain simple types of 'taxis', or direction of movement or of disposition of the body relative to the environment, can be characterized by laws of the form, 'if the light source moves in such and such a way, the animal will make such and such movements', but this is not true of the directing of such activities as 'picking up the inkwell', 'pushing down the lever', or 'catching the ball'. Nor is it true of the phylogenetically 'higher' forms of 'taxis'; e.g., a dog, in chasing a rabbit, can allow for the direction and speed of movement of his prey in the pursuit.

Now it might be thought that these higher forms of sensorimotor co-ordination differ from the simpler taxis only in their greater complexity. It might be thought, for instance, that the stimuli directed the behaviour in a greater number of ways, that is, that variations of the stimulus in a greater number of respects were correlated with variations in the behaviour. Thus, whereas for the bug, the position of the light is everything, for the dog, not only the position, but the velocity (direction and speed of movement) of the rabbit determines his course. But, at this level, the notion of a directing 'stimulus' is beginning to lose its

[1] *The Study of Instinct.*   [2] Ibid., p. 82.

meaning. To take the case cited by Tinbergen,[1] of flight to safety: When the mother herring gull utters an alarm call (releasing stimulus), her chicks run for the nearest shelter (directing stimulus). Now to speak of 'directing stimuli' here is doubly misleading. For that a certain space constitutes shelter for the animal is not necessarily dependent on its giving rise to a particular set of stimuli; shelter may be recognized in a great number of ways; and that the direction towards this spot constitutes the direction towards the nearest shelter, or the most accessible shelter, is not a function of the features of this part of the environment alone but of the whole. There are therefore no stimuli which can be isolated in this case as the 'directing' ones, and the introduction of this expression takes us no farther than this: That the response is directed by the whole situation in such a way that the animal is hidden as quickly as possible.

But there is something more seriously wrong with the conceptual scheme which posits 'directing' and 'releasing' stimuli. For the limits of a 'response' may be wider than those of a single motor habit. That is, when an animal has been trained to emit a certain response, i.e., bring about a certain goal, the goal may not only determine which variation of a given motor pattern will be emitted in the situation, but also which motor pattern will be used. We have already seen this in the case of 'getting the lever down', where the rat may use teeth, right paw, left paw, chin, etc. Thus if we train a rat to depress a lever, an action which he usually performs with his teeth, and if we then muzzle him, he will straightaway use his paws. What the rat has been trained to do is to 'get the lever down', and he will choose the best of a number of possible ways of doing this. It is useless to try to account for this by 'response induction', the rule to the effect that there are certain groups of responses which always grow together, such that when one is reinforced, and others are also. For this 'explanation', as in the case above, begs the question, as MacCorquodale and Meehl[2] partly realize. For it cannot be said that paw movements and teeth movements in general go together: The animal doesn't run with his teeth or chew with his paws; but only that some such movements are in a relation of mutual induction, and these turn out to be those movements which have in common a certain result. For the muzzling of a rat will not

[1] Op. cit., p. 82. [2] Loc. cit.

induce just any paw movements but only those which have the effect of depressing the bar.

Similarly, the attempt of MacCorquodale and Meehl to explain this by a principle of 'secondary' or learned response induction cannot meet the case. This is a law to the effect that whenever R_1 and R_2 are conditioned to S_1, then, when R_1 is conditioned to a new stimulus S_i, R_2 will also tend to be evoked by S_i. In this way the 'transfer' from teeth to paws would be seen as a result of learning. At some time in the past, the animal learned both responses to some object, and therefore the conditioning of one brings on the other. Now this is, to say the least, wildly implausible. Supposing the jaw-movement required was different, because of the shape of the lever, but this had no effect on the paw-movement; would the muzzled animal fail to improvise or describe some irrelevant movement with his paw? And suppose we train an animal in a maze where either one of two paths to separate goals is rewarded, and then train him to discriminate by rewarding only one, will all reinforcement of the 'positive' path also strengthen the response to the negative path, and will this link hold for all similar situations in future?

But, quite apart from these difficulties, it is clear that Mac-Corquodale and Meehl's hypothesis is still predicated on the assumption that 'he pressed the lever down with his paws' describes an effector-defined movement. In fact the animal may on different occasions use a different paw or different movement depending on initial stance and so on. Thus the 'induction', whether learned or innate, is not to *a* movement, but to the use of the paws for whatever movement is required to bring down the lever. It is clear that, once having acquired the skill in using his paws, an animal does not need to learn which paw movements will bring about what, i.e., it is not necessary in order that he use his paws to bring down a lever that this movement have been conditioned; for we have seen that an animal can easily emit a movement not found in the 'conditioning' period if this is required—indeed, it is possible that only a small proportion of the movements he might be induced to use have appeared in the training period.

But then it is hard to see what the role of learning could be here. In fact, it could only be to familiarize the animal to the potentialities of using the paws for those jobs which can also be done with the teeth. Now training can play such a role with some skills, as we have seen with the case of the chimpanzees in their use of 'tools', but this is hardly the type of learning to which MacCorquodale and Meehl subscribe. Nor could even this be invoked in the case of the skill of using the paws, for this results from growth, not training. The principle of 'secondary induction' is thus totally misplaced.

Now we said above that to say that an animal has learned to emit R to S is to say that, on the occurrence of S, he will do whatever is necessary within certain bounds to encompass G, where G is the goal by which response R is defined. It is now clear that the 'bounds' concerned can be wider than those set by one motor activity; the animal may have several in his repertoire from among which to choose, so that if one is inapplicable, another will be tried. Thus Tinbergen's model, according to which a releasing stimulus is required to set off a motor activity, which is then steered by directing stimuli, is very misleading. For the role of a 'releasing stimulus', if such can be found (in this case S, the conditions on which the response is emitted), will simply be to set off activity in the direction of a particular goal; both the choice of the motor activity and its direction will be dictated by the requirements of the situation. We do not need to assume a particular releasing stimulus for each motor activity. The notion of a specific releaser may seem plausible for behaviour sequences low on the phylogenetic scale. But as we direct our attention higher up, it begins to suffer the same fate as the 'directing stimuli' did: Ultimately the 'releaser' becomes simply 'a situation in which this particular motor activity is required for the attainment of the goal'.

Thus, in Tinbergen's example of the instinctive response sequence in mating in the three-spined stickleback, each stage must be 'set off' by a particular reaction of the partner. But it is difficult to see how this analysis could be applied to the 'appetitive' behaviour (i.e., behaviour prior in the sequence and preparatory to the 'consummatory act') of phylogenetically higher creatures. We may take such a sequence as that of the food-seeking behaviour of animals which hunt. For instance, the peregrine falcon[1] begins by random flight, then on sighting its prey, say, a flock of birds, it delivers a number of sham attacks until one of the birds is

[1] Tinbergen, op. cit.

isolated from the flock, then it delivers the final swoop, captures, kills, plucks and eats. What is the releasing stimulus for the swoop? A bird apart from the flock? But is this a 'stimulus', or are we really talking about a situation which can be recognized in a number of different ways? The falcon swoops at great speed and may do himself harm if he attacks a bird in a closely packed flock; he thus waits for one or some of the birds to be sufficiently spaced out. Perhaps a 'releaser' then is simply a situation where a bird is far apart enough from the rest to avoid harm. The notion of a releasing stimulus is even less appropriate higher on the phylogenetic scale. Thus, when a lion hunts, e.g., goes through the sequence of stalking and charging, what 'releases' the charge? Is it a particular size or distance, or smell? Surely where the lion will charge from will depend on the lie of the land, what cover there is, the distance and potential speed of the prey. In short, the lion will charge from the point where, all things considered, the prey can best be seized.

We can see this even more clearly if we consider not just activities which follow each other in sequence, but those which are alternatives at the same stage, as it were, such as pressing the lever with paws or teeth, getting the banana with stick or box. What 'releases' one of these activities rather than another? Plainly here the selection of the motor activity is as much dictated by the requirements of the situation granted the goal, as is the selection of the particular variation within the motor pattern. The particular type of motor response, in other words, is correlated not with any particular stimulus elements, but with a state of affairs where it is needed in order to reach a goal. Thus, once an animal has 'caught on', a stick is used in those situations where it is needed in order to get at the food. The releasing situation can only be defined in teleological terms as one which requires it. Not even the presence of the stick need be a condition, as we have seen.

But we do not need to draw a sharp line between behaviour sequences which are low and those which are high on the phylogenetic scale. Even such lowly creatures as birds and wasps can display in the instinctive sequence of nest-building variations in the way they go about repairing damage to the nest,[1] and the most rudimentary motor responses are directed in some way by

[1] Cf. Thorpe, *Learning and Instinct in Animals*, pp. 34–43.

the environment. The phylogenetic scale, in fact, shows a gamut of behaviours in which there is a gradual transition from the more 'rigid' to the more 'plastic'. At one limit few, or only one, motor activities are available to effect a given response; behaviour is therefore 'stereotyped'. At the other the animal has a wide range of effectors at its disposal, and behaviour can be highly varied. Similarly, low down on the scale the animal relies on 'abstract' signs, that is, whether a situation is judged propitious for a given response depends on a few cues only in a rigid way. Thus animals on this level are easily 'fooled', as Tinbergen has shown with the fighting response of the stickleback male. At this level, therefore, a notion like that of 'releasing stimulus' has application. But higher up, a response is correlated not with certain abstracted features only but with a whole situation of a certain type. The animal is more difficult to fool, and when we succeed, can rapidly disabuse himself. The notion of 'releasing stimulus' then becomes doubly inapplicable: Not only because there is no particular range of stimuli which is crucial to the animal's recognition of the situation, but also because the situation which will evoke a given motor activity can often only be characterized as one which, granted the potentialities of the animal, requires this response for a certain goal. But the transition between rigid and plastic behaviours is gradual.

The growth of behaviour in ontogenesis shows some analogous features. Obviously it is the animals with the most 'plastic' behaviour whose behaviour undergoes most change as a result of learning. Some motor functions, however, like, e.g., walking or flying, seem to be innate, in the sense that they do not seem to require any training but develop regardless of practice at a certain point. But the development of higher animals, whether through growth or training, shows the same transition between the rigid and the plastic. In mammals, the original stereotyped response to the abstract cue of a pressure on the cheek, viz., turning the head and sucking, gives way to eating, and then to finding or hunting and killing food as well. It is a feature of ontogenetic development, whether by training or growth, that the animal gradually acquires and perfects motor habits, and the discriminations and co-ordinations which go along with them, so that rigid behaviour gradually gives way to plastic. The S–R notion of ontogenesis, that certain innate connexions (sUr's) are gradually supplemented by learned ones (sHr's), is therefore incorrect. For development does not consist of conditioning new movements to new releasing stimuli, but of developing a new motor activity directed towards the same goals. For example, the development from the infant stage of eating a given food when given it (either because this food is innately selected by the species or as a result of training) to the stage of going to fetch it is not one which can be accounted for in terms of the conditioning of new movements. What intervenes is the development of the motor skill of walking. But as we have seen, once the motor skill is acquired, the animal does not need any special training to learn which walking movements will take him towards which points in the environment. It suffices that eating this kind of food is a goal for him to seek and fetch it without further training once he can move. And if this food is naturally selected, or he has been trained to eat it in infancy, then it is such a goal. But then we cannot explain this development by the conditioning of a new response.

In short, learning a new motor skill is learning how to use it for whatever purposes the animal may have. It cannot be conceived as the acquisition of a new type of movement, and then the conditioning of movements of this range to stimuli. The new activity is already 'directed' from the beginning by the goals of the animal. Indeed, we can frequently see that it is directed by a goal during the period of its development. Thus the ape may develop his skill in stacking boxes while attempting to get to some fruit. The movements of a child who is learning to feed itself are plainly directed to this goal, even though clumsy and failing of their target at first. Thus to the extent that learning is involved in the acquisition of new motor skills, it is definitely learning of the kind envisaged by the ordinary teleological view, that is, learning which increases the capacity of the animal to seek certain goals, which 'facilitates' responses but doesn't condition (i.e., determine) them. S-R theorists can only maintain their theories of learning by avoiding the consideration of phenomena of this kind.[1]

[1] Cf. H. W. Nissen, 'Description of the Learned Response in Discrimination Learning', *Psychological Review*, 1950. Nissen refers in passing to the 'integrations' which 'are either innate or acquired in early ontogeny'. The question, how learned? is not raised. And it is hard to see how it could be

4. RESPONSE AS ACTION

The upshot of this discussion is that the notion of response as it is used in the correlations which are found to hold between environment and behaviour is that of an element of behaviour identified by its goal, and not by its topography. Indeed, the topography may vary widely, for several different motor activities can sometimes be used to effect the same response. Thus with a correlation to the effect that a given response will occur in certain circumstances, we are saying that activity within certain bounds will occur which will be directed towards a certain goal. What movements are emitted in the particular case will be a function of what is required in this case to achieve the goal. In this sense the response is selected by the goal, and this is the justification of speaking, on the molar or 'peripheralist' level, of 'action' or behaviour which is elicited 'for the sake of', or aimed at a goal.

Now it may be that certain physiological mechanisms will be found to lie at the base of this adaptive behaviour. The prospect is held out by some theorists that more detailed research into neuro-physiology will yield some non-teleological explanation of a 'centralist' kind. The likelihood of such a discovery is beyond the scope of this discussion. But what seems clear is that a centralist theory would have to start from the fact that on the molar level, the level of correlations between observable environmental and response elements, the response is selected by the goal, and try to account for this by some intervening mechanism.

That is, it seems clear that, on a molar level, a place must be given to a teleological form of explanation, for the basic level correlations between environment and behaviour are generally teleological in type. The nature of the response must, at least in part, be accounted for in terms of the goals, or learned sub-goals (such as, e.g., pressing the lever), in relation to which the animal's activity will vary in such a way as to bring them about. That a

---

within the confines of S–R theory, for the type of learning involved here is quite different from that involved in learning about the environment; but S–R theory only allows one type of learning, and this is one of the features which distinguishes it from 'cognitive theory' or Gestalt, (cf. E. C. Tolman, 'There is More than One Kind of Learning', *Psychological Review*, 1949; and Kurt Lewin, *Field Theory in Social Science*); and from common-sense.

notion like 'goal', and therefore a notion like 'action', must play some role in a 'peripheralist' account of behaviour seems, therefore, undeniable. The only question concerns the scope of this role.

Now it is possible that the model of innate or conditioned connexions can account for some aspects of behaviour, but it certainly cannot account for all. Let us take as an example food-seeking behaviour in the 'open' situation, that is, a situation in which the goal-objects and the paths to them are fully visible. Now we may perhaps account for the fact that a given object is in fact sought as food by the animal in terms of an innate tendency to select this food, or in terms of past eating behaviour which was followed by 're-inforcement', in other words, the animal's selecting this food could perhaps be made a function of his behaviour history. But we cannot account for his behaviour in getting the food by a theory to the effect that the movements he exhibits are conditioned to certain stimuli. For these movements are not a function of his behaviour history. On the contrary, they are a function of what is required in the situation in order to get to the goal. For we have seen that they do not need to have been exhibited before in order to appear now: It is only necessary that the animal has acquired a general capacity to emit a motor activity of this kind. And we have seen that the acquisition of this motor capacity is not the conditioning of new responses to stimuli, but the development of a new way of effecting a response defined by its goal. Thus, while it may be that we will have to explain the ape's seeking of the banana by the previous occasions on which he ate bananas and by the satisfaction which then resulted, we cannot so explain his reaching, jumping, climbing, use of stick or box, etc., etc.

This means, of course, that the whole notion of S–R 'conditioning' is seriously misleading. If, for example, an adult animal comes to discover that a new substance is edible and pleasing to the taste by trying it, and thereafter seeks it, we cannot say that eating this has been 'conditioned' (that a response of eating has been conditioned to the stimuli connected with this substance). For what will follow from this is not that a certain range of movements will be emitted when this substance appears (and in certain other conditions, e.g., when the animal is hungry), but that a large and indefinite range of movements will appear which have in common that they are directed towards getting and eating this substance. But then we should more properly speak of this substance not as an 'eliciting' or 'releasing' stimulus, but as a goal-object, that is as something which is the object of a consummatory act which act is a goal for the animal under certain circumstances.[1] However we explain the selection of particular goals or goal-objects, the direction of behaviour cannot be accounted for in terms of the conditioning of stimulus–response connexions.

With this in mind, what can we say about the 'special' case of the animal's oriented behaviour in the 'closed' situation? Can this be explained by historically acquired connexions, or must it be explained by the goals the animal is seeking? Now it is clear, after what has been said about the open situation, that the explanation could never wholly be in terms of connexions between stimuli and movements. For the closed situation is bounded by an open one; the behaviour sequence in the maze, for instance, can be seen as a series of acts in a temporal chain of 'open' environments. And these constituent unit-responses, at least, must generally be seen as directed towards a sub-goal. Thus when we say that an animal is trained to take the lighted path, we are not saying that he will emit certain movements, but that he will do what is necessary to get into this path and follow it—he may even surmount obstacles to do so—just as in discrimination learning, or the training of animals in a 'Skinner-box', the response trained is one defined by result. The question then is one about the nature of the response the animal is emitting: Is it simply 'going left, going right', or should it also be described as 'going to the food'? That is, must we account for the fact that the animal seeks the sub-goals 'going right' and 'going left'[2] by his behaviour history, or can we account for it in a teleological way in terms of the goal of seeking food? On the first hypothesis, as we have seen, the

---

[1] This apart from the fact that it may not be the presence of any particular cues, but that of the object which sets off the behaviour; that is, the animal may not be relying simply on 'abstract' cues.

[2] The use of this term 'sub-goal' here and elsewhere in this chapter may seem to beg the question at issue. But whatever our conclusion we would still be justified in distinguishing such 'goals' as 'going right' and 'pressing the lever,' from, e.g., getting food or drink; for the former can easily be trained in or out, and will not long survive once they are no longer the means of the latter. Cf. the analogous distinction in S–R theory between 'primary' and 'secondary' rewards.

animal's behaviour in the maze can be characterized as following a series of 'directions', in the second case as truly oriented behaviour; for in the second case the explanation assumes that the animal knows where the food is.

Now we have seen that the evidence of oriented behaviour itself seems to point to the second hypothesis. But, in addition, what we have discovered about the role of goal-objects in behaviour lends weight to this view. For, if the animal's behaviour in the open situation can be accounted for in a teleological way by invoking the presence of a goal-object like food, there is nothing necessarily outlandish or 'mystical' in accounting in like manner for, say, improvisation behaviour in a maze run to food reward, once training has provided the necessary orientation. Why should we refuse to do so? In other words, why should we account for the complex behaviour sequence in a different way from that in which we account for the responses which we pick out as its constituent 'units'?

Now there may be two reasons for this. It may first of all be because of the learning process involved. For the teleological explanation assumes that the role of learning is to facilitate response, not to condition it; that is, it makes a number of adaptive responses possible but these cannot be made a function of the responses appearing in the learning history. The belief may be, then, that orientation learning resembles more the learning involved in discovering a new food, where present responses might be considered to be a function of past ones, than it does the acquiring of a new skill. Now in the case of discrimination learning or that induced in a 'Skinner-box' where rats learn to press a lever to get food, it may be difficult to say what type of learning is involved. But it is difficult to see how orientation learning could be classed in this way. For orientation learning can take place in an open environment, that is, an animal can get to know an open environment better, and this can hardly be explained in terms of the conditioning of responses.

So we turn to the second reason. And this is simply that the closed situation is a closed one; in other words, that the goal-object is 'remote' and not present. Now S–R theorists naturally want to maintain a barrier between the open and the closed situations. Thus MacCorquodale and Meehl[1] wish to exclude in

[1] Op. cit., p. 231.

the characterization of responses all language 'which refers even implicitly . . . to stimulation *not present to the organism at the time the response is being emitted*'.[1] From the point of view of a theory positing connexions between stimuli, i.e., objects impinging on the receptors, and responses, this concern is understandable. But once we have seen that the function of a goal-object in behaviour may not depend simply on its giving rise to a certain set of stimuli, once we admit that an object, like a situation, which 'releases' an action, may not depend for its recognition on a number of 'abstract' cues, then there is no need to maintain this exclusion. If we do wish to maintain it we have the extremely difficult task on our hands of defining the boundary between the open and the closed situations. For example, how far does the open situation extend in time? Is what was seen a minute ago still part of it? Where exactly is the boundary between the seen and the unseen? Where on the gamut which runs from the open room through the elevated maze to the closed maze does the animal enter a closed situation? When we examine these questions we can see that a rigid distinction is virtually impossible to draw. Ordinary behaviour sequences are always running across it. What do we say in the case where the ape goes to get a box from the next room to climb on it? What is this response if it is not 'going to get the box'? If not, to what is the response of running into the other room conditioned? We would be more justified in assuming that training can extend the intentional environment, so as to make remote objects relevant; that the behaviour sequence, like the unit, is to be explained by its goal.

[1] The stress is theirs.

X

THE ENDS OF BEHAVIOUR

1. THEORIES OF MOTIVATION

THE upshot of the discussion in the last chapter is that a 'peripheralist' account of behaviour must make use of something like the notion of action. For the first-level correlations between environmental and behavioural events will be largely teleological in nature, and will require that a place be given to the notions of a goal and of a response emitted for the sake of a goal. But the question is, what place? What does this mean for the more basic laws of a 'peripheralist' science, those by means of which the selection of particular goals, the acquisition of particular links between environment and behaviour, the occurrence of particular actions are to be explained?

We have seen in the last chapters the ramifications which this conclusion has on learning theory, on our account of the way behaviour will alter in a given environment. But, if this conclusion is right, then learning of this sort, i.e., learning about the environment, will not alter the goals the animal pursues, but rather his efficiency in attaining these goals. The more fundamental question, why are the goals he pursues what they are? cannot be answered, therefore, by a learning theory, or at least not by one restricted to this type of learning.

What we are discussing, then, is the set of most general laws determining the goals the animal will seek, the behaviour he will emit in different circumstances. It is this set of laws which are usually discussed under the heading 'motivation' in psychology text-books, where the problem is attacked of explaining the arousal and direction of behaviour and its persistence in a given direction.[1]

Now an explanation in terms of purpose is one, as we have seen, where the basic laws set out the natural tendencies or basic purposes of the being or species under consideration. The force of speaking of 'basic purposes' here is that the tendencies concerned are tendencies to engage in action of a certain kind or to pursue certain goals, that they determine the ends to which behaviour is directed. These may be of different kinds: The laws may set out an end-state to the attainment of which action is directed, or a consummatory act which the animal strives to accomplish, or they may specify a type of activity which is inherently desirable, which the animal in certain circumstances normally engages in. But in all these cases they delineate a type of action which the animal tends to exhibit. The question is, then, whether the basic laws of motivation are of this type.

We have seen that this type of explanation is implicit in our ordinary speech.[2] Now the fact that an explanation of a teleological sort is the rule in ordinary speech, of course, by itself cannot be taken as establishing that a scientific theory must also adopt this form. But it makes understandable the fact that the great majority of theories which have been devised to account for behaviour have been of this sort. With the modern era and specifically with Hobbes is born the ambition to account for the behaviour of organisms by means of a mechanical model, using the concepts of 'body' and 'motion', and even this has been relatively half-hearted until fairly recently; the 'mechanisms' were often mentalist in character, and the link between the 'ideas' and action was often surreptitiously teleological in form. Thus, as we have seen, Bain had to assume the idea or the anticipation of pleasure as one of the springs of action, and this comes very close to saying that the animal acts because he knows that the result will be pleasure, i.e., he acts for the sake of pleasure, or with pleasure as a goal. These theories had not solved the 'problem' of 'getting to' the response in a way which did not involve teleology. Until quite recently the great majority of theories of behaviour continued to account for action in terms of the purposes of men or animals.

But while these theories were influenced by common-sense

[1] Cf. Hebb, *The Organization of Behaviour*, p. 172.   [2] Cf. Chapter II.

notions of the form of explanation, they showed clearly by their extraordinary diversity that there is no such thing as the common-sense theory. The common-sense 'stopping points' of explanation were different from age to age, as they are from society to society, and even from milieu to milieu in one society. The notion of 'instinct' was often used as synonymous with 'basic purpose' here, and one commentator claims to have counted 6000 different instincts which have been canvassed by one theorist or another since the term was coined.

But among this plethora of theories it is possible to distinguish two basic types. Some theorists tend to remain fairly close to the naturalistic level of observation and postulate a large number of different instincts or purposes to account for the different kinds of behaviour exhibited by living species; McDougall is a case in point. They hold the view, to use Thorpe's phrase, that the animal under review is an 'instinct republic'. Others try to go below the naturalistic level and to find one or perhaps two basic overriding purposes which command all behaviour; such were, e.g., Bentham and Freud. The animal is considered to be an 'instinct monarchy', or perhaps 'duumvirate'. For the first, it is necessary to state not only what the instincts are, but their order of importance or urgency, that is, what purposes will take precedence over what others in what circumstances. (There may not be a fixed hierarchy valid in all circumstances; for instance, in some species, self-preservation seems to have first priority in general, but a mother may defend her young at the risk of her life if they are threatened.) But for the second, the fact of precedence of one activity or goal over the others can itself be explained teleologically in terms of the master purpose. The supercession of a given disposition is then like the sacrifice by a general of one of his units in battle; it is dictated by the general good of the whole. It is not necessary in a hypothesis of this kind, of course, to assume an intellectualistic model of calculated action, as, e.g., in the case of Bentham's felicific calculus.

Two of the most 'monarchical' theories of modern times have posited respectively survival and pleasure as the basic overriding goals. (For the latter, 'pleasure' is taken to include the absence of pain so that two goals were really here elided into one.) Both these theories are plausible. A large proportion of the activity of any animal species contributes directly to survival, conceived in the narrow sense as individual survival, and even more can be put under this rubric if we interpret the term broadly to include species survival. But to rely on this evidence is to confuse purpose and function. It may be that a certain activity has the biological function of contributing to survival, but that is not to say that this result constitutes its purpose. In order to make the latter claim, we have to show that the end-result can be used to explain the activity, that the activity will vary in the way required in order to bring about the result; in other words, that the activity is a function of what is required by the situation in order to bring about the result. And this does not necessarily follow. Thus, in the case of reproductive behaviour, we have no evidence for saying that the mating behaviour of many species has as a goal the continuation of the species. This behaviour is 'adaptive' in the sense that it biologically 'works' and results in young being produced, but there is no question here of the activity varying with what is required for this biological result, although it does vary in such a way as to bring about the 'consummatory act' of mating. This act can be considered the goal, then, but we have to distinguish this from function. This might be thought, perhaps, to be an unfair example, since there is no question here of varied circumstances for the normal animal; mating always leads to conception. But many other examples can be found. Thus Tinbergen relates[1] that certain birds show an instinctive (unlearned) flight reaction to the moving shape of a bird with a short neck. The shortness of the neck here is the crucial stimulus, the other features of the bird can vary without apparent result. This tendency happens to be very useful since this characteristic is in fact possessed by the predators of this species. But we cannot account for the flight reaction in terms of this essential function, for the reaction is unlearned, and operates even where it is of no use, e.g., in Tinbergen and Lorenz's laboratory.

Thus the notion of goal or purpose must be distinguished from that of function or survival value. An action may have both purpose and function, but the two are not necessarily the same. Where it is not, we cannot explain the action by the function as long as we are trying to account for the behaviour of the species as it is today, that is, in terms of its contemporary determinants.

This last qualification is important because we still have to

[1] *The Study of Instinct*, p. 162.

account for the co-incidence of purpose and function. This, however, cannot be done on the level of the individual in his lifetime, but only on the level of the species through some evolutionary span. And here, of course, an analogous question to the one we have been discussing is posed: Can we explain the co-incidence of goal and function in terms of a teleological tendency of the species over time to adapt itself, or do we rely on 'natural selection', the view that the coincidence of goal and function in any species can be explained by other, non-teleological laws, and that the coincidence in general among all surviving species is due simply to the fact that without this no species could survive? The question about the inheritance of acquired characteristics is also involved here as a necessary, although not sufficient condition of the truth of the first view.

The problem of explaining adaptation through evolution is, of course, not restricted to that of accounting for the coincidence of goal and function. We have also to account for the special capacities of various species which enable them to attain their goals in their environment. For, as was said above, to say that anything is a goal for animals of a given species is to say that they will do whatever is necessary *within the limits set by their motor capacities* to attain it. The acceptance of a teleological explanation for behaviour does not imply, as many theorists seem to think,[1] that no further questions need arise about how behaviour comes about. Thus evolutionary theory must not only account for the adaptive coincidence of goal and function, but also for the adaptation of capacity to goal.

Once the survival theory has been shifted to the evolutionary context, the other major monistic theory, that of hedonism, begins to look more plausible. For there are many activities which may have survival value, but which obviously do not have survival as a goal. The most striking example are those activities which are 'intrinsically' motivated. These are cases in which the purpose of the activity is not some end-state which is only contingently linked with the activity, a result that could have been brought about in another way, but it is the activity itself. Thus sometimes we explain an action by saying that it contributed to the survival or power or prestige or well-being of the agent, and sometimes we say simply that a given type of activity is desirable in itself,

[1] Cf., e.g., Tinbergen, op. cit., pp. 3-4.

e.g., all forms of play, exercise, cultural pursuits, and so on. These actions are those which we say are not done 'for any other purpose', that is, other than themselves, and *a fortiori* they are not done for the purpose of survival.

It is here that the hedonist story seems to be plausible. For, as a matter of fact, we often say—at least when talking of human beings—that we engage in intrinsically motivated activities 'for pleasure'. But, on reflection, this very same consideration seems to rob it of its value. For pleasure is not a result which is only contingently linked with the activity which we enjoy. For to take pleasure is to take pleasure in something, and to enjoy is to enjoy something, and the pleasure or enjoyment is not separably identifiable from what is being enjoyed; that is, we cannot know that we are experiencing pleasure, and be in ignorance of what we are taking pleasure in. In this way, as Ryle points out, pleasure is asymmetrical with pain; for it is a fact to be discovered by induction what gives us pain, but a search of this kind doesn't make sense in the case of pleasure. True, there are some apparent counter-examples.[1] Thus someone might say that he enjoyed the play but wasn't sure whether it was the acting or simply the speed at which it moved which made it so delightful. The answer could supposedly be discovered inductively by trying it again in slow motion. But this is not a real counter-example. For the thesis is not meant to deny that for any event or activity enjoyed there are not causes which are contingently linked with our enjoyment of them, and which therefore could be discovered by induction. Thus I may enjoy my back being scratched without knowing who or what is doing the scratching. Or it might be that I enjoy a party because I had a lot to drink, and this I might discover by induction. But whatever the contributory factors, what is clear is that consciousness of pleasure is non-contingently linked with consciousness of what the pleasure is in, e.g., either the back-scratching or the party, such that one couldn't have one without the other. And similarly, in the above case, there is no doubt that the man enjoyed the *play*; all that is in question is whether the acting or the speed is a condition of this enjoyment, that is a condition of the object enjoyed giving pleasure. In a similar way we might discover by induction that a certain colour

[1] I have borrowed much here from a discussion in an earlier unpublished version of A. Kenny's book *Action, Emotion and Will*.

scheme was pleasant, that our pleasure depended on a certain combination of colours, but this would not mean that we had to discover that it was the colour scheme which we enjoyed.

A second set of putative counter-examples arise in cases of self-deception. Someone might believe that he was enjoying doing his duty in punishing another, whereas he was actually enjoying the inflicting of pain. But the point about this case is that it *is* one of self-deception. Thus the man wouldn't need *inductive* evidence to discover the truth. Typically, we might convince him of it by showing such facts as 'you continued longer than you needed to according to the law'; but the link between enjoying an action and prolonging it is not a contingent one. But, above all, our ultimate evidence for this assertion would have to be his avowal, and not a grudging admission based on inductive observations of cases like himself, but on the ordinary non-inductive grounds by which we usually know what we take pleasure in. For an avowal of this kind would clinch the question in favour of the hypothesis, whereas the more evidence we amassed which went to show that he was not self-deceived, e.g., his ability to talk about it openly and without violent resistance to the hypothesis, the less certain we would be of our view.

Pleasure is thus not a separable end-state, but is non-contingently linked with the source of pleasure. This can also be seen from the following reflection. If pleasure were an end-state contingently linked with the sources of pleasure, as, e.g., survival and well-being are, then the pleasure from drinking, say, that is, the pleasure we have when we drink with pleasure, should be only contingently linked with drinking, such that we could plausibly conceive that this pleasure could occur whenever we play whist, while the pleasure of hearing, say, Beethoven's Fifth Symphony occurred when we listened to a raga, and vice versa. It is difficult to see what could be meant by this hypothesis.

But if this is so, then it is a serious setback for a hedonist theory. For if pleasure is not separately identifiable from the things that give pleasure, then saying that men seek pleasure is simply saying that they do those things which give pleasure. Thus a monistic hedonist theory becomes equivalent to a 're-publican' theory positing that men tend to engage in a certain list of activities, the list consisting of those activities which they find pleasurable. But surely a hedonist theory says more than this, it also says that if any of these activities happened to cease to be pleasant, they would drop from the list, and, if any others became pleasant, they would find a place on it. It would thus not be purely a theory setting out a number of basic purposes. This is true, but it would be of little help, for we would still have to find out *a posteriori* what activities had ceased to be or become pleasant, and though the theory would allow for change, it would not be able to predict it. If, however, there were a way of identifying pleasure independently, then this would no longer be the case; we could say beforehand whether something would result in pleasure or not, as we can say whether something will result in survival or not, and the list of actions which would tend to be emitted could be derived from this single principle. This is what hedonist theories have usually meant, and if it is true that pleasure is not separably identifiable, they are robbed of much of their value even if true.

I say, 'even if true', because they are not robbed entirely of their content by this fact. Thus the theory, so shorn, would be incompatible with the view that any of our actions were extrinsically motivated, except when the goal was some pleasure. Thus it would rule out any attempt to account for behaviour in terms of some other extrinsic purpose, like well-being, or survival, and so on. And it would also rule out the view that desire for any action could have any other genesis but the pleasure to be found in it, that is, all intrinsically motivated action would be motivated by pleasure. Now it might be thought that both these claims were empty; for the only way of establishing that a given goal or end-state was pleasant would be to see whether it was sought or not. Thus some philosophers have concluded from the fact that pleasure is not a state separately identifiable from the activity or event that produces it that we cannot speak of pleasure as a specific type of end of activity, along with, and competing with other ends, like power, survival, etc. The function of the answer 'for pleasure' to a question of the form, why are you doing that? is simply to deny that the act has any of these other ends as its purpose, not to assert the end it has. Thus Nowell-Smith, in his *Ethics*, says,

'Enjoyment' is neither the name of a type of disposition nor the name of a type of occurrence. It is primarily a pro-word the function of which is to block the question 'Why did you do that?'[1]

[1] P. 115.

Now there is no doubt that 'for pleasure' or 'because I'm enjoying it' can function as a way of blocking further questions, even as a rebuff, but it need not always do so, and often doesn't. For pleasure, like any other purpose, can be the point of an activity, so that we can say whether it has succeeded or failed on the criterion of whether or not it gives us pleasure. Where pleasure is the point of an activity in this sense, we cannot say that the answer 'for pleasure' to the enquiry 'why are you doing this?' simply means that we are doing it for its own sake. For the action enquired about may succeed, that is, it may achieve the object by which it is defined, but there may be no pleasure, and in this sense the enterprise will be a failure. Thus, if I go to the seaside for pleasure, and I actually get there, it would be absurd to be surprised if I came back disappointed because I didn't enjoy it after all, on the ground that the action of going itself succeeded. Secondly, we can say of a man that he is seeking pleasure, that he is out for pleasure, that his only interest is pleasure. But this doesn't mean the same thing as seeking the gratuitous act.

Thus there is some empirical sense in hedonism even in its shorn form. But this consideration, like that cited above concerning intrinsically motivated activity, while seeming to support hedonism, is actually double-edged. For once given empirical meaning, the claims of hedonism seem to be less plausible. In fact, much of the plausibility of hedonism rests on an equivocation between a notion of pleasure with empirical content, like that which we use when we say that pleasure is the point of an activity, and a more general one in which it is considered a sufficient criterion for an act's being pleasant that it is undertaken. In this latter sense, the theory, of course, becomes one large empty tautology. But in the former sense it is open to grave objection. For one of the claims, as we said above, is that we can account for the desire for a given action in terms of the pleasure accompanying it. But in some cases we seem to have to account for pleasure in terms of desire. Thus, our pleasure in eating is enhanced when we are hungry, that is, when we want to eat. Even less favoured foods taste good. Perhaps we could account for this by some theory to the effect that pleasure depends here on certain physiological conditions. But this assumes that we can account for hunger, that is, the desire to eat, purely in physiological terms. But we might be biologically deprived and our appetite still dimmed by some bad news, say, and our pleasure would still be less. It would seem, therefore, that pleasure is a function of the desire to eat, and not only that the desire to eat is a function of pleasure. How can both be the case? It can be that we have to account for the desire to eat in other terms, but that that unimpeded fulfilment of this desire brings pleasure. This pleasure in the course of ontongeny becomes attached to certain foods more than others, so that, while our reasons for eating may generally be the original one, our reasons for choosing one dish rather than another is pleasure. It is possible that the Aristotelian notion of pleasure as the free unimpeded flow of desired activity can provide a correct account of the genesis of pleasure which later tends to fix itself to certain acts rather than others. But, in any case, it would seem that we have to admit that there are some things which are pleasant because they are wanted, as well as other things which are wanted because they are pleasant, whether or not the second category can be explained genetically in terms of the first. The evidence particularly of the 'biogenic drives', hunger, thirst, sex, and so on, seems to point to an order of dependence of the first sort; sexual pleasure seems more a function of sexual desire than vice versa, and there seems little doubt which of these two motives is basic in the sense of prior in time.

2. MECHANISM: THE HYDRAULIC MODEL

This seemingly endless debate between divergent views on the basic goals, or 'instincts', of man and animal, the seemingly insoluble puzzle of which one is to be taken as basic has been a powerful inducement to abandon this mode of procedure entirely, and, instead of searching for the goals of action, to try to establish 'objective', that is non-teleological, laws of behaviour. But this procedure has offered only apparent relief from the problems and perplexities of the older method. In reality the same questions have come up again in the new context. For the 'objective' theorists have themselves usually taken one of the existing teleological theories as their point of departure, modifying it along behaviourist lines. The major exception to this rule, the Pavlovian theory of conditioned reflexes is, for this very reason, notoriously incapable of accounting for most non-reflex behaviour of a directed sort. This is a testimony to the hold which teleological theories still have; although whether this is due to the nature of the phenomena to be explained or simply the hold of tradition we cannot judge before examining the different theories more closely.

A non-teleological theory has been developed by the German ethologists (notably, Lorenz and Tinbergen). Typically, having started from a wide range of naturalistic observations, this theory, or family of theories, is 'republican' in character; it posits a number of different instincts. These instincts are identified in part by the physiological conditions which facilitate a certain pattern of behaviour, that is, increase its intensity, and lower the threshold to its initiating 'releasing stimuli'; but in part also by the behaviour pattern itself. In this, the theorists have followed the usual common-sense notion of instinctive behaviour, and have distinguished food-seeking, reproductive, and so on, behaviour patterns. But, while starting from this they have tried to remove the teleological element. Thus the behaviour pattern itself is not characterized as a sequence of actions, but as a set of movements, each released by certain stimuli and steered ('directed') by the same ones or others. In Tinbergen's theory, the model seems to be a hydraulic one. The facilitating internal conditions provide a flow of energy which tends to activate the motor activities constituting the appropriate behaviour pattern; for instance, a certain hormonal condition tends to arouse the motor activities involved in fighting off other males, courtship, mating, perhaps also care of young, and so on. But these motor activities generally do not appear until the appropriate stimulus is present, e.g., that of a rival male, or of a possible mate, and so on. These stimuli then 'release' the activity, as it were, remove the block to it, and it appears.[1] Thus the facts which lie behind the ordinary common-sense notion of basic purposes, to seek food, reproduce, etc., are reinterpreted in a non-teleological way.

Now the facts assembled by ethologists like Lorenz and Tinbergen are immensely valuable to any science of animal behaviour, but it is doubtful whether the theory is adequate, for three reasons.

---

[1] Sometimes, however, if the pressure is high enough, it may appear without the stimuli, and this is referred to by Lorenz and Tinbergen as 'vacuum' activity, and sometimes when an activity is frustrated, another activity belonging to a different sequence may appear, the so-called 'displacement activities'.

First, we can not always delineate the internal conditions for a given pattern as clearly as is implied.[1] In the case of reproductive behaviour, it seems that this can be done. The great advances in endocrinology in recent years have shown the close correlation which exists in virtually all animal species between the presence of certain hormones in the system and mating behaviour, maternal behaviour, and so on. (The correlation is, however, much less close with man.) But, in the case, for instance, of exploratory behaviour, 'gratuitous' activity, problem-solving without re-ward,[2] the internal conditions cannot be delineated in this precise way. The conditions of behaviour of this kind, of course, include the absence of any other strong competing tendency to action, such as hunger, sex, and so on, and the absence of fatigue, but it does not seem that the conditions can be stated with any greater precision than this. There are, of course, other physiological conditions which can be cited, just as there are others than simply endocrinological balance in the case of mating behaviour. These behaviours can be impaired or eliminated by cortical lesions, for instance. But conditions of this kind, viz., that certain organs be in good working order, are not conditions specific to, say, exploratory behaviour, but affect the whole range of the animal's behaviour; and their presence is not simply a condition of the behaviour's appearing, but of its appearing in its normal form, for the effect of a lesion is often to disrupt behaviour, or render it less efficient, rather than to eliminate it.

Moreover, even in cases where there are selective internal con-ditions, it is not clear that these do not themselves involve a teleological form of explanation. In the case, say, of hunger and thirst, it is not clear that these internal conditions can be stated

[1] An attempt has been made to determine these internal conditions more exactly by Morgan and his associates: cf. Morgan, C. T., and Stellar, E., *Physiological Psychology*, 2nd ed., 1950; and Morgan, C. T., 'Physiological Mechanisms of Motivation', in M. R. Jones (ed.), *Nebraska Symposium on Motivation*, 1957; also Stellar, E., 'The Physiology of Motivation', *Psychological Review*, 1954. Morgan's theory resembles Tinbergen's in some res-pects, postulating a 'central motive state' (c.m.s.) which is connected with the initiation and perseverance of certain types of behaviour. But external stimuli play a more important role for Morgan, for they also act as 'arousers' and 'amplifiers' of a c.m.s. This, of course, means that the role of internal conditions is even less clear cut.

[2] Cf. cases reported by Harlow, e.g., 'Mice, Monkeys, Men and Motives', *Psychological Review*, 1953.

without any mention of the notion of a 'need' for food and water. There is a range of skeletal behaviour, within which eating and drinking fall, which is continuous in function with the autonomic self-regulatory activity of the organism, whereby certain states necessary for survival are maintained. This tendency of the organism to regulate itself towards certain norms is generally referred to by the term which Cannon put into circulation, 'homeostasis'. In many cases, however, the norms are restored not only by internal bodily changes or autonomic reactions, but by skeletal behaviour, which thus works in a way complementary to these reactions. Thus, for example, a tendency for body temperature to deviate from the norm will be counteracted in many species by shivering or sweating, or, to cope with the long term seasonal changes, by the growth of the coat. But the same conditions will also lead to remedial action of a skeletal kind, viz., the animal will seek the sun or the shade, migrate, and so on. Nor is it easy to draw a sharp distinction between behaviour which is 'automatically' regulated, and 'voluntary' responses; there is on the contrary a continuum between reactions like shivering which can barely be inhibited, through those like, e.g., breathing, defecating, sleeping, which can be inhibited but only for a time, to, say, eating which can be inhibited indefinitely by exceptional people and finally, in man, shading off into learned and highly developed activities, such as the building of houses, and so on, which can not be considered as in any sense 'automatic'.

These 'homeostatic' activities, then, replace or complement the self-regulatory functions of the organism, and are, like these latter, normally set in motion by the imbalances which they correct. The question of whether the effect of these imbalances on the following behaviour can be accounted for in a non-teleological way is continuous with the question whether homeostatic functions as a whole can be so accounted for. This question, still a disputed one in biology, is outside the scope of this enquiry; but we cannot assume *a priori* as many theorists do that the 'homeostatic' behaviours can be put on a footing with sexual behaviour in the sense that we can find antecedents for them which do not involve us in accounting for their occurrence by the introduction of further teleological laws; that is, that we can identify the conditions under which a given behaviour is prepotent in other terms than that this behaviour is required in order to maintain certain norms.

But whatever the answer about the internal conditions, where there are any, of a behaviour sequence appearing, a theory of Tinbergen's type is inadequate for a third, more serious, reason. This is the reason which we explored in the last chapter: It seems, in fact, impossible to account for these behaviour sequences in an entirely non-teleological manner. For even in the most stereotyped behaviour there is some variation of activity as a function of the situation which is teleological in character, that is, a variation with what the situation requires granted a certain goal. The notion of a 'directing stimulus' as we have seen does not provide a non-teleological explanation of this fact, but is simply a way of recognizing it in somewhat misleading terminology. With the higher animals, this 'adaptability' of behaviour is more marked, behaviour is more 'plastic', and we can speak of the 'consummatory act' which ends the sequence as its goal, and of the 'appetitive' behaviour which precedes it as being entirely commanded by the goal. Thus we will have to find a place for the notion of goal or purpose, and to take as our highest level laws postulates stating the basic purposes of the animal species in question as well as the type of behaviour they exhibit in seeking these goals, and perhaps the conditions in which these goals become prepotent in the animal's behaviour. But these internal conditions will now not be the facilitators of a certain movement or movements, but of directed motor activities commanded by a given goal; they will be conditions, that is, not only of the motor activities but of the operation of certain goals on the animal's behaviour.

Thus, if this argument is valid, then the crucial feature of Tinbergen's theory which makes it a non-teleological one will be found to be invalid. This is the hypothesis that behaviour can be accounted for without using the notion of a goal, but in terms of laws linking 'releasing' stimuli and motor activities, which in turn is linked with the view that the conditions for the arousal of psychic energy can be separated from those determining its direction. This seems to be the point of the hydraulic metaphor in Tinbergen; the flow is turned on by the internal conditions (endocrinological state, for instance), but it is directed by the channels which are set up in the organism and which only require certain releasing stimuli to be unblocked. Thus the hope is held out that the conditions for the direction of behaviour, viz., the various connexions between motor patterns, can be separately delineated and be shown to be quite independent of the conditions for its arousal. For the direction of behaviour would be entirely a function of the connexions between the different motor patterns and between them and the internal state which arouses the sequence, a function, to continue the metaphor, of the shape of the channels established. Now a complete separation of this kind between the conditions for arousal and the determinants of the direction of psychic energy is, of course, impossible on the premiss that the highest level laws of behaviour are teleological in form. For the content of these laws would be that the species in question tended to pursue certain purposes, that is, seek certain end-states or engage in certain activities. If there are any specific conditions for the arousal of one such tendency, it is also *ipso facto* a condition for the behaviour it arouses having a certain direction, that is, for its being directed towards the end-state in question, or for the activity to be of the kind in question. Of course the action emitted would also be determined by the situation and, in some cases, the history of the animal; but it could never be entirely determined by them, for the effect of history or environment on behaviour would itself be a function of the goal or purpose of that type of behaviour. To say, then, that the conditions for arousal and the determinants of direction can be separately delineated is to say that the highest level laws are not of the kind that is assumed in teleological explanation, but that the phenomena usually characterized by these laws can be accounted for in two distinct non-teleological sets of laws.

Now while no one would claim to have discovered the conditions determining the direction of behaviour, it would be a good step if we were able to discover non-teleological laws which held of the behaviour aroused by a given set of internal conditions. For in this case we would not have to assume that these arousing conditions were linked with behaviour defined by its direction towards a certain goal, and therefore that the arousing conditions were also partly determining conditions. Thus the attempt to account for behaviour in terms of releasing and directing stimuli is of vital importance if we are to think of Tinbergen's theory specifically as an enterprise, or the beginnings of an enterprise, designed to account for behaviour without using the notion of purpose, in a non-teleological way. Thus the evidence we have cited above against the validity of this attempt is also evidence against the viability of the enterprise.

3. MECHANISM: DRIVES WITHOUT DIRECTION

But in the field of molar behaviour theory there is another serious attempt to give a non-teleological account of behaviour by attempting to separate the determinants of behaviour from its conditions of arousal. This is the S–R reinforcement theory. One of the main features differentiating this view from the instinct theory of ethologists like Tinbergen is its concentration on the behaviour of animals higher up on the phylogenetic scale and hence on learned behaviour. And this difference is at the base of an important difference in approach. One of the weaknesses of the theory discussed above which was only implicitly stated was that in its concentration on fixed innate patterns of behaviour it gave little attention to the problems of learning. This weakness is corrected, indeed over-corrected, in S–R theory where the concentration on learning is intense and where learning theory is the most highly developed area of research. But precisely because of this concentration on learned behaviour, S–R theorists have believed that they are in a position not just to elaborate correlations descriptive of behaviour but to discover the determinants of the direction of behaviour. For a theory of innate behaviour these determinants must lie in the physiological make-up of the organism; but in the case of learned behaviour we can perhaps discover the conditions for behaviour having the direction which it has in the history of learning itself.

This, as we have seen in the last chapters, is the fundamental approach of S–R theory, to consider the behaviour emitted in any situation as a function of the behaviour emitted in the past in this or similar situations, a function that is, of learning history. The idea of reinforcement theory is that certain acts in certain situations are followed by physiological states which are 'rewarding'. When this happens, a connexion is established between this situation and this act, such that the former tends to evoke the latter in future. This process is known as the 'reinforcement' of an S–R connexion, and the rewarding conditions which bring it about as 'reinforcing states of affairs' or 'reinforcers'. The problem of what is to be considered a reinforcer is, of course, a vexed one. Some writers[1] have complained that the use of this concept involves one in a circle: A reinforcer is a state of affairs which strengthens a connexion, while a connexion is strengthened by a reinforcing state of affairs. But as Meehl points out,[2] this only involves a circle if 'strengthening S-R connexions' is one's only criterion for 'a reinforcer'. But it might be that one could discover in the first place what states of affairs were reinforcing by discovering what connexions were strengthened and then extrapolate from this to other cases, having established criteria for a reinforcing state of affairs other than the question-begging ones.

But S-R theorists have usually not followed this tedious route. They have usually borrowed their criteria for reinforcers—at least to start with—from common-sense. And this illustrates what was said above about the borrowing from teleological theories which is a feature of most 'objective' theories. For the choice of states of affairs which are to be considered reinforcing is like the choice of goals or purposes which one is attributing to the animal. For it is postulating what his behaviour will tend to be directed towards, even if this is explained in a somewhat different way.

In fact, although Thorndike started with a hedonist sounding notion, the 'satisfier', the S-R theorists who have borrowed his Law of Effect have tended to adopt a different starting point. They have been very much influenced by Cannon's description of homeostatic processes, and the paradigm notion of reinforcement is the reduction of some visceral need state, the restoration of a necessary bodily norm. Hull, for instance, adopts this view:

> Whenever an effector activity occurs in temporal contiguity with the afferent impulse, or the perserverative trace of such an impulse, resulting from the impact of a stimulus energy upon a receptor, and this conjunction is closely associated in time with the diminution in the receptor discharge characteristic of a need, there will result an increment to the tendency for that stimulus on subsequent occasions to evoke that reaction.[3]

[1] E.g., Postman, 'The History and Present Status of the Law of Effect', *Psychological Bulletin*, 1947.

[2] 'On the Circularity of the Law of Effect,' *Psychological Bulletin*, 1950.

[3] *Principles of Behaviour* .p. 80.

This, of course, runs into all the difficulties of the teleological theory which posited survival as the master goal. These difficulties have led the S–R theorists to alter the notion of a reinforcer somewhat. Hull adopted the view that *any* reduction of a stimulus was reinforcing, with totally untenable results.[1]

But, as was pointed out quite early on, learning isn't the same as performance. What an animal does it not purely a function of the learning history. Thus an animal might learn what to do in order to get food, but will not do it unless he is hungry. Thus the notion of 'drive' was introduced into S–R theory to account for the arousal of behaviour. A drive was a state of high general activity which was held to result from the existence of a need.[2] Thus a reinforcer was often identified as a drive-reducing state, and this terminology ran parallel with and often replaced that of need-reduction.

'Drive' is the key term in neo-behaviourist theory of motivation. Virtually all problems in this area are thought out in terms of rival drive theories, which, as we mentioned above, run alongside and parody the older disputes between teleological systems. The list of drives is becoming as long and fluid as the list of instincts used to be. We now have drives to know, to explore, for money, power, etc., etc. But the notion is, however, intended to be fundamentally different from that of instinct or purpose. For the notion of drive is meant simply to account for the arousal of behaviour, but not in any way for its direction. Thus Brown[3] makes quite clear that the only functions that can be attributed to drive are (1) that of 'energizing' or 'activating' behaviour, (2) that of increasing the probability that a given response will

[1] The thesis cannot survive the most obvious counter-examples where an 'increase in stimulation' is 'rewarding', e.g., infants in the dark.

[2] Later the notion of drive was extended like that of a reinforcer. It goes without saying that S–R theorists didn't intend to accept the teleological connotation of the term 'need'. A need implies a goal for which it is needed. They hoped to be able to establish in non-teleological physiological terms what the various need-states were which resulted in drives and whose reduction resulted in reinforcement; or failing this, to use the history of the organism as a criterion of need, e.g., whether it had been deprived of food and for how long. Cf. Skinner, *Science and Human Behaviour*, Chapter IX, for the operationalist argument in favour of this latter course.

[3] 'Problems Presented by the Concept of Acquired Drives,' in *Current Theory and Research in Motivation*, Univ. of Nebraska, 1953; and also *The Motivation of Behaviour*.

follow a given stimulus when their joint occurrence is followed by a reduction in drive, and (3) that of reducing the probability of this when it is followed by an abrupt increase in drive. Drive thus activates without directing.[1] The direction of behaviour is to be explained uniquely in terms of the notion of 'habit' or S–R connexion which is set up as the result of drive reduction, and thus the conditions and determinants of behaviour are held to be quite separate. Brown warns against the confusion of 'drive' and 'habit', which, as he sees, would frustrate the whole attempt of S–R theorists to devise a non-teleological theory of behaviour.

> Every case of directed behaviour is to be ascribed, not to drives or motives, but to the capacities of stimulus cues, whether innate or acquired, to elicit reactions.[2]

The theory of drive as an undirected activator of behaviour is designed primarily as was said above as an account of what we have called the 'homeostatic' activities. But, in addition, reproductive behaviour, where there is also a fairly well established physiological criterion for a 'drive-state' is usually cited. This leads to the notion, absurd in teleological terms, that the goal of mating activity is the reduction in tension which comes from coetus. It is perhaps right to attribute this immensely counter-intuitive conclusion to the Yankee Protestant cultural background of many of the prominent behaviour theorists. But whether this is so or not, the elision of sexual behaviour with homeostatic activities covers up important differences and helps to hide from view the weakness of the theory.

For the view that activity is aroused by 'drives' and directed by the habits built up in learning history cannot even account for behaviour in its home territory, i.e., among the 'homeostatic'

---

[1] The mechanism is variously seen. According to some theorists a drive 'sensitises' the animal to the stimuli which elicit responses. In this way, we could account for cases where an animal in a drive state may nevertheless be inert in a monotonous unchanging environment until other stimuli are introduced. Cf. Campbell, B. A., and Sheffield, F. D., 'Relation of Random Activity to Food Deprivation', *J. comp. physiol. Psychol.*, 1953: 'Starvation does not instigate activity; it only lowers the threshold for the normal stimuli to activity.' But the principle here is the same, for the 'sensitizing' or 'facilitating' role of drive, like its 'activating' role, is indiscriminate and affects all stimuli alike.

[2] Op. cit., p. 6.

behaviours. For it is immediately obvious that 'drives' cannot be restricted to the three functions which Brown has ascribed to them. The Hullian notion of drive as an *absolutely general* activator of behaviour is close to the absurd. When an animal is satiated for food and sexually aroused, he does not gorge himself, but goes in search of a mate. But this is not what he should do according to this theory. Nor do we have to take such fanciful examples. An animal, generally speaking, will eat when he is hungry, and drink when he is thirsty. (There may, of course, be some borderline foods which satisfy both hunger and thirst.) More, he can often discriminate and eat selectively those foods of which he is in need. Now, in face of this evidence, Brown and other S–R theorists have postulated a drive *stimulus*, accompanying but separate from drive, which helps to steer behaviour. For this stimulus is associated with the responses which have led to drive reduction in the past and hence tends to evoke them. In the absence of this stimulus, inappropriate action will therefore not tend to occur. But this is really another way of saying that drives have a directing function after all. For no such stimulus has been discovered. The earlier view that hunger depended on a few signs, such as stomach contractions, has long since been disproved, as has that that thirst depends on dryness in the throat. The drive stimulus is, at the moment, a pure fiction meant to retain the appearance of the non-directional nature of drive. The notion of drive stimuli becomes even more implausible when we reflect that the animal can often distinguish whether he is in need of one vitamin rather than another.

The fact that we have to give 'drive-states' a directing role as well has led some theorists to reject 'motivational' interpretations altogether in favour of a purely 'associative' one.[1] On this view the notion of drive as an activator is done away with altogether; the occurrence of certain behaviour (e.g., seeking food) when certain internal conditions (e.g., food deprivation) obtain is accounted for simply by the fact that certain internal stimuli connected with these conditions, and to which the behaviour is conditioned, become more prominent. Since the hypothesis is that the probability that a response will occur depends on the

---

[1] Cf. Estes, W. K., 'Stimulus-response Theory of Drive', in M. R. Jones (ed.), *Nebraska Symposium on Motivation*, 1958, and discussion in J. S. Brown, *The Motivation of Behaviour*, Chapter 4.

prominence of stimulus elements in the situation to which the response is conditioned,[1] this would account for the prepotence of the appropriate behaviour. In this way, the intractable problem of distinguishing the drive-state from its accompanying 'stimuli' is avoided.

But whatever view is accepted, it is clear that insofar as certain drives can be identified by their physiological antecedent conditions, they are linked not just with activity in general but with that activity which tends towards a certain result. This much must be admitted. But it may perhaps be possible to restrict the directing function of drives to this: A drive-state can pick out from among all the habits conditioned those which lead to its reduction. And this could be made compatible with S–R assumptions if we postulated hypothetical internal stimuli connected with the drive-state. Then what the animal does is still a function of his behaviour history in this or similar situations, but 'similar' here will mean 'similar in internal drive condition' as well as in external environment.

But even this won't do. For the evidence cited in the last two chapters goes to show that much of an animal's activity cannot be accounted for in terms of his behaviour history alone, but can only be accounted for by the goals towards which it is directed, such goals, precisely, as getting to food, or drink, and consuming it, or finding a mate. For instance the chimpanzee's behaviour in using the box could not be accounted for by a theory of conditioning, but only by the hypothesis that his action was directed to the goal of getting the banana. The role of learning here was not to condition behaviour but to facilitate it. This is true of the behaviour of most animals above a certain phylogenetic level in the open situation, and we have seen evidence that the same is true in the closed situation as well. Thus, insofar as hunger is linked to food-getting behaviour, i.e., tends to evoke it, we cannot account for this by saying simply that hunger evokes those reactions which in this or similar situations have led to food (and hence to hunger-reduction) in the past; it will be truer to say that hunger is linked generally with that behaviour lying within the capacity of the animal which will in the situation as he knows it lead to food. In other words, we have to accept 'drive' as a

[1] Cf. W. K. Estes, 'Towards a Statistical Theory of Learning', *Psychological Review*, 1950.

tendency to pursue a certain goal, and thus abandon the notion of a directionless activator of behaviour.

In these pages we have been discussing the S–R reinforcement theory; but it is clear that this conclusion weighs against the contiguity theory equally. For here, too, the fate of the attempt to separate the conditions of arousal of behaviour from the determinants of its direction depends—once the selecting function of drive is established—on our being able to account for behaviour in terms of the response history of the animal; and, if this cannot be done, then a non-teleological account of motivation, at least on a molar level, is impossible.

But while it is clear that we must often explain 'appetitive' behaviour, e.g., food-seeking, by the 'consummatory act' at which it is directed, in this case, eating the food, might we not try to account for the fact that this act is a goal in terms of the notions of drive-reduction and the consequent strengthening of habit? Thus, in the examples discussed in the last chapter, the chimpanzee's using the stick, the rats' taking the short-cut, and in general with animals' approach behaviour to food when they are hungry, we have to account for the behaviour in terms of the goal of getting the food and eating it. But how do we account for the fact that this act is a goal whenever the animal is hungry? It would seem that, according to Hull and other S–R reinforcement theorists, this has to be explained in terms of a habit built up by drive-reduction. True, the sucking reaction of mammalian infants is innate, but that this is followed in adult life by eating seems to be the result of learning on their theory, or at least of the selection from among a number of innate responses by selective reinforcement.[1] And Hebb, who is not a reinforcement theorist, seems to consider the connexion between hunger and eating to be learned as well.[2]

But it is difficult to see what the evidence is for this. Admittedly mammalian infants are cared for by their parents, as are the young of many non-mammalian species, and their development is thus controlled. Perhaps in special experimental circumstances one could show that eating was a learned response to hunger, but it is hard to see where on the continuum between infant sucking and adult eating one could draw the line between innate and

[1] Cf. Hull, *Principles of Behaviour*, pp. 79–80.
[2] Cf. *The Organization of Behaviour*, Chapter VIII.

learned. The evidence cited by Hebb in connexion with a neurological theory of acquired links seems very weak. He points out that a rat will eat less in unfamiliar surroundings than he will when he becomes accustomed to them. But that interest in the surroundings can distract from eating is not evidence to the effect that the connexion between food deprivation and eating is a learned one. Hebb also points out that extreme deprivation can reduce or sometimes do away with the desire to eat. But it is difficult to see why this should constitute evidence for his thesis either.

What is true is that we can explain the preference of men and sometimes animals for different foods, at least partly in terms of their early diet, that is, what has reduced hunger in the past. This is perhaps not the only element in food preference. But some of the results of P. T. Young's studies on this subject[1] seem to indicate that a food which has redressed a severe nutritional imbalance in an animal in the past tends to be selected preferentially in the future even when the nutritional element concerned has been abstracted. But whether we can account for the development of taste historically through hunger-reduction or not, this in no way indicates that the connexion between food deprivation and the consummatory act of eating is an acquired one.

And when we turn to the case of mating behaviour not even this much can be said. It doesn't seem possible to doubt that, for most species, the connexion between the state of sexual excitability which results from the relevant hormonal conditions and external stimuli and the consummatory act of mating is an innate one. Here, too, there are preferences as to 'goal-objects', i.e., mates, which in some species, notably man, can vary widely, even beyond members of the opposite sex, and indeed, beyond members of the same species, but it is clear that this 'canalization' of sexual drive cannot be accounted for in terms of habits built up in drive-reduction, and certainly not by that induced by coetus. The evidence is strong that many of the factors determining preferences of this kind are in operation before puberty. The false analogy between mating and the 'homeostatic' activities has tended to obscure the weakness of the drive reduction case when applied to anything other than eating and drinking, and the extent to

[1] E.g., Young, 'The Role of Affective Processes in Learning and Motivation', *Psychological Review*, 1959.

which a general theory of behaviour has been built on the evidence of a fraction of the total behaviour of organisms—and evidence which has been misunderstood at that.

It would thus appear that the connexion between, say, food and water deprivation, sexual excitability, and their appropriate consummatory acts is an innate one. But this is not a connexion between certain physiological conditions and certain movements, but between these antecedent conditions and certain goals. For the consummatory act functions, as we have seen, as a goal in behaviour; that is, much of the previous 'appetitive behaviour' which leads up to it can only be accounted for on the hypothesis that it is directed towards, that it occurs 'for the sake of' the consummatory act. Low down on the phylogenetic scale and early in ontogeny the behaviour connected with any need-state is very stereotyped, and a characterization in terms of movement is more plausible; but as we proceed higher, and as the animal grows, behaviour becomes more 'plastic'. This plastic behaviour is heavily dependent on learning, but the learning is not of the kind that can be accounted for by conditioning; it consists in the development of the sensori-motor co-ordinations connected with the animal's motor skills, and in an increase in orientation. Learned and intelligent behaviour grows out of innate, stereotyped behaviour, the actions that are often called 'instinctive' in ordinary speech, retaining the direction towards the same goal, but altering and extending the modalities of action.

Thus insofar as one can delineate physiological antecedent conditions for psychic energies of certain kinds, as is implied in the notion of 'drive', these are connected not with a generalized state of activation, but with action directed towards a certain goal. For it is not only the case, as the S–R theorists themselves admit, that the different drive states are linked with actions which have a certain result, e.g., that the state of food deprivation is linked with actions which have the result of meeting this need; but also that they are linked with actions which have to be seen as directed towards certain consummatory acts as their goal. These connexions seem to be innate, and therefore there seems little evidence for 'drive' conceived as directionless psychic energy. On the contrary the psychic energy which is aroused by these antecedent conditions seems always to be directed towards some goal. And this is what is implied, of course, in such ordinary language concepts as 'hunger', 'thirst', where the antecedent conditions of deprivation are linked to the tendency to perform the consummatory action in the meaning of the term. Thus we can speak of someone dying of hunger (i.e., food deprivation), while at the same time to be hungry means (i.e., implies) to want to eat. Thus even in these favourable cases where we seem to be able to identify a drive in terms of some specifiable antecedent conditions, we cannot separate the conditions for arousal from the determinants of direction of behaviour. For food deprivation, the hormone balance, and so on, seem to be inseparably both one and the other. And by the same token we have to accept as the basis of our explanation of behaviour laws which state the direction in which behaviour 'naturally' tends, that is, the goals or purposes for the sake of which it occurs.

4. THE MULTIPLICATION OF 'DRIVES'

Once we move outside the range of hunger, thirst and sex, the S–R reinforcement theory seems even less plausible. This is particularly clear when we consider the whole range of human social behaviour, that behaviour which we normally explain in terms of the desire for money, power, friendship, success, and so on. For here the model of a directionless drive which acquires the capacity to direct behaviour only because reductions in it reinforce the stimulus–response connexions which concurrently occur has not even the semblance of validity. S–R theorists themselves find themselves forced to adopt a notion of directed psychic energy when they begin to identify the various 'secondary' drives as the drive 'for money', or 'to achieve', and so on.

The attempt to force this area of recalcitrant facts into the drive reduction mould has led to a flock of largely verbal theories of what is called 'secondary motivation'. An attempt is sometimes made to account for, e.g., the desire for money in terms of the notion of 'secondary reinforcement'. A secondary reinforcer is a stimulus which, having evoked an action which itself leads to primary reinforcement (drive-reduction) itself acquires the power to reinforce, that is to increase the probability of occurrence of those S–R connexions which lead to its occurrence. This was originally used to account for the learning of fairly long sequences of responses, such as, e.g., in a long and complex maze, where, according to the 'gradient of reinforcement' (the time which must elapse between a response and the reward for this to be reinforcing), the 'stamping in' of the earlier members of the sequence could not be accounted for by the primary reinforcement alone, which occurred much later. These earlier responses would then be reinforced by the choice-point stimuli which evoked the later responses. There has always been some doubt as to whether secondary reinforcers were meant to reduce drive themselves or whether their powers sprang from some other source. But in any case it is this *ad hoc* extension of the notion of reinforcement which has provided some justification for the accusations about the circularity of the Law of Effect. But, whatever the validity of this criticism, it is clear that the principle of secondary reinforcement will not help us much here. For it is notorious that the desire for money, friendship, power, and so on may often continue long after it is no longer necessary in order to achieve any other 'primary' gratifications; whereas the 'rewarding' value of choice-point stimuli will decline pretty rapidly if the food in the goal-box is removed.

S–R theorists have therefore generally turned to another stratagem; the invention of supposed drive states which are relieved or reduced by the attainment of the goals, power, money, prestige, etc., in question. Frequently these drives have been referred to as 'anxiety'. The liberal use of this notion seems mainly intended to save the S–R theory from the phenomena which, to say the least, cast doubt on it. Mowrer, one of the best-known theorists in this field hints at this when he says:

> Moreover, by positing anxiety as a kind of connecting link between complete well-being and active organic discomfort or injury, it is possible to reconcile the fact that much, perhaps most, of the day to day behaviour of civilized human beings is not prompted by simultaneously active organic drives and the fact that the law of effect (learning through motivation reduction) is apparently one of the best established of psychological principles.[1]

Seward shows the same concern:

> Meanwhile it may help to face squarely the issue before us. Experiments strongly imply that the chief sources of motivation are a few bodily needs, a variety of ways of satisfying them, and

[1] *Learning Theory and Personality Dynamics*, p. 26.

a large number of fears. Common experience, on the other hand, suggests that the bulk of our activity is directed towards things we want rather than away from things we don't want, and that many of the things we want have little to do with bodily needs. How can these conflicting lines of evidence be reconciled?[1]

But this 'reconciliation' is purely verbal. This can be seen clearly from a sample drive-reduction analysis of social behaviour, taken from Dollard and Miller's *Personality and Psychotherapy*.

A child who has experienced severe pain and other forms of discomfort when away from the mother and who has had the close presence of the mother associated with relief will be expected to learn to feel anxious when separated from the mother and safer when closer to her. Thus motivated he will learn to approach the mother by turning to the left to the cue of seeing her to the left, to the right to the cue of seeing her to the right, and going forward to the cue of seeing her straight ahead. After he has learnt these relative responses (turning to the left or right or going forward) to the cues of relative differences in position, his behaviour will be oriented toward her as a goal. In short, he will respond to the cues of distance from the mother with the drive of fear and the cues of the relative direction with appropriate approach responses. In the same way, he may learn much more complicated habits of approach, such as going around or under obstacles and even taking buses and street cars to get home. The fact that the mother is the one stimulus object that will reduce his fear will cause his behaviour to be oriented toward her as a goal.[2]

Now stripped of its untenable assumptions, this means simply that the child acquires, through the importance of his mother in meeting his primary needs in early infancy, a strong desire to be with her, coupled with anxiety away from her. Whether or not this is the correct explanation of the genesis of love for parents is not to the point. The point is that this attempt to squeeze the child's behaviour into the drive-reduction pattern has not succeeded in finding a place for the notion of drive as psychic energy which is originally without direction. For the conditions of the arousing of the 'drive' or anxiety are also the conditions of the child's trying to get near its mother. The drive is from the beginning characterized by the goal towards which it is aimed.

[1] 'How are Motives Learned?,' *Psychological Review*, 1953, p. 101.
[2] Op. cit., p. 87.

Dollard and Miller's one attempt to show the opposite lies in the absurd claim that the child learns to go left when his mother is on the left and right when she is on the right, and so on. It can safely be said that learning of this kind never takes place. Whether the motor skills needed in spatial locomotion are due to learning or growth, they do not require for their proper use that, in addition to making the movements of walking, say, we also learn what direction the different movements will carry us in. Learning to walk is learning to get from place to place on foot; and this is a general capacity which cannot be accounted for in terms of a set of S–R habits. When a child learns to walk for the first time, after many attempts, in the process, say, of getting a rattle, he does not have to start all over again from scratch in learning the movements needed to get to some other object. Perhaps Dollard and Miller wish to claim not that the child learns any specific movements to execute, but that he learns 'by accident' as it were that getting close to his mother relieves anxiety. But the evidence for this is nil. From the earliest days, before the child is even capable of locomoting very efficiently to get to his mother, he will cry when she leaves, plead with her to come, and so on. It is clear that we are dealing here with a desire to be near the mother, which may be explained historically in some way, but which cannot be reduced to an undirected 'drive'-state which only acquires the capacity to direct behaviour through the acquisition of habits based on drive reduction. In other words, we cannot separate the anxiety, as the primitive phenomenon, and the desire or disposition to get close to the mother, as the derived result of 'trial and error' learning. The desire and the anxiety are the same phenomenon, the latter only being comprehensible as a reaction to the frustration or threatened non-fulfilment of the former.

Thus Dollard and Miller's flimsy attempt to find a use for the drive-reduction model, is insofar as it is not based on patently false assumptions, such as those about learning, merely a verbal covering over the embarrassing fact that we are dealing with desires, that is, psychic energy which is directed towards a goal, and that this fact is the primitive one in explanation. The device they use is to try to divide this disposition to seek a goal into an anxiety state caused by its absence on one hand, and a set of habits induced by the reduction of this anxiety on the other. But we cannot account for the goal-seeking behaviour in terms of a set of S–R habits, and nor is there any evidence to show that the anxiety is prior to the desire for the goal. Yet this is a common approach among S–R theorists. Thus Brown[1] puts forward the hypothesis that

> the important motivating component of many of the supposed acquired drives for specific goal objects is actually a learned tendency to be discontented or distressed or anxious in the absence of those goal objects.[2]

But this turns out to be another way—albeit a way which sounds more acceptable to S–R drive theorists—of saying that the person comes to want money, power, prestige, or whatever; and this is so because no criteria are given for the acquisition of the 'tendency to be discontented or distressed' which are separate from those for the acquisition of the desire. Thus Brown discusses the possibility of explaining the desire for money by an anxiety aroused in childhood by the parents' worry about money. Now, no doubt this may be an important contributing factor to the child's later attitude, and may give him, as Cortes said to Mocte-zuma, 'a disease of the heart which only gold can cure'. But we cannot separate the anxiety over the absence of money from the desire to make it or get it. The induced anxiety about money is an induced anxiety-ridden desire to get money, and we cannot explain the second by the first.

The very small degree of plausibility of this theory comes from the notion of anxiety, for this tends to subsume these goals under the class of 'aversions', inducing behaviour which is designed to avoid some evil consequence, rather than achieve some good, and thus to accentuate the similarity with activities which are 'need-reducing'. Now it may be that many of our desires are accompanied with anxiety, although more, one feels, in the culture circle to which most behaviour theorists belong than elsewhere. But anxiety cannot be used to provide an S–R account of this behaviour. For anxiety is generally not ignorant of what it is anxious about. As a psychic state it has a direction, and an explanation in terms of anxiety is also one in terms of desire, that is, an explanation of a teleological form.

[1] Loc. cit., in *Current Theory and Research in Motivation*, 1953.
[2] Op. cit., p. 12.

But this reliance on anxiety brings to light another important feature of S–R reinforcement theory. As was mentioned above, the 'objective' behaviour theorists have not avoided the types of disputes that beset teleological theorists in their advocacy of different sets of basic instincts or purposes. For their theories take their starting point from one of the established teleological theories and attempt to recast it in objective terms. And as teleological theories are heavily influenced by what the thinker or his milieu or culture consider important, so are the objective theories. Those who have discerned in the pages of S–R writers the heavy imprint of the Yankee Protestant anti-hedonistic work-ethic have perhaps not been far off the mark. In any case it seems to be assumed by all theorists of this school (1) that all activity is extrinsically motivated, i.e., that all action is done for some end which is separably identifiable from the action, and (2) that this end is the reduction in or removal of some evil or discomfort. Rat, and presumably human, life, as seen by an S–R psychologist, is a very gloomy affair, an endless struggle to fend off noxious or unpleasant stimulation.[1]

But the objections to this theory are more than aesthetic. The facts themselves cannot be twisted into this picture. For it cannot account for such activities as exploration, play, problem-solving in the absence of primary reward, and so on, which are intrinsically motivated. This has been repeatedly pointed out by such thinkers as Nissen,[2] Harlow,[3] Montgomery,[4] and recently White.[5] For in these activities there is no separably identifiable end-state and *a fortiori* no separately identifiable state of need- or drive-reduction. Activity of this kind seems to occur whenever the animal has no more pressing demand to meet, and appears purely gratuitous.

Various attempts have been made to press these phenomena as

---

[1] Recently there has been some criticism along these lines from within the school, e.g., Koch, 'Behaviour as "Intrinsically" Regulated', in *Nebraska Symposium on Motivation*, 1956.

[2] 'The Nature of the Drive as Innate Determinant of Behavioural Organization,' *Nebraska Symposium on Motivation*, 1954.

[3] Loc. cit., *Psychological Review*, 1953.

[4] Cf. the series of articles on 'Exploratory Behaviour', *J. comp. and physiol. Psychol.*, 1952 and 1953.

[5] 'Motivation Reconsidered,' *Psychological Review*, 1959.

well into the mould, e.g., those of Berlyne,[1] Montgomery[2] and Glanzer.[3] Berlyne and Montgomery's theories make use of a special newly invented drive, called 'exploratory drive' in one case, and 'curiosity' in the other. Glanzer relies on the notion of 'stimulus satiation', the hypothesis that after a while an animal ceases to respond to stimuli to which he has been exposed. The latter theory is, of course, incapable of accounting for exploratory behaviour; it can explain why the animal 'moves on' but not why he actively explores, why the opportunity of exploring can be a goal for him, as Montgomery and Harlow have shown. But the first two theories are not in much better case, and are largely verbal restatements of the phenomena.

This can be illustrated with Berlyne's theory, many of the same points applying to Montgomery as well. Berlyne[4] attempts to expound a theory of curiosity with two Hullian postulates. These are:

i. When a novel stimulus affects an organism's receptors, there will incur a drive-stimulus-producing response . . . (which we call curiosity).

ii. As a curiosity-arousing stimulus continues to affect an organism's receptors, curiosity will diminish.

There are a number of other corollaries, but this gives the nub of the theory. Berlyne means to maintain that exploratory behaviour is learned. (Corollary (i). An organism will learn to respond to a curiosity arousing stimulus with an activity which will increase stimulation by it.) Thus we can subsume this behaviour too under the drive-reduction model. But this subsumption is wholly verbal. The first question-begging expression is that of a 'novel stimulus'. In fact novelty can only rarely be accounted for in stimulus terms. Most of the time when the animal explores, it is not a new shade of colour, for instance, which elicits it, but a new object or situation, or a familiar object in an unusual place. For the same reason exploratory behaviour cannot be accounted for by the increase in stimulation from a

---

[1] 'Novelty and Curiosity as Determinants of Exploratory Behaviour,' *Brit. J. Psychol.*, 1950.

[2] Op. cit.

[3] 'Curiosity, Exploratory Drive and Stimulus Satiation,' *Psychol. Bulletin*, 1958.

[4] Op. cit.

particular stimulus, but only as increasing familiarity with the situation. For the rest the theory is pure verbiage. There is no evidence for the supposed 'drive-stimulus-producing response' beyond the banal evidence which sets the problem in the first place, viz., that animals tend to explore unfamiliar situations, and after a time, when they have become familiar with them, cease to do so. Moreover, the suggestion that we can account for exploratory behaviour as a set of stimulus–response habits is almost unintelligible. For the set of responses which an animal will use in exploration include a vast range, in fact a large proportion of those in his repertoire, running, sniffing, walking around, jumping on top, pushing with his paw. We cannot account for the emission of all these by saying that they are conditioned to stimuli having the property 'novelty', for the problem is of explaining *which one* will be emitted; the answer being, of course, the one which will constitute effective exploration in this environment. The 'Hullian' account of exploratory behaviour turns out to be an empty one. The facts just won't fit into the theoretical mould, and even less will those of playful activity and gratuitous problem-solving.

It is Nissen[1] who has seized the nettle, and postulated that this behaviour is 'autonomously motivated', i.e., just occurs for its own sake. Nissen holds that an animal tends naturally to exercise his capacities, and to explore. He sums this up under the slogan 'capacity is its own motivation'. But this, of course, is just another way of saying that the attempt to find a non-teleological explanation here is misguided. In fact we have to explain the behaviour by a natural tendency to engage in activity of this kind. Nissen virtually admits this in speaking of a 'drive to perceive' and a 'drive to know'. In fact under the unity of terminology with S–R theories, he is proposing a view of a radically different type, one where the basic factors motivating behaviour are identified by their direction, i.e., by the kind of activity they bring about.

5. THE CASE OF AVERSION

But one of the most telling objections against the S–R theory of reinforcement is that it cannot account for that paradigm case of an aversion, namely behaviour which is aimed at avoiding pain.

[1] Loc. cit., *Nebraska Symposium on Motivation*, 1954.

The procedure of this theory, as we have said, is to try to account for behaviour in terms of its history: That response will occur which has led to reward in the past. But in the case of avoidance, the usual state of affairs is precisely a non-recurrence of previous action—that is, if the animal 'catches on'. If a rat has walked across a grid, been shocked, and run off, he will not on the next occasion go on to the grid again; although no doubt the running response which terminated the pain was 'rewarding', he will not go through the sequence again so as to get this 'reward'. Now we might account for this case by assuming the complementary principle to that of reinforcement, as many theorists, including Thorndike, have done. That is, we might assume that any conjunction of stimulus and response which leads to an *increase* in drive will tend to be *weakened* or 'stamped out'. This will account for the fact that the rat will not repeat the action, i.e., running on to the grid, which led to shock. But this, too, isn't enough. For shock will not lead simply to a tendency not to repeat the actions which led to it, but also to a tendency to *avoid* the painful spot. Thus, a rat will not only fail to repeat the original action, but may also refrain from other actions which will have the same result. This is evident from the experiment of Tolman and Gleitman,[1] where rats, after training to food in a maze with two distinctive end-boxes, were introduced separately and shocked in one end-box; when placed again at the beginning of the maze, they took the path leading to the safe box. Now in this case, what led to shock was not an action on their part, but their being put by the experimenter in the shock-box. The action inhibited on the test trial, viz., running up the path to the shock-box, was not emitted on the 'training trial'; what the two processes have in common is simply that they result in the animal's being in the painful situation. Secondly, an animal who has been shocked in a given chamber will, if placed again in this chamber, tend to flee it: In other words, he has learnt not only that he shouldn't repeat the action which brought him there on the previous trial, but that he should avoid the spot in general, whether this involves not going there in the first place, or leaving it once placed there. Nor can this flight reaction be explained in Pavlovian terms as a response conditioned to the cues of the goal-box by the unconditioned stimulus of pain. For the animal may not

[1] 'Studies in Learning and Motivation: I,' *J. exp. Psychol.*, 1949.

repeat the same action when fleeing from the box as he originally emitted when fleeing the pain. Miller's experiment[1] has shown that a rat is capable of learning a new response in order to escape from a danger spot, which has been identified as such by a previous experience of pain there. Similarly, an experiment by Brogden, Lipman and Culler[2] with guinea pigs illustrated the same point. If a conditioned stimulus, say a buzzer or tone, occurred before the unconditioned stimulus of shock which evoked running, the former might also acquire the power to evoke running. But if the shock followed the signal in any case, that is, whether or not the animal ran, then the running tended to be abandoned; the animals 'gave up', braced themselves and waited. In those cases where the shock was made contingent on the animal's behaviour, that is, was not administered if they ran, they continued to run. In other words, the running cannot be explained as a conditioned response to the signal, or at most only in part; we must also see it as an attempt to get away, which is abandoned when it proves fruitless.

Thus it would appear that avoidance behaviour cannot be explained either by Pavlovian conditioning or by 'operant' conditioning, the stamping in or out of a response. For the effect of administering pain to an animal in a situation cannot, it appears, be accounted for in terms of an increased or reduced tendency to repeat certain responses emitted in the pain situation, but only in terms of the animal's acquiring a goal, that of avoiding the painful spot. But then the function of the pain is not the stamping in or out of certain responses, but a cognitive one, that of informing the animal that a certain spot is painful. We will therefore have to assume in explaining avoidance behaviour a general propensity of the animal to avoid pain, that is, ascribe avoiding pain as a purpose of the animal.

Now S–R theorists naturally wish to avoid this conclusion, and they have therefore tried to account for avoidance behaviour in drive-reduction terms by means of a special mechanism. Two of the foremost theorists who have tackled this question are Mowrer and Miller, and, though there are minor differences between their hypotheses, in substance their approach is the same.

[1] 'Studies of Fear as an Acquirable Drive: I,' *J. exp. Psychol.*, 1948.
[2] 'The Role of Incentive in Conditioning and Extinction,' *Amer. J. Psychol.*, 1938.

And the approach is naturally to assume a drive which is being reduced by avoidance behaviour, and which can therefore account for its being conditioned. This drive is naturally labelled 'fear'. It is accounted for as a 'stimulus act', that is, a response which produces characteristic proprioceptive stimuli. These function as a 'drive', that is, they play the roles outlined by Brown above; they activate behaviour, and they stamp in or out those responses which lead to their reduction or increase respectively. The notion is, then, that the drive-inducing fear-response becomes conditioned, on the occurrence of pain, to the stimuli associated with or adjacent to the pain. Mowrer and Miller differ on the relatively marginal question whether this conditioning can be itself accounted for in terms of reinforcement, or whether we have to invoke some Pavlovian law of conditioning. According to Mowrer,[1] they seem to be agreed in considering fear as an accompaniment to, or part of the innate pain-response which, unlike the rest of the pain-response, can become conditioned to the surrounding stimuli. Avoidance behaviour can then be explained as stamped in by the reduction of this drive.

According to Miller[2] the conditioning of fear to a new stimulus produces three results: (1) It brings with it the innate responses of fear, e.g., increase in stomach acidity, startle, etc.; (2) It 'serves as a cue to mediate the transfer of responses previously learned in other situations', that is, the internal stimuli produced by fear may have certain (flight) responses conditioned to them from experience in other situations, and these responses will therefore tend to be emitted; and (3) It 'serves as a drive to motivate (whereas fear-reduction serves as a reward to reinforce) the learning of new responses. This learning will be influenced by the preceding two factors through their role in determining which responses are likely to occur'.

But how does this learning work? The idea is that since the drive is produced by a response conditioned to the surrounding stimuli, any action which will stop these stimuli from impinging on the receptors will reduce drive and thus be rewarding. But avoidance behaviour is bound to be of this kind; and therefore we can account for this behaviour in this way. Mowrer[3] spells

---

[1] 'Two Factor Learning Theory Reconsidered,' *Psychological Review*, 1956.
[2] In S. S. Stevens, *Handbook of Experimental Psychology*, pp. 441-2.
[3] Op. cit.

this out in more detail. In the case where an animal refrains from doing an action which led to pain in the past, we can assume that the proprioceptive stimuli from doing the action have become fear-arousing. It is therefore rewarding to cease to do it, and perhaps we might postulate a mechanism which works more directly whereby the fear itself inhibits the action. In other cases, such as that examined by Brogden, Lipman and Culler, we can assume that fear is attached to the 'signal' stimulus, and that therefore any thing which carries the animal away from this will be rewarding.

> If the fear-arousing stimulus is external to the organism, behaviour will be reinforced if it carries the organism away from the stimulus; and if the fear-arousing stimulus is internal, i.e., response-produced, the organism will be relieved, rewarded, reinforced for discontinuing the behaviour which is responsible for such stimulation.[1]

But it is doubtful whether avoidance behaviour can be accounted for in this way. First, the theory assumes that avoidance responses are learned in each case by trial and error, those responses which reduce fear being stamped in. But very often a correct avoidance response will appear on the first trial after the shock; and this may differ from the response which terminated the shock, if any, on the previous trial. We have only to look at the case studied by Tolman and Gleitman, but there are many other cases. For instance, a rat may escape from shock administered in the path of a maze by running quickly ahead. On the next trial, he will stop and refuse to enter the path. Or conversely, a rat who has avoided shock by non-entry may, if the incentive is great enough, enter the path but try to run quickly through it. Here the 'avoidance' is only partial, but the rat is plainly aware that running quickly is a way to minimize the shock, and this without trial and error training.

Now Miller tries to account for this by the second supposed effect of fear conditioning, the transfer of flight or avoidance responses from other situations. But to invoke this just begs the question. For insofar as any avoidance responses are conditioned to the internal stimuli of fear, all avoidance responses which have been successful in the past must be. But these will vary widely

---

[1] Mowrer, op. cit., p. 116.

through the animal's repertoire, and include running forward, running back, jumping, stepping aside, and so on. The problem is to explain which one will occur in this situation, that is, what governs the selection among all the possible avoidance responses. And the answer seems to be that that response will be selected which in this situation is required to avoid the shock, which is another way of saying that avoiding the shock is a goal for the animal.

Of course, the theory might account for some of these cases. Thus, where the animal runs ahead to escape the shock, and then hangs back on the second trial to avoid it, one might say that the stimuli of the danger area become fear-arousing so that approach to them becomes drive-increasing, and hence tends not to occur. But this device cannot be used to account for the Tolman and Gleitman case. For here the rats ran up to the choice point where the two paths branched off and then went beyond it on the path which took them to the safe box. And this brings us to our second point, viz., that the whole model of avoidance in terms of fear aroused by certain stimuli is suspect. The model assumes that avoidance behaviour is like the behaviour involved in flight from pain. Fear is a pain-like affect (indeed, perhaps a part of pain) which arises on contact (although perhaps only visual or olfactory contact) with certain features of the environment which have become 'signals' of pain through conditioning, just as pain arises through contact with parts of the environment which are unconditionally pain producing. In both cases, the animal learns by trial and error which responses will reduce his distress and these become conditioned. Avoidance behaviour is thus fundamentally similar to flight from pain. The animal avoids the greater distress of shock because he is induced to flee from the lesser distress caused by fear which is conditioned to the surroundings. A reinforcement theory of avoidance is bound to adopt such a model. For it could not assume that the non-occurrence of the pain is itself a reinforcing state of affairs. This would reinforce every action not followed by pain and not just avoidance responses. The point is to explain why responses which do not end in pain are 'correct' only in cases where there is some danger of or possibility of pain. This is solved by interpreting avoidance responses as flight from distressing stimuli which are associated with or adjacent to the pain-inducing thing or area.

But there is no evidence that avoidance of pain is generally also flight or retreat from something else. We may interpret the facts in this way when the animal backs away from the path where he was shocked on the last trial; and this might account for this reaction even in those cases where he ran ahead on the shock trial. But avoidance may mean, as in the case of Tolman and Gleitman, just taking another path. There is no evidence here which will permit us to interpret this as a case of retreat or withdrawal from a distressing, because fear-producing situation. It might be retorted that withdrawal is not to be interpreted simple-mindedly as involving always advance and retreat. This we can easily concede, but the problem still remains of how it is to be interpreted so as to account for the phenomena of avoidance behaviour. In the Tolman and Gleitman case, for instance, what exactly are the fear-inducing stimuli? Are they the stimuli at the choice point? But the animal shows no tendency to withdraw from these; he approaches them and then goes up on the safe path. Withdrawal was really shown by one animal who took the wrong path, and then promptly turned around and tried to regain the main choice point. This animal also showed signs of fear. But in the case of the others, there is no evidence that their behaviour should be interpreted in terms of flight or withdrawal. Similarly with a great number of other avoidance behaviours. For instance, sometimes animals just fail to enter a situation which has been shown to be painful. Fear and withdrawal only show themselves in their resistance if they are forced towards it. Or again, avoidance behaviour can be shown when one goes through a routine with care where carelessness has been shown to result in pain or harm. This is the case of a man driving slowly over ice, or repairing an electric fixture with especial attention, or taking certain precautions beforehand, such as padding oneself before a rough game. Such actions can be explained in terms of the goal towards which they contribute, but not, at least *prima facie*, in terms of withdrawal from unpleasant stimulation.

It would seem that we cannot interpret avoidance behaviour as withdrawal for the point of avoidance behaviour is precisely not to have to withdraw, to avoid getting in a situation where withdrawal becomes necessary or desirable. The confusion between the two leads to the puzzles which arise for S–R theorists over the problem of the extinction of avoidance responses. Now an avoidance response is often very resistant to extinction; that is, once an animal has suffered pain in a situation he will often go on avoiding it for a very long time without any fresh experience of pain. But according to the S–R theory this should not be so. For although the avoidance response is itself constantly re-inforced through the withdrawal from the fear-inducing stimuli, the power of these latter to induce fear should steadily decline. For whether this is due to reinforcement in the form of the relief that follows the end of pain (as Miller thinks) or to conditioning of a Pavlovian type (as Mowrer thinks), the occurrence of the stimuli without subsequent pain should extinguish the fear response to them.[1] S–R theory is thus in flat contradiction to the facts.

It seems difficult to find a way out of this. Miller[2] points out that we might explain the resistance to extinction by the fact that 'avoidance responses reinforced by escape from fear often keep the subject out of the frightening situation'. Now this is un-doubtedly it. Avoidance responses extinguish slower than approach responses, because if avoidance is successful, the animal stays out of the situation and never discovers that it has changed. But this is either an admission that the S–R theory is misguided, or no explanation at all. If by 'keeping the subject out of the frightening situation' Miller means keeping him away from fear-inducing stimuli, then he is admitting that avoidance cannot be explained by escape from fear. If he means keeping him away from the pain, then the problem remains entire how the fear-inducing stimuli can still induce fear when they are not followed by pain. In other words, on S–R premises there is no reason why the non-entry of the shock area should have anything to do with the resistance to extinction of avoidance responses. This only becomes an explanation when we assume that the animal is acting on the 'hypothesis' that area X is a shock area. Then his successful avoidance of it means that he never has a chance to falsify this belief, even though the current may have been switched off. But then we are saying that the effect of the shock is to alter the animal's intentional environment, what he believes or knows about his environment, and we are thus accounting for avoidance

---

[1] Cf. the argument by Ritchie, 'Can Reinforcement Theory Account for Avoidance?', *Psychological Review*, 1951.

[2] Op. cit., p. 452.

behaviour in teleological terms, i.e., as behaviour emitted because in the animal's intentional environment it will have the result of avoiding shock, i.e., as behaviour emitted 'for the sake of' avoiding shock.

Thirdly, the S–R theory is open to objection on its use of the notion of fear. According to this view fear always accompanies avoidance; it is the drive that 'energises' avoidance responses, and its reduction is essential to their being stamped in and maintained as 'habits'. But the question is, what is meant by fear? Are the criteria for fear simply that an animal has (a) suffered pain, (b) takes evasive action? If this is so, the theory loses much of its empirical content; and what is left is highly dubious, as we have seen above. Miller, however, seems to want to take another line. He identifies fear in part in terms of certain characteristic responses or reactions, stomach acidity, pallor, startle, and so on. And this is what we normally mean by the emotion of fear. But if this is the case, then it seems that the thesis that fear is always involved in avoidance cannot stand. For there are many cases of successful avoidance where there are no signs of fear. Indeed, characteristically, when a routine of avoidance is well established and we have confidence in it, we feel no fear. There is generally speaking no fear involved in plugging in a light, although one is taking care not to get a shock. Similarly, Miller himself reports that the animals settled down into a routine of avoidance in which they showed no signs of fear. Now for Miller this is just the prelude to extinction, as his theory would imply, but this is by no means always the case. In the case studied by Miller, where the rats had to leave the danger chamber, extinction was more likely since it was possible for them to notice, by delaying slightly, that shock did not follow. But routines of avoidance which keep the animal out of the danger situation altogether can continue for a long time without any signs of fear whatever.

There is evidence, however, that fear can be revived if something goes wrong with an established routine which itself is run through without fear. Thus, when Miller introduced a hitch in the proceedings, the rats, who had been 'going through the whole process nonchalantly and seemingly without drive'[1] suddenly showed signs of fear. The evidence, corroborated by

[1] Op. cit., p. 451.

that of introspection for what it is worth, is that fear is a function of the danger felt, and that where an avoidance response is known to be perfectly adequate no fear is felt. Being able to do something effective in a dangerous situation reduces fear. This seems to suggest that far from explaining avoidance in terms of fear, we must account for fear in terms of avoidance. For if fear is not the function of certain fear-inducing stimuli—and it is hard to see how we could explain the recurrence of fear when our evasive action is blocked on this hypothesis—but of the danger of the situation (the danger as seen by the animal, of course), and an element in this danger is the possibility of evasive action itself, then it would seem that fear generally can only arise in cases where there is an object or eventuality which for the animal is to be avoided as painful or harmful. Thus fear is also a function of avoidance, the success of avoidance, that is, and not only avoidance of fear. Or rather fear arises concurrently with the desire to avoid; it cannot be considered as a case of undirected psychic energy whose results in behaviour can be accounted for in terms of the conditioning of S–R habits by reinforcement (i.e., the reduction of this energy), but as emotion or psychic energy directed towards avoidance. This, of course, is the implication of the notion 'fear' in ordinary speech. But, if this is true, then, like 'anxiety', which was discussed above, an explanation in terms of fear would be a teleological explanation.

6. THE HEDONIST OPTION

Our discussion of the S–R reinforcement theory thus seems to yield negative results all along the line. The aim of this theory is to provide a solution to the problem of motivation, to answer the question, why do animals behave as they do? But, not only this, the answer must be an 'objective' non-teleological one. To answer this question is to offer a set of general laws which set out the factors determining behaviour. For teleological theory as we have seen these are the goals or ends towards which the being concerned naturally aims. S–R theory rejects this path and attempts to account for behaviour in terms of the Law of Effect; that is, the factors determining behaviour are features of the animal's previous behaviour history. Where history is not enough to account for behaviour, there is invoked a generalized psychic energy, a general 'sensitizer' of stimulus–response habits, which activates whatever responses have been conditioned in the animal's history to this situation. The notion of drive is then made to do double duty as that of a condition whose elimination is 'reinforcing', that is strengthens stimulus–response habits.

But the theory runs into three main obstacles. First, since the behaviour emitted is a function jointly of the responses emitted in the past and the reinforcement which has followed them, S–R theory runs into trouble when it tries to account for behaviour which is intrinsically motivated, i.e., where the end of behaviour is not some separably identifiable state of affairs. For here there is nothing which can be identified as a reinforcer, no state of affairs such that if it follows a response of this type, the probability of that response occurring in the future is increased. The attempt to force this behaviour into the mould of extrinsic motivation doesn't seem to be successful. These activities, on the other hand, consist of actions not movements. The actions are 'pointless', that is, they have no end outside themselves, but they are still directed to a goal. The dog running and catching the ball, the monkey solving the puzzle, the cat exploring the room, all direct their action towards an end, and their movements can only be accounted for on this assumption, even though the end-state they achieve is not the point of the activity—the dog loses interest in the ball once caught, the monkey in the puzzle once solved—but only the action of achieving it. It seems necessary therefore to invoke the hypothesis, as Nissen does, that animals naturally tend to engage in activities of this kind.

Secondly, it doesn't seem possible to identify a source of psychic energy or 'drive', either by its physiological antecedent conditions (as in the case of hunger, sex, etc.) or by the autonomic responses connected with it (as in the case of fear), which is not 'directed'— that is, psychic energy which is available only or mainly to actions which tend towards a certain goal (e.g., the consummatory acts of eating and mating, or the avoidance of harm). And this direction seems original and irreducible.

And thirdly, and this is a point which overlaps with the preceding one, there are a great many cases in which the thesis that behaviour is a function of behaviour history seems to be falsified in the most direct way; that is, behaviour occurs in conditions where the putative conditions in the animal's behaviour history cannot be found. We have discussed examples of this kind in the last chapter, and we can add the phenomena of avoidance behaviour discussed in this. These actions, however, can be explained on the hypothesis that the animal's behaviour is directed towards certain goals.

It would seem that behaviour science, at least on the molar or 'peripheralist' level, cannot replace or derive from higher level non-teleological laws, those laws which state the tendency of animals of a given species to pursue ends of a certain kind, that is attempt to perform consummatory acts of a certain kind (e.g., seeking and eating food in conditions of deprivation), or seek a certain end-state (e.g., the avoidance of pain or harm, protection of the young) or engage in activity of a certain form (e.g., exploration, gratuitous exercise of capabilities). Thus behaviour must be accounted for, or a great range of it in any case, either by saying that, in the case of consummatory acts or 'gratuitous' activities, this is the kind of action which beings of this kind normally do, or by saying that it is required for a certain consummatory act or a certain end-state which the animal naturally seeks to encompass. In either case we have a teleological form at the apex of explanation.

Now we have considered in this last section only the S–R reinforcement theory; and this is not the only theory in the field of behaviourism, nor the only possible one. We certainly cannot state *a priori* that no behaviourist theory will succeed where the drive-reduction theory has failed, but it can readily be seen that many of the objections made to this latter apply to other views which are canvassed among S–R psychologists. The three main difficulties outlined here would apply to any reinforcement theory, and not only to one which took drive- or need-reduction as its reward. For it would still attempt to account for behaviour historically (difficulty three) and could not account for new adaptive behaviour or for avoidance, which involves precisely replacing the old response of flight or withdrawal with the new adaptive response of avoidance. And it would be just as incapable of discovering a form of undirected psychic energy or of accounting for intrinsically motivated behaviour. For any reinforcement theory must posit a separably identifiable reinforcing state of affairs, on pain of circularity, not to say vacuity.

Similarly S–R 'contiguity' theory would not be much better

off. It runs into the third difficulty, viz., that much of adaptive action cannot be accounted for in terms of conditioning of responses to stimuli in past experience, and its performance on avoidance learning is rather worse than reinforcement theory, since on the postremity principle the animal should do the same thing again and run right into the shock. For the rest, contiguity theorists are no nearer to showing that the consummatory actions connected with 'drives' are learned by association than the S–R theorists are to showing that they are learned by reinforcement, and the evidence that these actions are goals which the animal naturally tends to seek in the appropriate circumstances weighs against their theory as well. Nor is it clear how they could give any more plausible account of gratuitous activities.

A quite different approach, however, to the normal S–R type is represented by the neo-hedonism of theorists like McClelland and Young. These thinkers strongly criticize the drive-reduction theorists for ignoring or distorting all the types of behaviour which cannot be fitted into the homeostatic pattern. They concentrate attention on the fact that behaviour can be carried out for its own sake and not because of some extrinsic end-result. But having removed behaviour from the homeostatic strait-jacket, they propose to confine it to the equally ill-fitting garment of hedonism. For McClelland there are 'two basic objectives—to approach or maintain pleasure and to avoid or reduce pain'.[1] Thus, although it might seem that hedonic theory can overcome the first difficulty, that of accounting for intrinsically motivated behaviour, it is likely that it will run into trouble in accounting for other types of behaviour.

But the trouble seems to start even with intrinsically motivated behaviour. In fact, there is a great deal of unclarity in the works of McClelland and Young on the subject of just how pleasure and pain direct behaviour. They seem to have little use for the notion of drive, i.e., that of a specific type of psychic energy identified by its physiological antecedent conditions. Their position seems to be that formerly adopted by Hebb,[2] that there is no special problem in accounting for the arousal of behaviour; the organism is usually active; the problem of motivation is the problem of explaining the direction of behaviour. Thus 'motive' in the writings of these thinkers shifts from the usual meaning it

[1] *The Achievement Motive*, p. 38.   [2] *The Organisation of Behaviour*.

bears among neo-behaviourists, where it is often used interchangeably with 'drive', and takes on the meaning of an anticipatory state set up by a cue. Thus Young:

> According to the need-stimulus theory of drive the source of
> motivation is found in persistent stimulation from tissues in need,
> such as the contractions of an empty stomach or the persistent
> pain pressure stimulations from the parched throat in thirst.
> According to the affective-determination theory persistent motiva-
> tion comes from the proprioceptors when the organism is in a set
> with expectant tension.[1]

This state is set up as a result of experience. All motives are
learned. McClelland and Young are emphatic on this point. But
it is very unclear how this comes about. The idea is basically that
the animal or human being learns by experience what things give
pleasure and what give pain and comes to seek the former and
eschew the latter. But what the learning consists in is hard to
understand. Young adds to the confusion by using the term
'learning' in an odd sense. Pleasure directs behaviour according
to two principles,[2] that of hedonic organization, according to
which 'an individual organizes neurobehavioural patterns that
enhance enjoyment and relieve distress', secondly that of exercise,
which 'modifies the neurobehavioural pattern in the sense that
it increases its probability of occurrence in the same or similar
situation, even when hedonic processes are no longer present'.[3]
The term 'learning' is to be confined to the latter process:

> It is necessary, therefore, to distinguish between learning through
> exercise (practice, drill, training) and the hedonic regulation
> of behaviour. Affective processes regulate and organize neuro-
> behavioural patterns in the sense that they determine what
> will be learned and what not; but such hedonic regulation and
> organization are not to be confused with learning through prac-
> tice. Learning is here defined as a change in neurobehavioural
> patterns that depends upon exercise. Affective processes do not
> *cause* learning. They are motivational in nature and they influence
> performance.[4]

[1] 'Food-seeking Drive, Affective Processes and Learning,' *Psychological
Review*, 1949, p. 109.
[2] 'The Role of Hedonic Process in the Organization of Behaviour,'
Psychological Review, 1952.
[3] Op. cit., p. 256.   [4] Loc. cit., *Psychological Review*, 1959, p. 123.

But this means that the interesting problem of learning, i.e., how we learn the instrumental acts that lead to pleasure and away from pain, how to get pleasure and avoid pain, is brushed aside and left unanswered, is not even given the name 'learning'. We are only told that a 'neurobehavioural pattern' is organized. McClelland is equally unilluminating on this score. Apparently pleasure leads to the cues associated with it acquiring the power to 'redintegrate a change in the affective situation'.[1] But how this leads to the appropriate action remains obscure. Sometimes McClelland speaks almost as though instrumental acts were 'stamped in' with pleasure as the 'reinforcer'. Thus[2] he explains how a dog might learn to make the right responses to the presence of a mate: A dog may pick up the smell of a bitch in heat; turning his head this way and that he will find that the pleasure increases or decreases, and thus will learn what to do. But generally he and Young speak as though the cue induced a set to make the appropriate response:

> An acquired motive is a preparatory set of the organism, aroused by stimulus cues, and containing a persistent tension from the proprioceptors and visceral structures.[3]

Young seems to attribute the strength of the motivation to the tension aroused by this set.

Now stripped of the neurological trimmings, for which no empirical basis is given, this means simply that an animal will tend to seek those experiences which are pleasant and avoid those which are painful. Now, in order to be used for predicting behaviour, such a theory, as we have seen, would have to have some criterion for pleasure or pain other than the approach or avoidance of the animal. With pain this is generally no problem. But with pleasure it notoriously is. How do we identify something as a state of pleasure *ex ante*? Young doesn't seem to have an answer for this question. But McClelland[4] proposes to use the expressive autonomic responses as a sign of affective arousal, although he feels he must rely on future behaviour to establish whether the experience was one of pleasure or pain. But if this

---

[1] Op. cit., p. 28.   [2] Op. cit., p. 91.

[3] Young, 'The Role of Hedonic Processes in Motivation', *Nebraska Symposium on Motivation*, 1955, p. 233.

[4] Op. cit., pp. 34–5.

is the criterion, then certainly we cannot maintain that all behaviour is motivated by pleasure and pain, for much of our
behaviour is not accompanied by any such reactions.

But McClelland also has a more sophisticated theory of pleasure
and pain as an autonomic response brought on by a discrepancy
between the experience of the organism and its 'adaptation level'
—roughly, what it expects; a mild difference is pleasing, a large
one painful. If there is no difference at all, the experience is, of
course, dull. McClelland adduces a number of plausible examples,
some of them drawn from Hebb (e.g., when one reads a detective
story for a second time, one falls asleep). But the thesis, of course,
is intolerably vague. There is no way of telling in general what
the adaptation level is and how much experience differs from it;
and since McClelland says that events can differ from expectations
on a variety of dimensions, it is always possible to find some ways
in which a pleasurable event fits the thesis. The theory thus
pushes towards the limits of vacuity where the effective criterion
for pleasure becomes that a thing is chosen. Thus McClelland
meets the traditional challenge against hedonism:

> What about the martyr, for example? Can he be seeking pleasure
> or avoiding pain? The answer is 'yes', in the larger sense in which
> positive and negative affect are defined here. If a man builds up a
> conception of the Universe—an expectation of the way in which
> moral or spiritual laws govern it and his place in it—which is
> sufficiently firm and well defined, it may well be that the anticipated
> nonconfirmation of such an expectation through transgression of
> those laws would produce sufficient negative affect so that a man
> would choose the lesser negative affect of burning at the stake.
> One of the virtues of our view of motivation is precisely that it
> permits the development of new, high level motives as experience
> changes the person's expectations or adaptation levels.[1]

Now, of course, here the notion of 'adaptation level' has been
shifted to accommodate the new case. For the martyr's *expectations*, in the normal sense of this term, are not in question here.
Indeed the martyr, if he believes in original sin, may expect the
laws to be transgressed more often than not, including by himself. What is required for martyrdom is not that transgression

[1] Op. cit., p. 66.

should be unexpected but that it should be eminently undesirable, and this is just what needs to be explained under the heading 'motivation'. The question is, why does the martyr *desire* a given consummation so much that he is willing to die for it? and this McClelland is a long way from explaining.

In the absence of a clearer criterion for pleasure, McClelland's theory cannot even offer an explanation of those activities which are undertaken for their own sake. And, as we have seen above, there are other considerations which make the hedonist theory implausible. In particular the view that all motives are learned runs counter to the evidence for an innate connexion between certain drive states and certain consummatory acts. If motivation is to be explained as a state which is aroused by a cue associated with pleasure *experienced in the past*, then sexual behaviour, for instance, will not fit the theory. But, in addition, we have seen that there is evidence for the belief that pleasure is itself partly a function of desire, and therefore cannot be the only factor involved in motivation. McClelland tries to close this gap by accounting, e.g., for the increase in the desire to eat which comes with increasing deprivation by saying that the cues which evoke the set to expect pleasure in eating get stronger. But what are these cues? If they are strong stomach cramp this is often accompanied by a reduction in hunger. A feeling of emptiness in the stomach? But this too does not invariably accompany hunger. In fact, as physiologists are constantly saying, the cues arising from food deprivation are extraordinarily hard to locate. Secondly, why does it follow from the fact that the cue is stronger that desire is increased? Thus, if the sight of a tasty dish is a cue arousing a motive, as it must be on McClelland and Young's view, does it follow that the desire is stronger if the cue is 'stronger'? The notion of 'strength' loses all meaning here.

The hedonism of McClelland and Young, then, when shorn of its neurological dressing, seems to be very similar to traditional hedonism: Its basic thesis is that animals and men seek pleasure and avoid pain. Like the traditional hedonism it seems to be teleological in form, although the hope seems to be entertained that one can account for the effects of pleasure in directing behaviour in terms of a molecular 'centralist' theory of 'neuro-behavioural organization'. Its principal claims are that all goals are learned and that pleasure can be identified separately from the actions which give rise to it, by means of the notion of 'adaptation level'. But in this latter enterprise it seems no more successful than traditional hedonism, and in the former claim it contradicts the facts. Neo-hedonism has yet to provide a non-purposive explanation of behaviour.

XI

CONCLUSION

IN the last chapters we have tried to examine the case for a 'peripheralist' account of behaviour which would not make use of explanation by purpose, that is, which would eschew the use of concepts involving intentionality and of teleological explanation. We have tried to see the types of correlation which a science of this kind would search for, and have tried to test whether the regularities which hold of the phenomena are such that correlations of these types can be found—or whether they are rather of the kind consonant with an explanation in terms of purpose.

In doing so we have gone on the assumption—although our account of explanation by purpose is mainly drawn from the concepts we use to describe and explain human behaviour—that this question can sensibly be asked not only of human beings but also of at least the higher animals. We have therefore drawn much—indeed most—of our evidence from the behaviour of these latter. The assumption of continuity between human and animal life seems to have been justified in the event. For many of the phenomena, of insight, orientation, improvisation, and so on, which we know to play an important part in human behaviour, also can be found in the behaviour of many animals, as we have seen, and even to a quite extraordinary degree among primates.

The phenomena we have studied, then, seem to point, for human and animal behaviour alike, towards an explanation in terms of purpose. Thus, in the field of learning the type of correlation which neo-behaviourism hopes to discover between learning history and post-learning behaviour does not seem to hold, nor can we account for learning behaviour by correlations linking environment and behaviour of the type which this theory demands, that is, between stimuli and responses. In addition, there is some indication, as we saw in Chapter VIII, that much learning cannot be accounted for in terms of a definite set of correlations, of whatever kind, linking environment and behaviour. Those cases where an animal learns a differential response to certain types of thing—the type of learning tested for in discrimination experiments—can perhaps be understood in this way, that is, as a set of 'directions' to respond in a certain way on the presentation of a certain cue. But in other cases, cases of what one might call orientation learning, no finite list of directions can express what is learned. It would seem more adequate to speak here of the acquisition of a general capacity to get around. Spatial orientation thus seems to be a type of 'know-how' and in this it has some affinities with a different type of learning of which many animals are also capable, the acquisition of new motor skills—a phenomenon which S–R theory doesn't seem capable of accounting for at all.

The evidence here, then, is that we have to introduce a range of notions connected with 'the way the animal sees the situation', or some analogous range, in any 'peripheralist' account of learning—whether or not this can in turn be accounted for by a 'centralist' theory which is non-teleological. This conclusion is strengthened by the fact that the first-level correlations which hold between environment and behaviour are such that the response must usually be defined in terms of its goal or achievement, so that a notion like 'action' seems to be indispensable here.

Thus it would seem essential that a peripheralist account of behaviour make use of explanation by purpose, or at least—if it is hoped that these can be derived from more basic 'centralist' laws of another type—of laws and notions closely analogous to those of this mode of explanation; and that, in particular, as we saw in Chapter X, it must make use of the notion of a natural tendency to engage in a certain type of activity or pursue certain goals.

The result is perhaps not surprising. Indeed, to some it will appear obvious. But the evidence of the literature is that to many, and particularly to many working in the field, this conclusion is far from obvious and is indeed resisted, even in the face of the most telling evidence. As a matter of fact, the startling thing is that the most important objections to their theories are often not seen at all by these thinkers, that for instance special hypotheses are put forward to cope with awkward counter-examples—such as the habit family hierarchy of Hull or the perception of likeness and difference of Nissen—which patently beg the question at issue; for antecedents cannot be discovered for these special factors of the type required by the theory any more than they could be discovered for the wayward phenomena —the taking of the short cut, or learning to match samples— which they were introduced to explain. S–R theory is rich in such question-begging special hypotheses, merely verbal solutions which leave the problem untouched—'conditional' cues, relative stimuli, sensory integration, acquired drives of all sorts—which, as we saw in Chapter V, are a usually reliable symptom of a theory's ill-health. The fact that these difficulties are not seen is perhaps a testimony to the strength among many theorists of the belief which we discussed in Chapter IV, the belief that the data language of psychology must not include psychological concepts. For if this is so then whatever law-like correlations can be found must hold between events characterized only in the 'physical thing' language, and the alternative to which the evidence points more and more, that some place must be given to concepts in-volving intentionality, is excluded from the start, so that the bearing of this on the question we have been discussing is never seen. It is laid down *a priori* that if a correlation has been found to hold it must be of the kind required, even if it relates such dubious elements as 'relative' stimuli or 'learning sets'.

The assumption of S–R theory is that in defending behaviour-ism they are defending the very possibility of a science of be-haviour, one whose propositions can be inter-subjectively verified.[1] But this assumption, as we have seen, rests on certain propositions in epistemology and the philosophy of mind which are far from being self-evident, and the conclusions drawn from them about the 'data language' are highly dubious. In fact the question we have been discussing is not whether a science of behaviour is possible, but rather, which direction should we

---

[1] Cf., e.g., K. W. Spence, 'The Postulates and Methods of "Behaviour-ism"', *Psychological Review*, 1948, reprinted in Feigl and Brodbeck (eds.), *Readings in the Philosophy of Science*.

proceed in in order to develop such a science? Can we do away with the notion of purpose altogether in explanation; or is it essential? There are a number of theories, notably those of psychoanalysis[1] which, while they are more precise than the common man's unsophisticated view, and may even shock him in many ways, make use of the notion of purpose and of related notions, such as 'action', 'insight', 'intentional description', and so on. The question is whether these represent the correct route for scientific enquiry to take, or whether this is to be found in the road mapped out by behaviourism. We cannot prejudge the question in favour of the latter alternative by according it the monopoly to the title 'scientific', particularly when the evidence seems to point to the former.

But there is another reason for making light of the contrary evidence. S–R theorists will often plead, in the face of objections, the complexity of the subject matter and the infancy of the subject. Now the plea of 'complexity' certainly has validity as a ground for uncertainty about the principles on which explanation should be based, and it is certainly true that we cannot conclude from the inadequacy of neo-behaviourist theories to that of all accounts which eschew explanation by purpose. For, as we have said above, the possibility of a more 'complex' 'centralist' account remains open. And this is often what is meant in speaking of complexity. But if certain definite principles have been put forward, as in the case of S–R theory, then it will not help, if they come off badly, to say that the subject matter is complex, for whether it is complex or simple, they are inadequate to it.

As a matter of fact, 'complexity' in another sense, so far from being an extenuating factor, may be a sign of error.[2] For any subject matter is complex in the light of a wrong theory once we try to apply it, in that we are forced to complicate our theory with *ad hoc* hypotheses. If we are right and the subject matter is really that complex, then these hypotheses should be amenable to being tied down and, once they are, confirmed. But if they

[1] Freud, of course, in keeping with the scientism of his day, believed that all this could be explained at a more basic level in terms of a 'centralist' neurophysiological theory. But Freudians, including the master, do not seem ever to have taken this seriously enough to attempt it. Even the importance of physiological metaphor in the language seems to have diminished with time.

[2] Cf. the discussion above, Chapter V.

are not readily amenable to the test—and this is certainly the case with a great many of the vague and pliable hypotheses of S–R theory, e.g., 'response induction', 'afferent neural inter-action', 'fractional anticipatory goal response', and so on—or, worse, if they are themselves inadequate to the evidence, then complexity is not an excuse but a symptom.

As for the plea of 'infancy', one can only answer that it begs the question. For it may be that these theories are in their 'infancy' precisely because there is a fatal obstacle to their growing up, viz., that they are incorrect. The 'Galilean spirit' has been abroad in psychology for quite some time, and, if it hasn't produced anything very solid in experimental psychology, this *may* be because current approaches are wrong. The best way to settle this question is to test the validity of these approaches against the phenomena as we have tried to do. The fact that the subject is young may excuse the narrowness of scope of the hypotheses or the paucity of evidence, but it can be of no help to a theory which has failed to meet the facts and provides no ground for according it a special consideration. Indeed, we should, if anything, be more exacting in the early days, for this is the period when, notoriously, mistaken approaches can thrive.

But, whether surprising or not, the result of our enquiry is hardly spectacular. This was, as we indicated in Chapter IV, only to be expected. For the question which is of greatest interest to scientist and layman alike is the one which we raised at the outset, whether animate beings must be given a different status from inanimate things in that their behaviour can only be explained in terms of purpose. But in the nature of the case we could not, on the basis of the evidence reviewed here, have returned anything close to a final positive answer to this question (although if our results had been different we might have established the negative conclusion). For there still remain to be considered a whole range of 'centralist' neurophysiological theories, and perhaps theories of other ranges as well, e.g., the biochemical. Indeed, there is a sense, as we have said, in which no conclusive affirmative answer can ever be given, since the claim to special status involves a negative existential statement; that there is no mode of explanation which eschews concepts involving intentionality which will be adequate to that range of behaviour which we now account for by such concepts as 'action' and 'desire'. And although we may establish for a certain range of theories of this kind that they are inadequate, we can never affirm that these are all that there are, that this range exhausts the possibilities of non-purposive explanations.

But some progress can nevertheless be made, and some rational basis provided for the belief that animate organisms exhibit these special properties, if some of the theories which are founded on the opposite assumption can be shown to be inadequate. And this is the value of our results, if they are valid, that in marshalling the evidence against one false route for scientific enquiry, they may add some substance to a belief which has been the subject of debate for centuries and which will probably continue to be so for centuries to come; that in putting certain theories to the test, they may add a little to our understanding of a fundamental issue, which, even if, like many philosophical questions, it may never be finally decided to universal agreement, is nevertheless of fundamental importance and of perennial interest.

INDEX

International Library of Philosophy & Scientific Method

Editor: Ted Honderich
Advisory Editor: Bernard Williams

List of titles, page three

International Library of Psychology Philosophy & Scientific Method

Editor: C K Ogden

List of titles, page six

ROUTLEDGE AND KEGAN PAUL LTD
68 Carter Lane London EC4

International Library of Philosophy and Scientific Method
(Demy 8vo)

Allen, R. E. (Ed.)
Studies in Plato's Metaphysics
Contributors: J. L. Ackrill, R. E. Allen, R. S. Bluck, H. F. Cherniss, F. M.
Cornford, R. C. Cross, P. T. Geach, R. Hackforth, W. F. Hicken, A. C. Lloyd,
G. R. Morrow, G. E. L. Owen, G. Ryle, W. G. Runciman, G. Vlastos
464 pp. 1965. 70s.

Armstrong, D. M.
Perception and the Physical World
208 pp. 1961. (2nd Impression 1963.) 25s.

Bambrough, Renford (Ed.)
New Essays on Plato and Aristotle
Contributors: J. L. Ackrill, G. E. M. Anscombe, Renford Bambrough,
R. M. Hare, D. M. MacKinnon, G. E. L. Owen, G. Ryle, G. Vlastos
184 pp. 1965. 28s.

Barry, Brian
Political Argument
382 pp. 1965, 50s.

Bird, Graham
Kant's Theory of Knowledge:
An Outline of One Central Argument in the *Critique of Pure Reason*
220 pp. 1962. (2nd Impression 1965.) 28s.

Brentano, Franz
The True and the Evident
Edited and narrated by Professor R. Chisholm
218 pp. 1965, 40s.

Broad, C. D.
Lectures on Psychical Research
Incorporating the Perrott Lectures given in Cambridge University in 1959
and 1960
461 pp. 1962. 56s.

Crombie, I. M.
An Examination of Plato's Doctrine
I. Plato on Man and Society
408 pp. 1962. 42s.
II. Plato on Knowledge and Reality
583 pp. 1963. 63s.

Day, John Patrick
Inductive Probability
352 pp. 1961. 40s.

3

International Library of Philosophy and Scientific Method
(Demy 8vo)

Edel, Abraham
Method in Ethical Theory
379 pp. 1963. 32s.

Flew, Anthony
Hume's Philosophy of Belief
A Study of his First "Inquiry"
296 pp. 1961. 30s.

Goldman, Lucien
The Hidden God
A Study of Tragic Vision in the *Pensées* of Pascal and the Tragedies of
Racine. Translated from the French by Philip Thody
424 pp. 1964. 70s.

Hamlyn, D. W.
Sensation and Perception
A History of the Philosophy of Perception
222 pp. 1961. (2nd Impression 1963.) 25s.

Kemp, J.
Reason, Action and Morality
216 pp. 1964. 30s.

Körner, Stephan
Experience and Theory
An Essay in the Philosophy of Science
272 pp. 1966. 45s.

Lazerowitz, Morris
Studies in Metaphilosophy
276 pp. 1964. 35s.

Merleau-Ponty, M.
Phenomenology of Perception
Translated from the French by Colin Smith
487 pp. 1962. (2nd Impression 1965.) 56s.

Montefiore, Alan, and Williams, Bernard
British Analytical Philosophy
352 pp. 1965. 45s.

Perelman, Chaim
The Idea of Justice and the Problem of Argument
Introduction by H. L. A. Hart. Translated from the French by John Petrie
224 pp. 1963. 28s.

Schlesinger, G.
Method in the Physical Sciences
148 pp. 1963. 21s.

4

International Library of Philosophy and Scientific Method
(Demy 8vo)

Sellars, W. F.
Science, Perception and Reality
374 pp. 1963. 50s.

Shwayder, D. S.
The Stratification of Behaviour
A System of Definitions Propounded and Defended
428 pp. 1965. 56s.

Smart, J. J. C.
Philosophy and Scientific Realism
168 pp. 1963. (2nd Impression 1965.) 25s.

Smythies, J. R. (Ed.)
Brain and Mind
Contributors: Lord Brain, John Beloff, C. J. Ducasse, Antony Flew,
Hartwig Kuhlenbeck, D. M. MacKay, H. H. Price, Anthony Quinton and
J. R. Smythies
288 pp. 1965. 40s.

Taylor, Charles
The Explanation of Behaviour
288 pp. 1964. (2nd Impression 1965.) 40s.

Wittgenstein, Ludwig
Tractatus Logico-Philosophicus
The German text of the *Logisch-Philosophische Abhandlung* with a new
translation by D. F. Pears and B. F. McGuinness. Introduction by Bertrand
Russell
188 pp. 1961. (2nd Impression 1963.) 21s.

Wright, Georg Henrik Von
Norm and Action
A Logical Enquiry. The Gifford Lectures
232 pp. 1963. (2nd Impression 1964.) 32s.

The Varieties of Goodness
The Gifford Lectures
236 pp. 1963. (2nd Impression 1965.) 28s.

Zinkernagel, Peter
Conditions for Description
Translated from the Danish by Olaf Lindum
272 pp. 1962. 37s. 6d.

International Library of Psychology, Philosophy, and Scientific Method
(Demy 8vo)

PHILOSOPHY

Anton, John Peter
Aristotle's Theory of Contrariety
276 pp. 1957. 25s.

Bentham, J.
The Theory of Fictions
Introduction by C. K. Ogden
214 pp. 1932. 30s.

Black, Max
The Nature of Mathematics
A Critical Survey
242 pp. 1933. (5th Impression 1965.) 28s.

Bluck, R. S.
Plato's Phaedo
A Translation with Introduction, Notes and Appendices
226 pp. 1955. 21s.

Broad, C. D.
Ethics and the History of Philosophy
Selected Essays
296 pp. 1952. 25s.

Scientific Thought
556 pp. 1923. (4th Impression 1952.) 40s.

Five Types of Ethical Theory
322 pp. 1930. (8th Impression 1962.) 30s.

The Mind and Its Place in Nature
694 pp. 1925. (7th Impression 1962.) 55s. See also Lean, Martin.

Buchler, Justus (Ed.)
The Philosophy of Peirce
Selected Writings
412 pp. 1940. (3rd Impression 1956.) 35s.

Burtt, E. A.
The Metaphysical Foundations of Modern Physical Science
A Historical and Critical Essay
364 pp. 2nd (revised) edition 1932. (5th Impression 1964.) 35s.

6

International Library of Psychology, Philosophy, and Scientific Method
(Demy 8vo)

Carnap, Rudolf
The Logical Syntax of Language
Translated from the German by Amethe Smeaton
376 pp. 1937. (6th Impression 1964.) 40s.

Chwistek, Leon
The Limits of Science
Outline of Logic and of the Methodology of the Exact Sciences
With Introduction and Appendix by Helen Charlotte Brodie
414 pp. 2nd edition 1949. 32s.

Cornford, F. M.
Plato's Theory of Knowledge
The Theaetetus and Sophist of Plato
Translated with a running commentary
358 pp. 1935. (6th Impression 1964.) 28s.

Plato's Cosmology
The Timaeus of Plato
Translated with a running commentary
402 pp. Frontispiece. 1937. (4th Impression 1956.) 35s.

Plato and Parmenides
Parmenides' *Way of Truth* and Plato's *Parmenides*
Translated with a running commentary
280 pp. 1939 (5th Impression 1964.) 32s.

Crawshay-Williams, Rupert
Methods and Criteria of Reasoning
An Inquiry into the Structure of Controversy
312 pp. 1957. 32s.

Fritz, Charles A.
Bertrand Russell's Construction of the External World
252 pp. 1952. 30s.

Hulme, T. E.
Speculations
Essays on Humanism and the Philosophy of Art
Edited by Herbert Read. Foreword and Frontispiece by Jacob Epstein
296 pp. 2nd edition 1936. (6th Impression 1965.) 32s.

Lange, Frederick Albert
The History of Materialism
And Criticism of its Present Importance
With an Introduction by Bertrand Russell, F.R.S. Translated from the German
by Ernest Chester Thomas
1,146 pp. 1925. (3rd Impression 1957.) 70s.

7

International Library of Psychology, Philosophy, and Scientific Method
(Demy 8vo)

Lazerowitz, Morris
The Structure of Metaphysics
With a Foreword by John Wisdom
262 pp. 1955. (2nd Impression 1963.) 30s.

Lean, Martin
Sense-Perception and Matter
A Critical Analysis of C. D. Broad's Theory of Perception
234 pp. 1953. 25s.

Lodge, Rupert C.
Plato's Theory of Art
332 pp. 1953. 25s.
The Philosophy of Plato
366 pp. 1956. 32s.

Mannheim, Karl
Ideology and Utopia
An Introduction to the Sociology of Knowledge
With a Preface by Louis Wirth. Translated from the German by Louis Wirth and Edward Shils
360 pp. 1954. 28s.

Moore, G. E.
Philosophical Studies
360 pp. 1922. (6th Impression 1965.) 35s. See also Ramsey, F. P.

Ogden, C. K., and Richards, I. A.
The Meaning of Meaning
A Study of the Influence of Language upon Thought and of the Science of Symbolism
With supplementary essays by B. Malinowski and F. G. Crookshank.
394 pp. 10th Edition 1949. (4th Impression 1956) 32s.
See also Bentham, J.

Peirce, Charles, *see* Buchler, J.

Ramsey, Frank Plumpton
The Foundations of Mathematics and other Logical Essays
Edited by R. B. Braithwaite. Preface by G. E. Moore
318 pp. 1931. (4th Impression 1965.) 35s.

Richards, I. A.
Principles of Literary Criticism
312 pp. 2nd edition. 1926. (16th Impression 1963.) 25s.

Mencius on the Mind. Experiments in Multiple Definition
190 pp. 1932. (2nd Impression 1964.) 28s.

Russell, Bertrand, *see* Fritz, C. A.; Lange, F. A.; Wittgenstein, L.

8

International Library of Psychology, Philosophy, and Scientific Method

(Demy 8vo)

Smart, Ninian
Reasons and Faiths
An Investigation of Religious Discourse, Christian and Non-Christian
230 pp. 1958. (2nd Impression 1965.) 28s.

Vaihinger, H.
The Philosophy of As If
A System of the Theoretical, Practical and Religious Fictions of Mankind
Translated by C. K. Ogden
428 pp. 2nd edition 1935. (4th Impression 1965.) 45s.

von Wright, Georg Henrik
Logical Studies
214 pp. 1957. 28s.

Wittgenstein, Ludwig
Tractatus Logico-Philosophicus
With an Introduction by Bertrand Russell, F.R.S., German text with an English translation en regard
216 pp. 1922. (9th Impression 1962.) 21s.
For the Pears-McGuinness translation—*see page 5*

Zeller, Eduard
Outlines of the History of Greek Philosophy
Revised by Dr. Wilhelm Nestle. Translated from the German by L. R. Palmer
248 pp. 13th (revised) edition 1931. (5th Impression 1963.) 28s.

PSYCHOLOGY

Adler, Alfred
The Practice and Theory of Individual Psychology
Translated by P. Radin
368 pp. 2nd (revised) edition 1929. (8th Impression 1964.) 30s.

Bühler, Charlotte
The Mental Development of the Child
Translated from the German by Oscar Oeser
180 pp. 3 plates, 19 figures. 1930 (3rd Impression 1949.) 12s. 6d.

Eng, Helga
The Psychology of Children's Drawings
From the First Stroke to the Coloured Drawing
240 pp. 8 colour plates. 139 figures. 2nd edition 1954. (2nd Impression 1959.) 25s.

Jung, C. G.
Psychological Types
or The Psychology of Individuation
Translated from the German and with a Preface by H. Godwin Baynes
696 pp. 1923. (12th Impression 1964.) 45s.

International Library of Psychology, Philosophy, and Scientific Method

(Demy 8vo)

Koffka, Kurt
The Growth of the Mind
An Introduction to Child-Psychology
Translated from the German by Robert Morris Ogden
456 pp. 16 figures. 2nd edition (revised) 1928. (6th Impression 1952.) 45s.
Principles of Gestalt Psychology
740 pp. 112 figures. 39 tables. 1935. (5th Impression 1962.) 60s.

Köhler, W.
The Mentality of Apes
With an Appendix on the Psychology of Chimpanzees
Translated from the German by Ella Winter
352 pp. 9 plates. 19 figures. 2nd edition (revised) 1927. (4th Impression 1956.) 25s.

Malinowski, Bronislaw
Crime and Custom in Savage Society
152 pp. 6 plates. 1926. (7th Impression 1961.) 18s.
Sex and Repression in Savage Society
290 pp. 1927. (4th Impression 1953.) 21s.
See also Ogden, C. K.

Markey, John F.
The Symbolic Process and Its Integration in Children
A Study in Social Psychology
212 pp. 1928. 14s.

Murphy, Gardner
An Historical Introduction to Modern Psychology
488 pp. 5th edition (revised) 1949. (5th Impression 1964.) 40s.

Paget, R.
Human Speech
Some Observations, Experiments, and Conclusions as to the Nature, Origin, Purpose and Possible Improvement of Human Speech
374 pp. 5 plates. 1930. (2nd Impression 1963.) 42s.

Petermann, Bruno
The Gestalt Theory and the Problem of Configuration
Translated from the German by Meyer Fortes
364 pp. 20 figures. 1932. (2nd Impression 1950.) 25s.

Piaget, Jean
The Language and Thought of the Child
Preface by E. Claparède. Translated from the French by Marjorie Gabain
220 pp. 3rd edition (revised and enlarged) 1959. (2nd Impression 1962.) 30s.

10

Piaget, Jean *(continued)*
Judgment and Reasoning in the Child
Translated from the French by Marjorie Warden
276 pp. 1928 (3rd Impression 1962.) 25s.

The Child's Conception of the World
Translated from the French by Joan and Andrew Tomlinson
408 pp. 1929. (4th Impression 1964.) 40s.

The Child's Conception of Physical Causality
Translated from the French by Marjorie Gabain
(3rd Impression 1965.) 30s.

The Moral Judgment of the Child
Translated from the French by Marjorie Gabain
438 pp. 1932. (4th Impression 1965.) 35s.

The Psychology of Intelligence
Translated from the French by Malcolm Piercy and D. E. Berlyne
198 pp. 1950. (4th Impression 1964.) 18s.

The Child's Conception of Number
Translated from the French by C. Gattegno and F. M. Hodgson
266 pp. 1952. (3rd Impression 1964.) 25s.

The Origin of Intelligence in the Child
Translated from the French by Margaret Cook
448 pp. 1953. 35s.

The Child's Conception of Geometry
In collaboration with Bärbel Inhelder and Alina Szeminska. Translated from the French by E. A. Lunzer
428 pp. 1960. 45s.

Piaget, Jean and Inhelder, Bärbel
The Child's Conception of Space
Translated from the French by F. J. Langdon and J. L. Lunzer
512 pp. 29 figures. 1956 (2nd Impression 1963.) 42s.

Roback, A. A.
The Psychology of Character
With a Survey of Personality in General
786 pp. 3rd edition (revised and enlarged 1952.) 50s.

Smythies, J. R.
Analysis of Perception
With a Preface by Sir Russell Brain, Bt.
162 pp. 1956. 21s.

van der Hoop, J. H.
Character and the Unconscious
A Critical Exposition of the Psychology of Freud and Jung
Translated from the German by Elizabeth Trevelyan
240 pp. 1923. (2nd Impression 1950.) 20s.

PRINTED BY HEADLEY BROTHERS LTD 109 KINGSWAY LONDON WC2 AND ASHFORD KENT